Selling the Sea

An Inside Look at the Cruise Industry

Bob Dickinson, CTC

Andy Vladimir

John Wiley & Sons, Inc.
New York   Chichester   Brisbane   Toronto   Singapore

Copyright © 1997 by John Wiley & Sons, Inc.

Library of Congress Cataloging-in-Publication Data
Dickinson, Robert H.
    Selling the sea : an inside look at the cruise industry / Robert H.
Dickinson, Andrew N. Vladimir.
        p.   cm.
    Includes bibliographical references.
    ISBN 0-471-12001-4 (cloth : alk. paper)
    1. Ocean travel.   2. Cruise ships.   I. Vladimir, Andrew
II. Title.
G550.D53   1996
387.2'43'0688—dc20   96-20420

Printed in the United States of America

10 9 8 7 6 5 4 3 2 1

*For Jodi and Ute
with love and appreciation*

Contents

Preface and Acknowledgments

It's no secret to anyone involved in travel and tourism that both of us love the cruise industry. Bob has spent most of his business career helping build the world's largest and most profitable cruise line. Andy has supplemented his full-time career in marketing and education by writing about cruising since he took his first cruise in 1970. Both of us have spoken on the subject extensively to a variety of audiences, and we have known each other for many years.

Since so many people today either have taken a cruise or intend to take one, and since no one has ever written a book on the business of the cruise industry, we thought it was high time to tackle this subject.

The North American cruise industry is a $7-billion-plus business that carries almost 5 million passengers annually and directly employs approximately 50,000 persons. It is projected that by the year 2000, as many as 8 million passengers per year will cruise. Some 200,000 travel agents sell cruises that average about $225 per person per diem. These same cruise passengers spend tens of millions of dollars on airline seats (to travel to and from their port of embarkation), hotel rooms (for pre- and post-accommodations) and are the prime source of income for jewelry stores, art galleries, attractions, and gift shops in major destinations all over the world. Moreover, tens of millions are spent on board the vessels in the bars, gift shops, shore tours, casinos, and so forth.

Cruising has been the fastest-growing segment of the vacation business for the last decade, beating land-based resorts, theme parks, and excursions. Studies show that whether they are first-time or frequent cruisers, the majority of travelers (63–66%) rate cruising as better than other vacation experiences. Ninety percent of them expect to take more cruises, and nearly 60 percent dream of taking a cruise some day.

Our purpose in writing this book is to share what we have observed and know about why cruising is so popular. We hope that anyone who buys or sells travel experience, or who works in the field, will be interested in the lessons we have learned and the practical advice we have to offer.

Of those whom we would like to acknowledge, a few stand out because they really helped launch this project. Rod McLeod was the Chairman of the Cruise Line Industry Association when we decided to take up our pens. His support, along with that of Jim Godsman, CLIA's President, was invaluable.

Much of our historical material was gathered at Florida International University's library, which contains a good collection of books on the history of steamships because its director, Dr. Laurence Miller, is also a steamship historian. Dr. Miller was very helpful in this area.

Jahn Maxtone-Graham's three books, *The Only Way to Cross*, *Liners to the Sun*, and *Cruising and Crossing* were veritable gold mines of information, and we would be remiss if we did not thank him for his special inspiration.

Without exception, all of the major cruise lines that we asked for help opened their doors and their ships to us. Ed Stephan, the founder of Royal Caribbean Cruise Lines, spent a good deal of time telling us about the early days of cruising. So did Micky Arison, Carnival's Chairman, who stood beside his father, Ted Arison, from the day the line started.

Others at Royal Caribbean who deserve recognition for allowing us to interview them who provide background include: Rod McLeod Jacques Bourguignon, Raul Calvo, Emil Graf, Heinz Neidemier, Sigi Konetzny, Tom Murrill, Margarita Navarrete, Nils Nordh, Gunner Oten, Paolo Pallone, Rich Steck, Tom Strom, Lou Vaccaro, Jean Pierre Venne, and Peter Whelpton.

We naturally expected everyone at Carnival to be helpful and without exception they were. But we want to mention a few who went an extra mile: Brendan Corrigan, Vitorio Fabietti, Vicki Freed, Glenn Fusfield, Tim Gallagher, Henry C. Hernandez, Roberta Jacoby, Cindy Jones, Everette Philips, Jennifer Shashaty, Terry Thornton, Mike Zonis, and Paul Zacharski.

At Princess Cruises we were welcomed as well. Our special thanks to Karine Armstrong, Julie Benson, Jill Biggins, Tim Harris, Mark Iannazo, Rick James, Peter Ratcliff, Nigel Stewart, Giuseppe Romano, and Dedrick Van Regemorter.

Kloster Cruise Limited (Norwegian Cruise Line and Royal Cruise Line) was very generous as well. President and CEO Adam Aron gave us more time then we asked for and contributed a good deal to our discussion of some of the more controversial aspects of cruise line marketing. We also need to thank Erik Baaken, Louis Back, Victor Barothy-Langer, George Drummond, Peter Grant, and Gunnar Mikkelsen.

At Holland America Line we are indebted to Kirk Lanterman, and members of his team including John Anderson, William Cruijberg, Larry Dessler, Joe Russo, and Hans van Biljouw.

There's a good deal in this book about Seabourn, which many consider the world's best cruise line. They couldn't have been any more helpful to us. Special thanks to founder Atle Byrnstad and Larry Pimentel, president, as well as Ernest Beyl, Norbert Fuchs, Jurg Inniger, Harold Langer, Johannes Moser and his charming wife, Larry Rapp, and one of the true legends of the cruise business, Warren Titus.

Celebrity Cruise Lines' Al Wallack is former Chairman of CLIA. He was supportive and helpful. So was Costa Cruises' Senior Vice President David Christopher.

We have Corrado Antonini, Chairman & CEO of Fincantieri—Cantaeri Navali Italiani to thank for telling us how his company builds some of the world's most elegant and largest cruise ships, and noted architect Joe Farcus for telling us how he designs them. Jon Rusten, who is designing the new Disney Cruise Line ships, was also very helpful.

Two industry consultants, Bruce Nierenberg and Ron Kurtz, who know much about starting successful cruise lines because they did, contributed stories and ideas. Some other industry leaders, observers, and experts to whom we are grateful are Joel Abels, Jack Estes, Janice Farmer, Dick Friese, Christopher Hayman, Michele Paige, Brook Hill Snow, and Douglas Ward.

Bill McFarland and Stuart Newman, both giants in their respective fields, contributed their wisdom about advertising and public relations. Gavin MacLeod shared his experiences playing Captain Merril Stubing of the Love Boat. Lucky Congdon helped us with information about the airline business, as did Jim Russell and Dan Bleich. Phil Davidoff, Lauraday Kelley, Graeme Clark, Bill Figge, and Brian Kravitz were outspoken about the travel agency business, and we listened to them carefully.

The title *Selling the Sea* originally appeared as the headline for a news story in the *Miami Herald* by Ted Reed on March 5, 1995. It is used with permission of the *Miami Herald*.

Finally we want to thank Micky Arison, Carnival's chairman, and Tony Marshall, dean of Florida International University's School of Hospitality Management, for their support and encouragement. Claire Thompson, senior editor of John Wiley and Sons, put her money where her mouth is and actually agreed to publish this book. Without her, our thoughts would never have seen the light of day, and we'll always be grateful to her for her confidence and interest.

After all was said and done, while we both take joint and full responsibility for every word in this book, there is a special person who spent countless hours at home on her own time coordinating and assembling this manuscript and dealing with the multiple edits both of us made. We owe a huge debt to Janet Simpkins whose fortitude and patience probably exceeded ours.

BOB DICKINSON AND ANDY VLADIMIR

Selling the Sea

Casting Off

The evolution from steamship transportation to cruising as a vacation

It isn't easy to state authoritatively when the first real cruise set sail or, for that matter, where it went. While almost everyone agrees that the first travel agent was Thomas Cook, who organized his first "Grand Tour" of Europe in 1856, historians disagree as to who organized the first cruise. There's little doubt, however, that it happened in the mid-nineteenth century when traveling to distant places was becoming safer and more fashionable.

The First "Cruises"

We support the claim of Peninsula and Oriental Steam Navigation Company that it invented cruising in 1844. The line, popularly known as P&O, ran ships from Britain to Spain and Portugal and to Malay and China. Today P&O operates cruises under the P&O flag as well as the flag of Princess Cruises (the "Love Boats").

P&O entered the leisure cruising business when, in 1844, the noted novelist William Makepeace Thackeray traveled to Malta,

Greece, Constantinople, the Holy Land, and Egypt in a series of P&O ship connections. He told of his "delightful Mediterranean cruise" in an elegantly written book, *Diary of a Voyage from Corn-hill to Grand Cairo*, which he published under the *nom de plume* of Michael Angelo Titmarsh.

Clearly Thackeray (not unlike most travel writers today) wanted to reward his hosts' hospitality but that was not easy to do considering that everyone aboard became seasick crossing the Bay of Biscay and again going from Gibraltar to Malta. However,

> . . . at last the indescribable moans and noises which had been issuing from behind the fine painted doors on each side of the cabin happily ceased. Long before sunrise I had the good fortune to discover that it was no longer necessary to maintain the horizontal posture, and, the very instant this truth was apparent, came on deck, at two o'clock in the morning, to see a noble full moon sinking westward, and millions of the most brilliant stars shining overhead. The ship went rolling over a heavy, sweltering, calm sea. The breeze was a warm and soft one; quite different to the rigid air we had left behind us, off the Isle of Wight.

That was the good part. Thackeray was a bit of a snob, and while he liked the cruise he didn't enjoy many of the sights on shore. In Athens he complained about the prices, the bugs, and the lack of pretty women. In Constantinople he complained that he didn't get to see the dancing dervishes or Saint Sofia or the harem or any of the royal palaces or mosques because it was the month of Ramadan and everything was closed. And in Egypt he climbed a pyramid but condemned "the swarms of howling beggars, who jostle you about the actual place. And scream in your ears incessantly, and hang on your skirts, and bawl for money." At the end however, he granted that he had had a good time. "So easy, so charming, and I think profitable—it leaves such a store of pleasant recollections—that I can't think but recommend all persons who have the time and means to make a similar journey."

P & O stopped cruising during the Crimean War but by the 1880s, after the British Medical Journal recommended sea voyages as curative, resumed them and in fact converted one of their ships, the *Ceylon,* to a "cruising yacht" that sailed around the world.[1]

The first American-origin cruise was probably the 1867 voyage of the paddle wheel steamer, *Quaker City,* from New York. Its organizer, an entrepreneur named Charles C. Duncan, advertised it as an "Excursion to the Holy Land, Egypt, the Crimea, Greece, and Intermediate Points of Interest." We know a good deal about this cruise because the advertisement caught the attention of Mark Twain, who promptly sent in his application, submitted references, and deposited 10 percent of the fare to join the trip along with 150 "select companions" who would sail from New York and return six months later. The idea that one could visit a number of different places in relative ease and safety appealed to Twain, as did the fact that 1867 was the year of the Paris Exposition. He anticipated that this cruise would be a "picnic on a gigantic scale" and wrote:

> They were to sail for months over the breezy Atlantic and sunny Mediterranean; they were to scamper about the decks by day, filling the ship with shouts and laughter—or read novels and poetry in the shade of the smoke-stacks, or watch for the jellyfish and the nautilus over the side, and the shark, the whale, and other strange monsters of the deep; and at night they were to dance in the open air, on the upper deck, in the midst of a ballroom that stretched from horizon to horizon, and was domed by the bending heavens and lighted by no meaner lamps than the stars and the magnificent moon—dance and promenade, and smoke, and sing, and make love, and search the skies for constellations that never associate with the Big Dipper they were so tired of; and they were to see the ships of twenty navies—the customs and costumes of twenty curious peoples—hold friendly converse with kings and princes, Grand Moguls, and the anointed lords of mighty empires.[2]

---

[1]For more about the history of P&O and its role in steamship travel we recommend David and Stephen Howarth's book *The Story of P&O,* published by Widenfield and Nicolson, London, 1986.

[2]Mark Twain, *The Innocents Abroad,* New York, Harper & Brother. *The Complete Works of Mark Twain,* Volume 2, 1875–1928.

The trip did not turn out as advertised. The *Quaker City* had no sooner cast off and sailed when a storm forced it to anchor for two nights in the foot of New York harbor. Twain was proud of the fact that he did not get immediately seasick in the heavy weather. "We all like to see people seasick, when we are not, ourselves" he observed. After the steamer finally left the harbor, the seas eventually calmed down and a more normal pattern of activities emerged. Every evening after dinner, for example, guests would promenade the deck, sing hymns, say prayers, listen to organ music in the grand saloon, read, and write in their journals (low-cost entertainment by today's standards). Sometimes dances were held on the upper deck to the music of a melodeon, a clarinet, and an accordion, which Twain did not particularly like. "However," he wrote, "the dancing was infinitely worse than the music. When the ship rolled to starboard the whole platoon of dancers came charging down to starboard with it, and brought up in mass at the rail; and when it rolled to port, they went floundering down to port with the same unanimity of sentiment. The Virginia reel, as performed on board the *Quaker City* had more genuine reel about it than any reel I ever saw before." Other forms of entertainment consisted of a mock trial where the purser was accused of stealing an overcoat from a passenger's stateroom and passengers were appointed to serve as judges, lawyers, witnesses, and jury.

Among other countries the group visited Morocco, France, Italy, the Greek Islands, and Turkey, where they took a shore excursion to Ephesus and had their pictures taken there just as modern tourists do today. Then they continued to Jerusalem, Egypt, and finally back to New York six months later.

Twain had mixed feelings about the cruise upon his return. He found the passengers to be too somber and too old for his taste, with three-quarters of them between 40 and 70 years old, and no young girls, which at Twain's stage of life was a distinct disappointment. He wrote about this historic voyage in his 1869 book *The Innocents Abroad*. A year later, writing about the trip from his home in San Francisco, Twain's view had become somewhat more positive: "If the *Quaker City* were weighing her anchor to sail away on the very same cruise again, nothing could gratify me more than to be a passenger." He particularly liked the fact that he did not have to pack and unpack at every new city, and that he could chose friends he had made on board to accompany him on excursions and not be dependent on strangers for companionship. Clearly, while cruises have become a good deal more comfortable and entertaining since those early days, some of the main attractions a cruise has to offer have stayed the same.

The current popularity of cruise travel can probably be traced to those original ideas articulated by Twain—that cruise travel is relatively hassle free because you pack and unpack once, it's safe, and you can make new friends. Twain's notion of cruising as a grand picnic suggests the nonstop, diverse festivities (dining, dancing, entertainment, etc.) that characterize today's cruises.

There is little doubt that in 1977, when the television series "The Love Boat" was launched and broadcast all over the world, the public awareness of cruising as a romantic and relaxing vacation increased. Nevertheless, the thought of chucking it all and escaping the workaday world by going to sea is a fantasy that most of us have entertained at one time or another, so it's no surprise that one of Carnival's most popular ships is called the *Fantasy*, while Royal Caribbean invokes these deep-seated stirrings with the *Legend of the Seas*. Noel Coward's song *Sail Away*, expresses an almost universal sentiment:

> When the storm clouds are reigning in the winter sky, sail away.
> When the love light is fading in your sweetheart's eyes, sail away.
> When you feel your song is orchestrated wrong why should you prolong your stay?
> Sail away.[3]

The Growth of Transatlantic Travel

From the time of the *Quaker City* up to the late 1950s, far more people crossed the Atlantic because they had to rather then for

---

[3]Noel Coward, *The Lyrics of Noel Coward*, Heineman, London, 1965.

pleasure. Late nineteenth- and early twentieth-century ocean travel was dominated by immigrant traffic between Europe and America and between Great Britain and Australia and New Zealand. But this era of immigration contributed nothing to the romance of the sea. Immigrants were not tourists, shipboard conditions were miserable, and a long ocean voyage with no intermediate ports of call was something to be endured, not enjoyed. People regarded the ship purely as a means of transportation, carrying them away from political, economic, or social repression to new lands of opportunity.

As commerce between Europe and North America developed in the 1900s, increasing numbers of people took transatlantic voyages. While the elite traveled in the grand style in first class accommodations on luxurious ocean liners, for others the second- and third-class accommodations were spartan at best: four berths, six berths, and dormitory living with crowded public toilet and bath facilities. Moreover, the rough seas of the North Atlantic, particularly in the winter, combined with top-heavy vessels prone to pitching and rolling, caused many to fear or experience severe seasickness. (Remember, this was before modern hull designs and stabilizers.) For those travelers the voyage lived up to their worst fears, and they hated every minute of it.

The stories of both rich and poor contributed to the dual image of ocean travel today. On one hand we have the reality that an ocean voyage embraces food, service, entertainment, and ambiance on a grand scale; on the other, the false perception that ocean travel is, by definition, an uncomfortable experience.

Even the earliest promoters realized that a major part of the problem of popularizing ocean travel was the ocean itself. Because of their fears of the unknown, many people wanted to forget that they were at sea. Ships were therefore designed to nurture the illusion that one was not at sea and to shield passengers as much as possible from even being aware of the extremes in weather they might encounter. English architect Arthur Davis, who began designing the great Cunard liners in 1907, put it this way:

> The people who use these ships are not pirates, they do not dance hornpipes; they are mostly sea sick American ladies, and the one thing they want to forget when they are on the vessel is

that they are on a ship at all. . . . If we could get ships to look inside like ships, and get people to enjoy the sea it would be a very good thing; but all we can do as things are is to give them gigantic floating hotels.[4]

This illusion of being in a gigantic floating hotel was of course created only for those who were able to afford it, and so it was the glamorous experience of first class steamship travel that became responsible for the legend of cruising as one of the most luxurious of all vacation experiences.

The Race for Market Share

Because of the strong British maritime tradition, the first regularly scheduled steamship service across the Atlantic was a British concern. In 1840 Samuel Cunard inaugurated regular passenger service when he formed the British and North American Royal Mail Steam Packet Company, which later took its founder's name and became the Cunard Line. The British were mainly interested in was building safe, fast, and reliable ships. Comfort was important but only after the first three conditions had been satisfied.

By 1897 the German empire was looking with an envious eye at British outposts worldwide. The Germans pursued an expansionist strategy, launching a fleet between 1897 and 1907 that would beat the British on all fronts. By 1903 they had the four fastest ships on the Atlantic. These vessels were small by today's standards, averaging only 15,000 to 20,000 gross tons, but they could achieve a speed of 23 knots. Typically they held around 2,000 passengers, of which 700 were first class. Despite the best efforts of their designers, however, the German vessels were not very comfortable. Hamburg-Amerika's *Deutschland* and *Kronprinz Wilhelm* rolled a good deal because they were built to ride high out of water. As a result, all of the furniture had to be bolted down to keep it in place during inclement weather.

But speed was what counted, and in 1900 the *Deutschland*

---

[4]John Maxtone-Graham, *The Only Way To Cross* (New York: Collier Books, Macmillan Publishing Company, 1972), p. 112–113.

won the Blue Ribband, a prestigious award recognizing her accomplishment as the fastest ship to cross the Atlantic. Not surprisingly, it took a good deal of machinery to propel this vessel at 23 knots, and much of her interior space was taken up by engines and coal bunkers. In fact, only three decks were completely open to the public, and there were just eight cabins with private baths. The *Deutschland* did offer some dining tables for two, which was a break from the English tradition of putting everyone at rows of long communal tables.

But the ship's design, with three large funnels rising from the engine room to the top, made it impossible to incorporate any grand salons except between the funnels, which limited their size.

Excursion Voyages—the Precursor to Cruising

While most steamship lines of the time were focusing on the highly competitive North Atlantic run, some took older ships that were no longer competitive for this service, refurbished them, and sent them on one-of-a-kind excursions. North German Lloyd, Hamburg Amerika, and Royal Mail were the first lines to initiate this practice toward the end of the nineteenth century. The excursions were clearly a forerunner of modern-day cruising: They still went from point A to point B (like their North Atlantic brethren), but rather than the convenience of round trip, the customer appeal was a touring vacation experience, not just transportation.

Other early forays into cruising included Hamburg Amerika's initiative of temporarily converting two three-class liners to a one-class cruise service. These ships, the *Cleveland* and *Cincinnati*, did extended cruises each winter, including one 125-day world cruise each year. The world cruises were so successful that in 1914 the company began advertising two simultaneous world cruises from New York—one leaving January 16 and the other January 31, 1915. However, the subsequent outbreak of World War I meant that German passenger ships were banned from the seas and so the cruises never got off the ground. Cunard, Canadian Pacific, and Red Star Line also offered world cruises each winter in response to a fall-off in seasonal demand as well as to avoid icebergs.

Up until World War I, the only cruise or excursion activities available were offered by very old ships or during the winter season by transatlantic liners. Trips offered by older ships represented attempts to develop some meager revenue for outdated vessels. These were secondary revenue sources for the lines involved—in theory it was better then laying up the vessels for good.

One of the first significant year-round commitments to the cruising concept was the conversion of the *Deutschland* to the *Victoria Louise* in 1912. The Hamburg-Amerika Line invested significant sums to remove half of her engines, install much more spacious public rooms, and paint the hull white (a first in those days). White was chosen because it better reflected the heat (keeping the ship cooler), as the ship was destined now to sail in the sunny Caribbean rather than the colder climates of the North Atlantic. White vessels are still favored today because of their superior heat-reflecting qualities and their fundamental attractiveness. After all, what is more alluring than a sparkling white ship on an azure sea?

The Pacific Gets into the Act

Liner operations in the Pacific also contributed to the early excursion cruise phenomenon. Canadian Pacific had three express liners, *Empresses of Japan, China*, and *India,* constructed in Britain to sail between Vancouver and China. Because it had to position the ships in the Pacific ocean, the line organized round-the-world excursions in connection with each ship delivery. These excursions began in Britain, transited the Suez Canal to India and China, and then sailed to Vancouver. There the passengers disembarked and boarded a Canadian Pacific train across Canada to Montreal, where they embarked on yet another Canadian Pacific vessel for the return home.

Positioning voyages provided a revenue stream to offset the positioning cost. The continue to be a common practice today—rarely profitable to the lines but still helping defray costs. Such "one-off" cruises generally offer terrific consumer value because the lines price them very attractively, not wishing to spend significant marketing dollars to promote them.

The Pacific operation of the P&O Line, because of its unique weather and seasonal demand pattern, created the need for seasonal cruise and excursion activities to utilize ships during periods of slow demand.

Meanwhile . . .

Back in the North Atlantic the British were not about to lose their superiority to the Germans. To regain their lead they commissioned two new ships, the *Lusitania* and the *Mauretania* (Cunard liked to name its ships after Roman provinces), that were to be a new generation of express liners. Each was over 30,000 tons, so there was space to do something with the interiors besides house machinery to propel the ship. More space meant more elegance. It also meant more money.

Britain's maritime pride was suffering and she was militarily vulnerable. Given the times and rising German militarism, the British government became aware of a need to have armed merchant cruisers and troop ships in event of war. Cunard offered to build the *Lusitania* and the *Mauretania* to Royal Navy specifications, incorporating a speed of $24^1/_2$ knots, a double hull, and strong decks to mount guns if needed. An important innovation on the *Mauretania* was a new kind of propulsion system that had been used experimentally before on a few smaller ships, including Cunard's *Carmania*. This was a steam turbine, invented by Charles Parsons, that not only was much more efficient than the conventional steam engine, but had much less vibration and was quieter as well. When launched in 1906 into the Tyne River, the *Mauretania* showed the amazing capacity to run at a maximum speed of 26 knots. Britain was now able to regain her lost crown, and the *Mauretania* held the Blue Ribband for the Atlantic speed record for 22 years until 1929.

The *Mauretania's* exterior design of four evenly spaced funnels in a row was another unique feature—the Germans used two pairs side by side, but the new design gave the British ships a more streamlined look.

An interesting side note—there was a perception among both passengers and observers that the more funnels the better. Funnels equaled power and speed and they looked good. In later years when only three funnels were needed to vent more efficient power plants, some ships continued to use a fourth as a dummy because designers felt it added to the vessel's overall favorable impression.

The *Mauretania* also exhibited design innovation that was to have a major impact on cruise ships up to the present day. Before her time the stern of a vessel had been considered the premium space for all living accommodations. But, with the *Mauretania's* four propellers and giant steam turbine engines, for the first time the midships area was quieter and had less vibration, and this was where the best cabins as well as the major public rooms were located.

Even with this spacious layout, however, Cunard did not forget the basic principle that had guided it since Samuel Cunard started a speedy transatlantic mail service—speed always took precedence over comfort. Indeed, speed sold more tickets than comfort back then because people didn't want to be at sea any longer then they had to. So while luxury had been given a higher priority, passengers were still forced to share tables and public space was sparse. Moreover, the four funnels spaced along the length of the ship and running from top to bottom meant that there could be no grandiose public rooms. Clearly there was still room for improvement, opening the door for Cunard's biggest British competitor, the White Star Line.

The Titanic

White Star's strategy was to build even bigger and safer ships that would offer a quieter and more stable ride than ever before but be somewhat slower than the *Mauretania* and two other new Cunard liners, the *Luisitania* and the *Aquitania*. The new White Star vessels would not shake or roll in normal seas, and passengers could truly forget (except in times of nasty weather) that they were at sea instead of at their country homes in Oxford or Bath.

White Star decided to build three new ships—over 40,000 tons each—quieter, more stable, and more luxurious than anything that had been sailed the transatlantic route before. It was a bold scheme and an expensive one—since no facilities to build a ship of that size yet existed, nor were there any piers on either side of the Atlantic big enough to hold them. The ships, to be named the *Olympic*, the *Titanic*, and the *Britannic*, were to be veritable "floating palaces" with a noble and majestic profile and a good deal of open deck space (the nautical equivalent of palatial gardens). Both requirements were feasible only because safety regulations at the time called for only enough lifeboats to carry half the number of people aboard. More than that might have caused unsightly lines or occupied valuable deck space much more suitable for strolling around on a pleasant day to take in the sea air.

Although these ships were less than 100 feet longer and only 4 feet wider than the *Mauretania*, they appeared to be much larger. This illusion was accomplished by purposely abandoning the goal of setting new speed records. The company thereby freed itself of all kinds of constraints, such as weight and power, and public space and cabin size could be expanded dramatically. If you were one of the lucky 700 first-class passengers, there was always room for everything, whether it be a private corner to share a brandy or an intimate table for two in the opulent dining room or Ritz Restaurant. Indeed, a table for two was an innovative and prized amenity. The dining rooms were the largest afloat and the first to offer small private dining alcoves. The ships would also boast the largest athletic facilities afloat—electric bodybuilding equipment, a squash court with a spectators' gallery, and an indoor pool and sauna.

The maiden voyage in 1911 of the first ship of the trio, the *Olympic*, was a roaring success. She was hailed as an unprecedented event in maritime history, the dawn of a new era of sea travel. By the time the *Titanic* was ready to sail on her maiden voyage the following year, the word was out and the rich and famous were lining up to be part of the inaugural celebration. Benjamin Guggenheim was aboard, as was John Jacob Astor. They were accompanied by Bruce Ismay, White Star's managing director. One writer called the event "the millionaire's special"

The *Titanic* sailed from Southampton on April 10, 1912, with 2,228 passengers and crew. Only 705 passengers survived the voyage after the ship struck an iceberg in the North Atlantic on the night of April 15th and sank—the saddest day in the history of passenger shipping. A woman who survived the tragedy later wrote about that Sunday evening in her diary:

We dined the last night in the Ritz Restaurant. It was the last word in luxury. The tables were gay with pink roses and white daisies, the women in their beautiful shimmering gowns of satin and silk, the men immaculate and well groomed, the stringed orchestra playing music from Puccini and Tchaikovsky. The food was superb—caviar, lobster, quail from Egypt, plover's eggs, and hothouse grapes and fresh peaches. The night was cold and clear, the sea like glass. But in a few short hours every man in the room was dead except J. Bruce Ismay, Gordon Duff, and a Mr. Carter.[5]

The unthinkable had happened, the unsinkable *Titanic* had sunk, and the public and the media looked for a scapegoat. They found one in Ismay who did not go down with his own ship as did the captain, Edward Smith. Writing in the Chicago *Record-Herald* Ben Hecht composed these lines:

To hold your place in the ghastly face
Of death on the sea of night
Is a seaman's job, but to flee with the mob
Is an owner's noble right.[6]

In retrospect the *Titanic* accident should not have happened, and if anyone was to blame it was Captain Smith. In the true Cunard spirit of running on schedule, like their early mail boats, Smith decided not to slow down even when he was advised that icebergs were in the area. This breach of good seamanship and common sense caused the loss of more than a thousand lives—most of them second-class passengers and immigrants, who were kept below while the first-class women and children filled most of the seats on the few lifeboats provided.

After the *Titanic* disaster, a number of changes affecting passenger safety were instituted, including the shifting of the

---

[5]Ellen Williamson, *When We Went First Class* (p. 112). Cited in *Hospitality Today*, by Rocco M. Angelo & Andrew N. Vladimir, (East Lansing, MI, Educational Institute AH&MA 1994).

[6]John Maxtone-Graham, *The Only Way To Cross* (New York: Collier Books, Macmillan Publishing Company, 1972), p. 76.

transatlantic routes to a more southerly course, the raising of watertight bulkhead levels, and the addition of more lifeboats.

The Germans Pull Ahead

Meanwhile, in Potsdam, Kaiser Wilhelm II, a grandson of Queen Victoria, was not at all pleased with the idea of Germany losing the superiority of the seas that it had won with the *Deutschland* in 1903. He understood that having the fastest or largest navy was not enough; passenger ships were an important part of the equation that gave the British their sea power and prestige. Hamburg-Amerika's management, as frustrated as their Emperor, realized that to compete Germany would need passenger ships that were bigger, more luxurious, and, in view of the *Titanic* disaster, safer than anything the British had afloat.

To achieve their goal the Germans engaged the services of a top British hotel architect, Charles Mewès. Working with famed hotelier Céasar Ritz, Mewès had designed the famous Paris Ritz Hotel on the Place Vendôme and the Ritz in London. He had also collaborated with Ritz on an earlier German ship, the *Amerika*. If people who were crossing the Atlantic wanted to travel on a world-class floating luxurious hotel, Hamburg-Amerika, with the backing of Kaiser Wilhelm and the help of Mewés, would give it to them and recapture the prestige of the seas for Germany.

The first of these new ships, *Imperator*, was completed in 1912. Since the *Titanic* disaster had occurred before her maiden voyage, the *Imperator*'s builders implemented additional safety regulations, including more secure watertight measures and more lifeboats. Another piece of new technology, a stabilizing system using water ballast tanks, was also installed to make the ship less susceptible to rolling.

This huge ship, the largest yet built, carried a maximum of 4,000 passengers and 1,100 crew. Mounted on her prow was a grotesque bronze eagle clutching a globe with its claws and the Hamburg-Amerika slogan, *Mein Feld ist die Welt* ("My field is the world"). At a time when Prussian imperialism was already a concern many felt that there was more than a little political significance to this figurehead (which in fact looked out of place because the *Imperator's* architect had made no provision for it).

Inside the ship the decoration was pure eighteenth-century French palatial with a Teutonic flavor. Because there were only three funnels instead of four there was room for a huge social hall with a 30-foot-ceiling where all 700 first-class passengers could gather for tea or conversation. From the grand lounge, diners ascended a wide staircase to enter the Ritz-Carlton restaurant in grand style. There was not much formal entertainment on the ship. Listening to music, dancing, reading, people watching, conversation, and shuffleboard were the main forms of recreation.

By the following year, 1913, the Germans had launched the second ship in the trio the *Vaterland* (Fatherland). However, in 1914, the breakout of the war disrupted passenger shipping. The *Vaterland* was in New York at that time and was seized and converted to an American troop carrier. Some British ships, such as the *Mauretania* and the *Britannic*, were converted to armed merchant cruisers, but others continued to carry passengers. One of these, Cunard's *Luisitania*, was torpedoed and sunk by the Germans, occasioning a national holiday in Germany.

The *Imperator* was in port in Hamburg when the war broke out. The third ship in the series, the *Bismarck*, was still under construction and so all work was stopped. At the end of the war the British received the *Imperator* and the *Bismarck* as reparations, while the United States kept the *Vaterland*, which was renamed the *Leviathan*.

Michael A. Musmanno, a lawyer from Philadelphia, traveled home from England aboard the *Leviathan* in 1958 and gives us an account of the ship's cuisine in those days:

> In all the history of good eating, not even King Henry VIII feasted more felicitously than I did during that five-day journey between Southampton and New York. At seven-thirty each morning fruit juice and black coffee appeared like magic in my stateroom. At eight-thirty, in the ship's dining room, I attacked a matinal repast of cereal, eggs, bacon, potatoes, and hot cakes. At noon the table glowed, smiled, and chuckled with soup, steak, vegetables, salad, dessert, and coffee. At four o'clock tea, little sandwiches and cakes refreshed the oceanic afternoon,

and at seven each evening a royal banquet unfolded in the large dining hall where one's eyes dilated as his belt yielded to appetizers, smoked oysters, celery soup, roast fowl, vegetables, salad, nuts, fruit pie, ice cream, and demitasse. At ten o'clock— I skipped the chaffing-dish supper available to those trenchermen who had the capacity for it. . . . The voyage added nine pounds to my sparse frame.[7]

Post-War Changes in Transatlantic Travel

After the war, transatlantic traffic resumed on many of the same ships, which were refurbished for peacetime use. However, in the 1920s the United States curtailed its open-door immigration policy. Not everyone who was tired and poor was welcome and so could not be customers of steamship companies. Even though first-class passage produced pages of news, the major lines had earned most of their money from immigrants. When that business dried up they needed to find new passengers to fill their ships—a marketing problem aggravated by a post-war over-building of fleets. Cunard and other lines replaced war losses with more and larger ships in anticipation of an immigration business that never materialized. Thus, there was a major change in the kind of passengers these vessels carried.

Fortunately, the Great War had created a major interest in visiting Europe. With a strong marketing thrust immigrants were replaced by teachers, students, and tourists who wanted to visit the sites of famous battles or gaze upon Paris, Berlin, and London, cities they had viewed for the first time in war newsreels. There was another incentive for transatlantic travel: Prohibition had dried up America in 1919. For those who craved a martini, a scotch, or glass of champagne a transatlantic voyage was a trip to nirvana!

To take advantage of all of these trends, minor changes in design were necessary. What had been immigrant quarters were

---

[7]Michael A. Musmano, *Verdict! The Adventures of The Young Lawyer In the Brown Suit*, Doubleday, a division of Bantam, Doubleday, Dell Publishing Group, reprinted from *All In The Same Boat*, edited by Robert Wechler (Catbird Press, 44 North Sixth Avenue, Highland Park, N.J., 08904 1988) p. 186.

turned into "third-cabin" or "tourist-class" accommodations. Additional bars and cocktail lounges were added, and brochures prominently featured the availability of all kinds of alcoholic beverages on board.

The large luxurious ships were still the most prestigious and patronized by the rich and famous. Society columns published travel plans of celebrities and it was not uncommon for social climbers to book passage hoping to reserve a deck chair or a dining room table next to one of them. With luck, ambitious parents might light the spark for a suitable marriage. Even if one could not meet eligible companions by sitting or dining next to them there were other opportunities: Passengers organized deck tennis, billiards, potato sack races, and a host of other silly pastimes in which anyone who was willing could participate. Masquerade balls were particularly popular (and still are on some ships), and some guests spent long hours designing and making elaborate costumes with materials brought on board specifically for this event or supplied by the ship's crew.

There were no casinos on board post–World War I ships, but waging bets on everything from the outcome of games to the ship's daily mileage was a common activity. Professional gamblers soon discovered that a five-day voyage with people of means was an easy way to make a living, and lines warned their guests not to play poker with strangers. Nevertheless, these suave, sophisticated adventurers added a certain aura of excitement to the voyages and helped build the image that a large ocean liner was an exciting place to be.

In short, spending a week at sea was no longer something to be avoided but was turning into *the* fashionable thing to do. This newfound cachet was enhanced by the widespread press coverage of the lavish (and expensive) first-class life-style, where one could eat lavishly, drink and party into the late hours, and form significant relationships with desirable companions. Thus, transatlantic voyages during this era attracted the rich, powerful, and famous from all over the world. They were now the grandest of travel experiences.

What a phenomenal transformation! In a matter of a few short years ocean voyages went from a dreaded, uncomfortable, and life-threatening experience, to a wonderful trip. And the clientele went from the downtrodden to high society.

Sadly, however, the pendulum swung too far. Because of all the press and public interest on the first-class voyage experience, the broadest perception was that this type of type of travel was only for a very few. Moreover those few, to the common man, were stuffy swells, intimidating or boring or both.

More Cruises Are Offered

The Great Depression, which began in 1929, prompted many companies such as Holland America and the Italian Line to minimize their losses by sending their ships on cruises, thereby reducing unneeded transatlantic capacity. Given the state of the economy and prohibition, the market was ripe for short cheap "booze" cruises to Nova Scotia, Nassau, and Bermuda. The ships offering these excursions were not really suited for cruising. They were obsolete and could no longer compete with the newer ocean liners. They lacked the necessary air conditioning for cruising in warm waters, and their dark, enclosed design discouraged sunbathing, swimming, and other resort-type activities.

By the end of the thirties short, inexpensive cruises were but one segment of an even larger cruise market. Fancier and more modern ships were deployed cruising, and thus longer, more expensive, and more lavish itineraries were fashioned. Unfortunately, these more elaborate cruises reinforced the elitist image that had evolved from the first-class transatlantic voyages of the twenties. One can just imagine the passenger composition when the French liner *Normandie* sailed in 1939 from New York to Rio de Janeiro on a month-long cruise chartered by American Express.

Regarded by many as the most beautiful ship of all time, the *Normandie* was the quintessential ocean liner. She was built in 1935 at an extravagant cost, and featured the grandest staircase at sea entering an air-conditioned dining room 400 feet long. Original art commissioned by the French Line for the *Normandie* was the most expensive sea-going collection. Every stateroom was uniquely decorated—one was even done in sparkling stainless steel—and the suites featured grand pianos and, of course, more original works of art.

With the fall of France in 1939 the *Normandie* took refuge in New York harbor. While she was being converted to a troop ship renamed the *Lafayette*, she caught fire, capsized, and was lost.

Credit for glamorizing warm-weather cruising goes to the Italians. Specifically, the Italian Line built two large ships, the *Rex* and the *Conte di Savola*, which began operations with transatlantic cruises from New York to Italy. These itineraries necessarily entailed several days of warm-weather cruising in the Mediterranean, and so the ships were lighter-toned, more open, and thus more resort-like. With unusual marketing savvy, Italian Line posters were the first to portray gaily dressed passengers pursuing vacation activities. At the same time the Germans lines showed serious-looking businessmen and their fashionable spouses strolling the decks.

Despite the fact that the focus was now shifting from crossing the Atlantic to cruising, and that passengers were mostly Americans, the steamship business was still dominated by European interests. American companies were generally not trendsetters, since they had never seriously competed for the transatlantic market.

There were, however, several niches that American-owned steamship companies filled nicely. The Matson Line offered service from San Francisco to Hawaii and the South Pacific; the Grace Line sailed to the Caribbean and South America; Moore McCormick also sailed to South America; and American Export Lines managed to offer transatlantic voyages as well as extended cruises to Mediterranean.

On the other side of the Atlantic the cruise business was being developed for the same reasons it was in America—too many ships and not enough passengers and immigrants to fill them. Seasonal cruises went from England, France, Italy, and Germany to Scandinavia and the Mediterranean. Had World War II not intervened, cruising in Europe might have become far more developed than it is today.

There were also a series of annual world cruises by Cunard, Canadian Pacific, and the Red Star Line, a subsidiary of the same group that owned White Star. The brochures for these world cruises stressed the ports to be visited rather than the experience of being aboard. Cole Porter and Moss Hart went around world on Cunard's *Franconia* in 1935. This was one of the ships built to replace war losses.

One pivotal ship during this period was the 40,000-ton *Empress of Britain*. Built by Canadian Pacific, she was the first major liner built for a dual purpose: in the winter a world cruise carrying only 400 passengers; in the summer express service from Southampton to Quebec with a passenger load of 1,100, many of course traveling second and third class. The *Empress* was a truly elegant ship, influenced by the design characteristic of Canadian Pacific's grand hotels built during the same period. Her amenities included a full-sized tennis court. Unfortunately, her funnels were not long enough and often scattered soot all over the passengers. Canadian Pacific also used the *Empress of Australia* for her world cruises. This was one of the ships taken from Germany as part of war reparations.

Britain's largest passenger shipping company in those years was the venerable Cunard Line. Among its extensive trans-atlantic fleet were its two largest and notable liners, the *Queen Mary* and *Queen Elizabeth*. The *Queen Mary*, built in 1934, had the ambiance and glamor of a stately London hotel. Today she is a major tourist attraction berthed in Long Beach, California, and though somewhat modified she can still provide the flavor of crossing the Atlantic in the thirties. The *Queen Mary* is the only surviving liner from this era.

Her sister, the *Queen Elizabeth*, launched in 1940 was the largest passenger ship ever built. At 80,000 tons, that distinction has already been lost however, since Carnival launched the first 100,000-gross-registered-tonnage cruise ship, *Carnival Destiny*, to be followed by a 106,000 ton vessel, the *Grand Princess* of Princess Cruise Lines, as well as a Carnival sister to the *Carnival Destiny*, the *Carnival Triumph*.

World War II and the Post-War Boom

With the outbreak of World War II, all of the major steamship lines converted their ships to troop carriers or stayed in port. Only the Swedish Line, whose country was neutral, continued as usual. Eventually however, everything afloat was taken over for troop transfer. Even the Swedish Lines *Gripsholm* was sold to the United States. Crossing and cruising closed down for the duration and would never be the same again.

Americans Join the Fray

After the war came the boom. The rebuilding of Europe spurred a growing demand for transportation to Europe for both tourists and business travelers, and there were many refugees to be resettled in the United States and Canada. The steamship business became enormously profitable, but all the profits were going to Cunard, the French Line, and other European lines. Why was the United States left out of the picture? The answer is simple: The European lines were operating ships whose construction had been heavily subsidized by their governments. The United States had no significant passenger fleet because government shipbuilding subsidies applied strictly to the U.S. Navy. Nevertheless, the war had clearly demonstrated the need for ships that could be quickly converted to troop carriers. Something had to be done.

The United States realized it might need additional troop ships and so began subsidizing the building and operation of new vessels. American Export Lines built two ships, the *Independence* in 1951 and the *Constitution* at Bethlehem Steel's Fore River Shipyard in Quincy, Massachusetts. These were 30,000-ton vessels, specifications for which required that they be able to sail at 25 knots from Norfolk, Virginia, to Capetown, South Africa, without refueling.

American Export quickly established itself as a luxury American ship line. While the *Independence* crossed the North Atlantic and cruised the world, the *Constitution* cruised from New York to Italy, visiting the ports of Gibraltar and Cannes en route. In 1956, when actress Grace Kelly became the Princess of Monaco, she sailed on the *Constitution* with her wedding party.

These two ships were retired from service in 1967 when American Export discontinued its passenger service. Both ships were sold, refurbished, and one still sails today—the *Independence*—on inter-Hawaiian island cruises under the flag of the America Hawaii Line.

In 1951, Congress appropriated the funds to subsidize the building of a state-of-the art Transatlantic liner, the *United States*, which was designed with two purposes: to provide fast troop ship capability after quick conversion and to display superior (albeit delayed) American ingenuity and technology to the world. The *United States* was one of our country's more significant ego trips. Many of her design and performance details were kept confidential to ensure that other governments would not try to steal her thunder. However, because she was designed and built to be faster then any other passenger ship afloat, concessions had to be made. Despite the owners' desire to make her a luxury liner she was in fact quite austere. She offered little open deck space (which obviously would be of little use on a troop carrier), and her watertight doors were not disguised or concealed, which contributed to her spartan look. Even so, she could do 40 knots, and on her first crossing in the summer of 1952 she beat the *Queen Mary's* record by a full 10 hours, completing her eastbound voyage in 3 days, 10 hours, and 40 minutes. As a result, she secured the Blue Riband for the United States, which we retain to this day because of that singular performance.

By the 1950s the future of the steamship business seemed clearly established. Companies like Swedish American built new ships with spacious cabins and marketed them heavily to the tourist trade. Another American line, Moore McCormack, launched the *Argentina* and *Brazil* in 1957, both of which sailed on liner and cruise routes to South America. The Grace Line also launched passenger-cargo ships, all of which carried the "Santa M" nomenclature The *Santa Maria* and the *Santa Mercedes* later operated as the *Veendam* and *Volendam* for Holland American, the *Monarch Sun* and *Monarch Star* for Monarch Cruise Lines (now defunct), and the *Enchanted Isle* and *Enchanted Seas* of Commodore Cruise Lines.

Transatlantic passenger boardings built steadily after World War II, reaching their peak in 1957. In 1958, however, Pan American offered the first nonstop transatlantic crossing when its Boeing 707 jet left New York's Idlewild airport in the evening and touched down early the next morning. This seminal event effectively sounded the death knell for the transatlantic steamship business. While a few ships after 1958 were built the transatlantic market (most notably the *Empress of Canada* in 1960, the *S.S. France* in 1962, the *QE2* in 1967, and the *Mikhail Lermentov* in 1973); the majority of new ship construction now had cruising in mind. Examples include Holland America's *Rotterdam* (1959,

38,645 tons) and Norwegian American's *Sagafjord* (1965, 25,147 tons) and *Vistafjord* (1973, 24,492 tons). Other cruise-specific vessels included Incres' *Victoria* and Chandris' *Amerikanis*.

As transatlantic boardings declined in the 1960s the companies that did not redeploy their fleets began to take on water. The list of fatalities include Canadian Pacific, Furness Bermuda, United States Lines, Hamburg-America Line, and Swedish American Line.

The Advent of Modern Cruising

Ted Arison, a young Israeli from Tel Aviv, had fought in Israel's War of Independence as a colonel in the Israeli army. In 1966, retired after starting and then losing two air cargo businesses, he was calling on friends in the shipping business who owned two car ferries that were under charter as cruise ships in Miami, the *Bilu* and *Nili*. The charterer was a Miami cruise pioneer, Leslie Frazer.

While Arison was visiting, a telex from Frazer came in advising that his business was not doing well and was facing serious financial problems. Arison volunteered that this was clearly a negotiating tactic by Frazer to secure a lower charter fee and suggested to the ferry owners that since he knew the charter business he would be glad to go to Miami to take over their ships and run them. "He was basically bluffing" recalls his son Micky, now Carnival's Chairman, "because he in fact knew nothing about the passenger cruise business." Sure enough, a day later Frazer sent another telex asking for a lower fee. Rather than accept this, the owners canceled Frazer's charter and Arison flew to Miami to manage the ships.

As in Arison's other ventures, lady luck was not with him, and his Israeli partners went bankrupt from losses in business interests in Europe. The Israeli government, which held a first mortgage on the ships, foreclosed and ordered the ships back to Israeli waters, where they would be available in case of military emergency. This move left Arison with a cruise line consisting of a sales and marketing organization and no ships.

While perusing a stack of trade publications—the remnants of his now defunct shipping business—he saw a picture in *Travel*

Weekly of a brand-new ship, the *Sunward*, which had been pur-pose-built by a Norwegian, Knut Kloster, to sail to Gibraltar. However, Gibraltar was having political difficulties and the ship was unable to operate. Arison called Kloster and explained that Kloster's ship was very much like the *Nili*, which he, Arison, had just lost and that he had future passenger bookings but no ves-sel to carry them. He suggested that if Kloster would send the *Sunward* to Miami they could both make some money. Kloster agreed but only on the condition that Arison guarantee him a half a million a year in profit. Arison agreed and sent Kloster a telex guaranteeing him the sum.

Of course, Arison didn't have that kind of money, but Kloster didn't know that, so the *Sunward* moved to Florida to offer 3- and 4-day cruises, entering service on December 19th, 1966. This arrangement between Arison and Kloster was really a partner-ship between Arison Shipping Company, Arison's management company, a general sales agency, and Kloster Rederi, Knut Kloster's Norwegian firm, which owned the *Sunward*. While they did business under the name Norwegian Caribbean Lines (NCL), in reality there was no such entity.

By 1968 business was doing well enough that a second ship, the *Starward*, was added to the fleet. It had two decks of ferry space, so cruise passengers were located on the outer part of the ship near the portholes and the inner spaces were utilized for a roll-on roll-off cargo service between Florida and Jamaica. Busi-ness continued to expand and two more ships were added: the *Skyward* in 1969 and the *Southward* in 1971.

With her fleet of four modern cruise ships operating regu-larly from Miami on a year-round basis, NCL's enterprise repre-sented the beginning of the cruise business as we know it today.

From the start, Arison and Kloster realized that a national marketing campaign would be a key to their success. There were simply not enough prospects living in Florida to fill their cabins every week. The large (at the time) weekly capacity of 3,000 plus berths forced NCL to reach out for prospects in other parts of the country. In so doing, NCL transformed South Florida con-temporary cruising from a regionally marketed hodgepodge of very old ships, built originally to weather the North Atlantic wa-ters, to a nationally marketed contemporary vacation product featuring brand-new vessels designed for Caribbean cruising.

The Competitors

Like any successful new concept, this fast-growing market quickly attracted competition. Sandy Chobol, a Miami real estate developer and hotelier, recognized the potential for converting hotel landlubbers to sailors and founded Commodore Cruise Lines. He brought in a new combination ferry-cruiser, the *Boheme*, in 1968 on year-round 7-day cruises. The *Boheme* was built in Finland and owned by Olaf Wallenis, a ship owner, who liked opera names for his vessels. At the time she was called the *Aida*. Chobol and his general manager, Ed Stephan, did not like that name and changed it to *Boheme*. This was also the name of an opera, but it suggested a carefree, bohemian way of life. The ship was an overnight success.

After leaving Commodore Cruise Lines, Ed Stephan decided to pursue a dream to found his own line. Stephan, originally from Madison, Wisconsin, had started as a bell captain at the Casablanca Hotel on Miami Beach and had worked his way up to General Manager of the Biscayne Terrace Hotel. He also taught hotel management at Lindsey Hopkins Vocational School. In time he was offered the job of General Manager for Yarmouth Cruise Lines by Jules Sokoloff, a Canadian living in Jamaica who had two ships, the *Yarmouth* and the *Yarmouth Castle*. (History buffs may recall that on November 13th, 1962, the *Yarmouth Castle* burned and sank, killing 89 people. While the cause of the fire was never pinpointed, several officials believed it was the work of an arsonist. This belief was based on cross-referencing employment records, which revealed that one crew member on board the *Yarmouth Castle* had previously worked on other cruise ships that had also experienced unexplained fires. Fortunately, this was the last major catastrophe involving cruise ship passengers in North American waters. The ship was old, built in 1929, and of largely wooden construction. It would not have been allowed to sail, let alone carry passengers, given today's much tougher safety standards.)

While between jobs, Stephan produced some designs and plans for a new cruise line. In 1967, at the suggestion of a ship broker employed by Fearnley & Egar, Stephan took these plans to Oslo, Norway, where they impressed two prominent Norwegian shipping executives, Sigor Skaugen and Anders Wilhelmsen. The two decided to invest in Stephan's concept, which was the beginning of another industry giant, Royal Caribbean Cruise Lines (RCCL). Later Gotaas Larsen, a subsidiary of International Utilities in Canada, bought a one-third share of RCCL. "Harry Larsen, the chairman, had to pay one-third of all expenses since the beginning of the company to consummate the deal," recalls Peter Whelpton, RCCL's Executive Vice President.

RCCL quickly launched a modern fleet of three vessels destined for year-round Caribbean sailings from Miami. These vessels incorporated Ed Stephan's design innovations, including a sleek, yacht-like profile and an observation lounge located in the ship's funnel, high above the superstructure, which was inspired by Seattle's Space Needle. The first, *Song of Norway*, entered weekly service in 1970, followed by the *Nordic Prince* and the *Sun Viking* in 1971 and 1972.

The latter ships originally offered 14-day cruises departing from Miami on alternate Saturdays. From an operation and marketing standpoint, the plan was simplicity itself: Every Saturday two RCCL ships debarked and embarked passengers in Miami. Travel agents and customers alike quickly realized that each and every week you could take a one- or two-week Royal Caribbean cruise. The marketing was further simplified by several other innovative ideas. First, unlike previous entrants into the market, Royal Caribbean started promoting her ships a full year before the first one went into service. This provided enough time to fill the ships well before they operated. In contrast, the *Sunward* had had only a few weeks of advance marketing.

Next, rather then scattering their promotional efforts over a large area, Royal Caribbean concentrated on two major markets. This allowed for maximal efficiency of sales and promotional efforts and reduced costs by chartering and filling back-to-back, widebodied aircraft departing weekly from Los Angeles and San Francisco. RCCL passed on these savings to their guests, thus creating a terrific travel bargain for the time.

While Royal Caribbean Cruise Lines was building ships for cruising in the Caribbean, another group of Norwegian investors, headed by Bergen Line, decided to launch a new line with three luxurious ships built especially for world travel. They recruited Warren Titus, the first president of P&O Lines in

North America, to found their company, which was to be called Royal Viking Line. The concept was worldwide cruises that were expensive but luxurious. Royal Viking soon had a fleet of three ships, the *Royal Viking Star*, brought into service in 1972, and the *Royal Viking Sky* and *Royal Viking Sea*, which began sailing in 1973. Unlike the other lines operating at the time, says Titus, "our marketing approach was based not only on tapping existing markets but going after and rewarding those people who cruised with us repeatedly." Their method was to introduce the Skald Club at the very outset, which offered special programs for repeat passengers. (Remember, this was ten years before the first airline frequent-flyer program.) Titus recalls that by the time he left the company in 1987 to found Seabourn Cruise Lines, Royal Viking's repeat factor was well over 50 percent per cruise and 65 to 70 percent on longer cruises.

An incredibly complex web of relationships spawned the rapid growth of the cruise line industry. The *Yarmouth* of Yarmouth Cruise Lines, had been acquired from a Canadian-born Seattle businessman, Stanley B. McDonald, who ran package tours combining a cruise with land options—California to Oregon, British Columbia, and the Seattle World's Fair (which is where Stephan first saw the Space Needle when he acquired the ship). McDonald's venture had been so successful that it inspired him to try winter cruises to Mexico. In 1965 he chartered another ship, Canadian Pacific's 6,000-ton *Princess Patricia*, and named his company Princess Cruises. During the winters of 1965 and 1966 the "Princess Pat" pioneered cruising to Mexico's West Coast and became an overnight success. After two highly successful seasons and demand far exceeding the capacity of the small vessel, Princess Cruises chartered the newly completed Italian ship *M/S Italia* and renamed her the *Princess Italia*.

By 1972, Princess had added two more ships to their fleet, the *Princess Carla* and the *Island Princess*. But then came the recession and the Arab oil embargo. The cash-strapped company was saved by a takeover bid from the London-based Peninsular & Oriental Steam Navigation Company, the same P&O that in 1844 had pioneered the business by offering the world's first cruise. P&O decided to keep the newer *Island Princess* but replaced the older ships with two newer ones, the *Sun Princess* and the *Pacific Princess*.

Cruising's Revolutionizers

In 1977, an event occurred that would make Princess the best known cruise line in North America and, at the same time, popularize the idea of cruising as a mass-market vacation to such extent that virtually every cruise ship afloat at the time benefited. A television production company, Aaron Spelling Productions, had the idea that a luxury cruise ship would be an ideal setting for a TV series. They approached Princess, which was located on the West Coast near Hollywood, and Princess agreed to make their two ships, the *Island Princess* and the *Pacific Princess* available for the show. Veteran actor Gavin McLeod (also known for his portrayal of Murray on the Mary Tyler Moore Show) was cast as Captain Merril Stubing. "Stubing" was picked by a writer who was a baseball fan and remembered a great ball player with the same name. "Thank God, I hit a home run," McLeod says.

The producer, Douglas Cramer, told McLeod that every episode would consist of three stories, one sophisticated, one a farce, and one poignant. McLeod liked the idea but insisted that every story in every show have a happy ending because as the captain, he wanted to be the paternal figure who at the end made everyone feel good. He felt then, as he does today, that television should offer programs that help people who are trapped at home in dull jobs to escape, to travel, and become vicarious adventurers. "There's nothing on TV today that makes me cheer," he says wistfully.

McLeod, who had never set foot on a cruise ship, recalls that when filming began the experience exceeded his expectations. He was absolutely astounded that the ships had real elevators. "The Love Boat" attracted a worldwide audience and created a public-relations bonanza for Princess and the fledgling cruise industry. "It made you feel good" says McLeod, "and that's very important." The series continued in production for ten and a half years and is still in syndication all over the world.

Another revolutionizer of the cruise business in the early days was a company that traces it roots back as far as 1860, to an Italian olive oil producer named Giacomo Costa. The Costa family's business prospered so much that by 1924 they had bought their first freighter to ship their olive oil, and in 1948 they entered the passenger business with the *Anna C.*, the first post-war Italian luxury liner. In 1959 the company moved into the American market with the *Franca C.*, offering 13-day cruises from Miami.

By 1968 Costa was firmly established in the U.S. market and decided to reposition the *Franca C.* to San Juan, Puerto Rico, to offer lower Caribbean cruises from there. There was only one problem that needed to be solved—how to induce people from the Northeast to go to San Juan to embark on a cruise. The answer was logical and earthshaking in its ultimate impact: Sell the cruise together with the airplane trip as an air/sea packaged vacation. Costa did just that by teaming up with Simmons Group Journeys of New York and pioneering weekly air/sea programs from Puerto Rico.

Air/sea programs are without doubt a key component in the success of today's cruise industry. They are now offered by virtually all cruise lines in one form or another. Basically, the cruise is packaged with a round-trip air fare between the passenger's home city and the port of embarkation. A hotel room is also included if necessary because of flight scheduling, as are ground transfers between the airport and the seaport.

While the year-round cruising business was building a steady stream of regular customers from the East Coast, in the western part of the country a young tour operator named Chuck West was building a seasonal cruise operation along Alaska's Inside Passage. A former bush pilot for Wein Airlines, West had originally founded a travel agency to promote Alaska tour packages. He soon realized that the best way to see Alaska was by sea, so he first chartered and then bought a fleet of ships under the banner "Alaska Cruise Lines," which departed from Vancouver, British Columbia, and visited Glacier Bay and other ports in combination with a railway trip through the mountains. West's cruise line was part of his overall tour operation, which he called Westours.

By 1970, West was popularly referred to as "Mr. Alaska" (a title he still retains in the industry). He was also president of the American Society of Travel Agents and owned four small cruise ships, a motorcoach company, and several Alaskan hotels. West had opened up Alaska not only to mass tourism but also to the cruise industry as visitors returned with stories of seeing up close icebergs "calfing," bald eagles nesting, and herds of moose grazing contentedly . . . from their vantage points on cruise ships.

Unfortunately, by expanding so rapidly, West had overextended himself and by 1970 he was over his head financially. His controller, Kirk Lanterman (now President of Holland America Line), was forced to chop personnel by one-third and institute other cost-saving measures, but they were not enough. West had a million-dollar payment due on his newest ship, the *West Star*, and no funds to make it with.

The 1970 World Congress of the American Society of Travel Agents (ASTA), over which West presided, was held in Amsterdam. During a social event, West met Nico Van der Vorm from the venerable Holland America Line, who expressed an interest in buying Westours. "The Dutch possessed the one cruise-tour component that was vital to the future of Westours and I had not been able to supply—large efficient ships," says West. "They knew how to manage those ships economically and profitably." West sold his company to Holland America that same fall and left the company shortly after. He remains in the cruise tour business in Alaska with a new company called Alaska Sightseeing/Cruise West, headed by his son Richard.

The Rise of Carnival

In the summer of 1971 Knut Kloster served notice that NCL intended to terminate Ted Arison's ten-year contract at the end of the year. The contract stipulated that if Kloster didn't make $1.5 million for two years in a row, he had the option to cancel the deal. Jealousy had been forming in Miami between Kloster's Norwegian employees and Arison's Americans. According to Ted's son Micky Arison, even though the Norwegian company was very profitable they felt their American partners were making too much. So, it was alleged, the Norwegians, aware of the contract provision, decided to sabotage Arison's profits by purchasing needed equipment such as deck chairs and engine parts and then throwing them overboard. This ensured that the inventory would not exist on the ship, throwing a shadow on Arison's integrity and guaranteeing that he would not be able to deliver the agreed-on profit because the nonexistent inventory would not show up on the balance sheet. These allegations later came out in the discovery process of a lawsuit between the two parties. In any case, Arison did not meet his profit for the second year and Kloster, as predicted, canceled the contract.

Because Arison Shipping Company's cash flow stemmed from NCL's advance ticket sales, Arison quickly moved to protect himself by seizing all advance moneys on hand at the various NCL sales offices around the country. He believed that the cancellation of his contract was not valid and that he was entitled to his commission, which amounted to 18 percent of the gross revenue. The lawsuit was eventually settled out of court, with Arison agreeing to return half of the funds he had seized. The rest legitimately belonged to him as a result of the Norwegians actions.

As 1971 was drawing to a close, Arison once again found himself with a cruise line but no ships. So, with the funds he had withdrawn from NCL bank accounts, he immediately set off for Europe, where, he had learned, two older Cunard ships, the *Carmania* and *Franconia*, had been retired from service and were laid up in England. Wasting no time, he prepared ads for his new "golden fleet" of two ships. He asked his employees to stick with him and have faith, as he would soon start a new company, but most didn't believe him. Micky Arison remembers standing with his father on the last day of business as former employees and friends filed out of the building. Only a handful took Arison at his word; the others knew Kloster had the ships and they wanted to get paid at the end of the week. A few loyal employees, including Mike Zonis, now Carnival's Senior Vice President of Operations, decided to abandon the security of Kloster-NCL for the uncharted waters of a nameless, shipless company.

Arison was unable to work out a deal with Cunard and his plan had to be abandoned. Depressed, he talked to his friend Jacob Victor, of Technical Marine Planning, a firm of naval architects (which Carnival retains to this day). Victor suggested he look at another laid-up vessel, the Canadian Pacific liner *Empress of Canada*. Lacking the capital to buy it, Arison turned to his old schoolmate and pal from Israel, Meshulam Riklis, an ultra-successful entrepreneur at the time who chaired a multibillion dollar conglomerate, Rapid American Corporation. Riklis was also the principal shareholder in a Boston-based travel operation, American International Travel Service, which operated group and individual tours to Hawaii, South America, Europe, and other destinations using the name *Carnival*. There was a Hawaiian Carnival program, a Rio Carnival program, and others.

Arison convinced Riklis to set up an AITS subsidiary, Carnival Cruise Lines, to own and operate the *Empress of Canada*. The line would be financed by the $1 million Arison had seized from NCL. The subsidiary renamed the ship *Mardi Gras*, consistent with the Carnival name. Arison's sales and marketing team, remnants of the NCL management, positioned her as "the Flagship of the Golden Fleet" on the basis of their expectation of obtaining the two Cunard ships, which were painted yellow (and two of them could be considered a fleet). Unfortunately, the *Empress of Canada* wasn't golden, she was white, and of course there was no longer to be a fleet, but it was too late to change anything.

When the *Mardi Gras* entered service on March 7, 1972, she ran aground on her maiden voyage in Government Cut, at the tip of Miami Beach. She sat there, ignominiously, for 24 hours in plain view of thousands of vacationers who crowded the beach to gawk at her before she was refloated. On her maiden cruise, because of nonexistent cash flow, Ted Arison didn't have the funds to refuel her in San Juan for her voyage home. After unsuccessfully wining and dining his Puerto Rican suppliers hoping to obtain credit, he actually collected money from the bar cash registers on board and had the advance deposits for future cruises wired to him from Miami to purchase the fuel he needed to send the *Mardi Gras* home.

For the first year and a half, two of the four decks of the *Mardi Gras'* passenger cabins were being converted from two-class transatlantic service to one-class cruising. This entailed sailing while a crew of several hundred plumbers and carpenters installed compact showers and toilets. During this period, the company lost millions of dollars as the *Mardi Gras* sailed on a sea of red ink. In the late fall of 1973 the "Golden Fleet" positioning was scrapped as inappropriate shortly after Bob Dickinson arrived at the company. The question then became what slogan or positioning to replace it with.

Dickinson gathered all the cruise brochures then on the market and noticed that one stood out: Commodore's "Happy Ship," the *Boheme*. This idea appealed to Dickinson because the cruise slogan applied to a specific ship and not the company. After all, the ship, not the company, is what people buy. "Happy" was taken and it sounded kind of wussy anyhow! What is the one universal question—the one ingredient everyone wants in their vacation, FUN! And, fortunately, the *Mardi Gras*, at the time backed up that idea. Being 50 percent larger than her competition, she had the space to provide activities and entertainment choices for everyone. With the "Fun Ship" positioning, the ship itself became a destination and the ports of call became green stamps.

This was a total reversal of previous cruise marketing. Up to that time, cruise promotion had been destination driven. But less than 1 percent of the public had been on a cruise, and the vast majority were leery of this unknown concept. By focusing on the ship rather than the ports of call, Carnival could communicate to the public what the experience of the ship and cruising on her was all about. Thus, the "story" of what a vacationer could expect on board was a very saleable one. Moreover, Micky Arison recalls, because the *Mardi Gras* was very old, Carnival was forced to price her low, and these low prices attracted a younger crowd that had not been able to afford to cruise and were drawn to the fun experience of Carnival. They viewed it as a departure from the typical idea of stodgy ships whose average passenger age was deceased. The repositioning worked, and Carnival turned its first profit in 1975.

Like a man on a roll at a craps table Ted Arison took the profit and immediately bought the *Mardi Gras'* sister ship, the *Empress of Britain*, putting her into service on February 7, 1976, as the *Carnivale*. To make room for her at the port of Miami, Carnival shifted the *Mardi Gras* to Sunday sailings. This was a very controversial move at the time. No one had offered Sunday departures before because the conventional wisdom said there would be little demand. Yet today about half of the 7-day cruises sailing from North American ports depart on Sunday.

Incredibly, the *Carnivale* made money in her first year of operation. Once again, Arison, ever the optimist, began scouring the world for a third ship. He found the *S.A. Vaal*, a South African passenger/cargo vessel, and bought her sight unseen, negotiating with the Japanese to have her rebuilt in Kobe.

This was the first time that the Japanese had built or rebuilt a deep-water cruise ship, and taking advantage of their eagerness to get into the business, Arison negotiated an extremely favorable price of $16–18 million, to be paid in Japanese yen.

However, by the time Carnival took delivery the cost had risen to $30 million. "We learned our lesson on currency fluctuation," Micky Arison recalls. "We lost money tremendously because we didn't hedge the yen and I'm sure they did." At the same time, Carnival was negotiating with the Kobe yard on another building project for about $40 million. Again, because of the movement on the yen, by the time the project was finalized in 1978 the cost was more like $80–90 million.

This was simply too expensive, and Carnival was forced to turn to Europe for its shipbuilding needs. Since that time, Carnival has spent over $4 billion in European shipbuilding contracts, and the Japanese yards have built only one ship for the North American market, the *Crystal Harmony* (owned incidentally by a Japanese firm, NYK Industries). Carnival executives believe that as much as they've tried, Japanese shipyards are still not competitive with European yards in terms of price and quality.

Sitmar and Cunard

At about the same time that Carnival Cruise Lines was being formed, John Bland was charged with the unenviable task of establishing a new cruise North America brand, Sitmar, with two large ex-Cunard vessels refurbished and renamed the *Fairwind* and *Fairsea*. As president of this fledgling operation, Bland had little time or money to accomplish the task, and as a result early voyages of these 900+ passenger vessels sailed with few guests. A marketing gimmick was needed and Bland devised a great one. He priced his one-week cruises with air supplements that were so much lower than the cost of the airline ticket that prospective vacationers could easily grasp the value. Sitmar's air add-ons from New York to Fort Lauderdale, for example, were $20 per person, about 10 percent of the ticket price. The ships filled almost overnight, and the Sitmar brand gained recognition because of this pricing deal. Once on board the two Sitmar vessels, passengers quickly appreciated the Italian food and service. Successfully launched, Bland was able to ratchet up his rates over time and make a profit. Through pricing actions and a great product, Sitmar was transformed from a "bottom feeder," priced below the Miami-based cruise lines (the contemporary or mass-market segment of the business), to a high-priced, traditional, upscale line.

Cunard, of transatlantic fame, decided to enter the cruise business on a year-round basis by building two 600-passenger vessels, the *Ambassador* and *Adventurer*, in 1970 and 1971. These ships operated one-week contemporary cruises from Fort Lauderdale and San Juan, competing with NCL, Royal Caribbean, and later Carnival. Recognizing that the ships were too small to be particularly profitable, Cunard replaced them with the 800-passenger sister vessels, the *Cunard Countess* and *Cunard Princess*.

Cunard had a unique marketing challenge, as these ships carried the same brand name as the only other ship in their fleet at the time, the *Queen Elizabeth 2 (QE2)*. The hardware was decidedly different and, because of the lower price point, so was the software (food quality, service levels, entertainment, and other amenities).

Home Lines and the Fall of New York

From 1966 onward, New York was slowly and inexorably losing its grip as the number-one passenger port in the United States. The Port of Miami garnered this honor in 1974 and has held it ever since. A good lesson in the demise of the Port of New York is Home Lines, which in its heyday in the sixties and seventies offered seven-day Bermuda cruises on the *Homeric* from May to November (some including Nassau as a unique extra destination) as well as longer cruises to the Caribbean during the fall and winter. Home Lines identified itself as a Manhattan-based line—not only were its headquarters there but so were the departures of all of its ships. However, the market shifted to Miami (which was much closer to the popular Caribbean destinations) the line was slow to reposition its vessels southward.

The Miami-based lines had a huge geographical advantage— being two to three days steaming time closer to warm weather. Moreover, they didn't have to traverse the rough seas of the North Atlantic on their way south. Sailing from Miami, ships are in the lee of the Bahamian islands, which protect them from the possible swells of the open ocean.

On the other hand, folks from the Northeast had to fly to Miami. This was not what New York–area cruisers were used to, having always driven to their ships. Also, travel agents didn't view these people as willing to fly, which is why the Miami-based cruise industry had had a very difficult time penetrating the New York market. The breakthrough came when the Miami lines stopped targeting the New York cruisers and went after the fly/land vacationers.

Moreover, and perhaps more important, during the late seventies and into the eighties, Home Lines focused its marketing and sales efforts in their traditional area, the Northeast, and, critically, to their past passengers. Naturally their market eventually died! Today, New York continues to be the seasonal home for Bermuda-bound cruises as well as a few seasonal cruises to New England and the Canadian Maritime Provinces. But its days as the hub for transatlantic travel and the cruise capital of the world are long gone.

Florida remains the cruise capital of the world as this book goes to press, and it probably will continue as that well into the future. Even so, nothing is forever, and cruise ships, unlike hotels, can be moved as new ports develop, as ships are redeployed, and as the infrastructure of new home ports evolves. In the meantime, many of the preemptive strikes in the battle for a larger share of the vacation dollar will be launched by the cruise industry from the Port of Miami and its sister ports of Fort Lauderdale, Cape Canaveral, and Tampa.

2

Coming About

The foundation of the modern cruise industry

Somehow, without too many people noticing, cruising has grown phenomenally in the last 25 years—from a mere half a million passengers a year in 1970 to over 5 million in 1995. During this time cruising has been far and away the fastest-growing segment of the entire travel and tourism industry in the United States—outpacing hotels, restaurants, and theme parks. Thousands of people who hadn't the foggiest idea of what a cruise ship was, or what happened aboard one, who had never seen an ocean before, and who had never left Fargo, North Dakota, or other urban and rural communities, are now finding themselves at sea.

Cruising in the Seventies

In the early 1970s, what few cruise passengers there were came from large—typically coastal—cities. If you lived in New York or Los Angeles, because of your proximity to the ocean, you might well have been able to imagine a trip across that limitless horizon, and even have some familiarity with deep-water vessels, even if they were only the ferries to Staten Island or Sausilito.

The early passengers were something like pioneers, we suppose, the first to try out this new-fangled product. Their primary motivation was to see new places that they had only read about or seen pictures of in *Life, Look,* and *National Geographic*—the fabled pink-sand beaches of Bermuda, the great sugar plantations of Jamaica, and the old Spanish forts and rain forests of Puerto Rico. And there were bargain prices to be had on perfumes, cognac, and champagne from France, watches from Switzerland, and of course rum distilled on the islands. (The Bacardi Distillery is still one of the most popular tours in Puerto Rico).

Cruising in those days was viewed primarily as a novel way to travel to interesting places, conferring at the same time a certain status on the travelers, who were often the same people to acquire the first color television sets among their circles of acquaintances. The ship itself, however, was merely a by-product of what was basically a sightseeing vacation. Although early slogans promised that getting there was half the fun, in truth much of this was largely wishful thinking. Getting there was often rough if the weather was inclement, crowded as the ships were small, and even boring if there were not enough activities on board. Cruise lines hawked their wares by touting the ports of call—Port au Prince, where you could shop for crafts in the Iron Market; banana and coconut plantations in Montego Bay; and even an active volcano in St. Lucia. There was little said about the cruise itself.

Changing Lifestyles; Changing Passengers; Changing Cruises

Veterans of this business observe that while early cruises were different from those of today, many things remains the same. "We do today essentially what we did then," says Rod McLeod, Royal Caribbean's Executive Vice President of Marketing, Sales, and Passenger Services. "The only things that have changed are the type of people we do it for and the way that we do it." He adds, "We have to do it differently because the people have changed. One example is how we handle smokers. There was no issue then, for instance, about smoking in the dining room."

Smoking

Smoking is a single but dramatic example of the changing life-style of American consumers in the last 25 years and its impact on all segments of the hospitality business. But it is an issue that the cruise industry is still wrestling with. Unlike being in a hotel or restaurant, if you are on a ship you can't get very far away if cigarette smoke bothers you. You are in a relatively confined space for an extended period of time.

Twenty-five years ago over half the adult population smoked; today it's under 20 percent. This change has been gradual, and the cruise industry response has been equally measured. About 15 years ago, the first "no smoking" signs appeared in designated sections of some public rooms on a few ships—most notably the dining room and main lounge. At first, these designated areas were quite small, but, as demand grew the number of seats for nonsmokers grew proportionately. Finally, in the early 1990s smoke-free cabins and dining rooms appeared. At Carnival, the decision to introduce smoke-free dining rooms on all the vessels was made with a certain amount of controversy and anguish. Some executives were concerned about passionate backlash from the remaining smokers. In a business whose trademark is hospitality inviting people on board and then telling them that they can't smoke hardly seemed hospitable.

Carnival's managers felt that many avid smokers would respond by canceling their reservations, refusing to sail with Carnival again (or for the first time), and even demanding their money back on the grounds that they were not aware that their smoking on board would be restricted. With the exception of those who complain vocally (and many don't; they just don't come back) in the cruise, hotel, and restaurant businesses, you can't easily measure how many guests would have returned and didn't.

Competitive Advantage

This is one of the reasons that cruise and hotel executives fail to define or delimit their product offerings: They are afraid to make choices. Michael Porter of the Harvard Business School, whose specialty is competitive strategy, has written extensively on competitive advantage. He believes that any successful business strategy focuses on particular market segments and then creates value for customers by delivering added-value services that the customers in those specific segments consider important. Since it is impossible to create a product or service that will appeal to everyone, Porter points out successful strategies involve choosing which market segments you are going to pursue and recognizing that you are going to lose some customers—those who, by definition, are in the least desirable segments. Thus, you hope that the customers you lose will be replaced by the ones you want to attract.[1]

While it is true that you can't know how many people would have bought and didn't, you can measure cancellations and read the mail. When Carnival made their no-smoking decision , they monitored both activities very closely and tested the impact. One 3- and 4-day vessel and one 7-day vessel were selected for the test. Less than 30 days notice was given to travel agents so that they didn't have time to negatively influence their client's buying decisions. And everyone in a guest-contact position, both on ship and ashore was presensitized to any negative reactions.

During the test period, there were fewer than a dozen cancellations on a base of tens of thousands of passengers, although several irate guests wrote blistering letters or complained to the hotel managers of the ships involved. If Carnival had responded to the degree of emotion expressed by these individuals, the no-smoking decision would have been quickly and quietly rescinded; but the few passionate dissenters represented a very small market segment that Carnival and other lines could not serve without disturbing the vast majority, who, it turned out, were very appreciative of the no-smoking rule. A few smokers were observed *in flagrante delicto* in the dining room. They were discreetly approached by the ship's staff, and all were willing to suffer the slight inconvenience of leaving the dining room to smoke—realizing how much more comfortable it made their fellow passengers. It's amazing the extent that all of us respond to peer pressure!

---

[1]"Michael Porter on Competitive Strategy," Harvard Business School Video Series, 1988. President and Fellows of Harvard College, A Nathan/Tyler Production.

It is true that McDonald's has now banned all smoking in their restaurants, but it would be difficult for any cruise line to market a smoke-free ship. After all, McDonald's customers are not for the most part on vacation, they aren't planning to spend more than few dollars, they typically spend less then thirty minutes in the building, and of course they can take their meal outside and smoke there.

Even so, while a majority of cruise lines still have segregated smoking and no-smoking sections in their dining rooms, we suspect that most dining rooms and other public rooms will be smoke-free by the turn of the decade. Royal Caribbean's reservations department reports that 70 percent of passengers request no-smoking tables, and Majesty Cruise Lines has designated some smoke-free cabins as well on their ships. Princess Cruises chairman, Tim Harris, told us that he would not be surprised to see entirely smoke-free ships (except outside on the decks) by the turn of the century—mainly due to concerns about the effects of secondhand smoke.

Public and Private Spaces

Another difference between early cruise ships and those of today is that there was relatively little public space on the older vessels compared with modern ships that carry many more passengers. One of NCL's original ships, the *Skyward*, was only 16,000 gross registered tons (GRT) and carried 724 people for a space ratio of 22 tons per passenger (gross tonnage in the cruise ship business has nothing to do with weight—it is the amount of usable space per passenger on a ship. By definition, 1 gross registered ton is 100 cubic feet of volume.)

Travel writers often refer to the "space ratio" of a ship, which is simply the number of tons divided by the basis two occupancy of the vessel. Since there are normally two passengers in each cabin, a ship containing 1,000 cabins, for instance, and carrying 2,000 passengers is 100 percent occupied. In other words, in the cruise industry, unlike the hotel business, capacity is not expressed in rooms or cabins but in double-occupancy passenger capacity. In our hypothetical example, if this 2,000-passenger ship (basis two to a room) is carrying 100 children in the third or

fourth berths of their parents' cabins, the ship is 105 percent occupied. The term *total occupancy* includes the usage of third and
fourth berths up to the lifeboat-carrying capacity of the vessel.
This explains how Carnival has been able to state in its promotion that its vessels have sailed in excess of 100 percent paying
occupancy for over twenty years.

On contemporary ships such as the *Crown Princess*, which at
70,000 tons, carries 1,590 passengers, the space ratio is more than
44. Princess' mega-ship *Grand Princess* is 104,000 tons and carries
2,600 passengers (basis two to a room), resulting in a space ratio
of 40. *Carnival Destiny*, a 100,000-tonner, has a space ratio of 39.
These mega-ship ratios are extremely comfortable and generous
for the contemporary or mass-market cruise segment.

When you move up significantly in price, you move up proportionately in expectations. In the ultra-luxury segment, for example, the *Seabourn Pride* and *Seabourn Spirit* are 10,000 tons
each and carry 200 passengers—for a whopping 50 tons per
passenger space ratio. This ratio is not apparent from the size
of the vessel alone. The Seabourn vessels are small, intimate,
and yacht-like—less then 10 percent of the size of the hundred-
thousand-plus tonners—yet more spacious on a per-passenger
basis. The majority of this additional space is found in the staterooms. All Seabourn staterooms are suites—277 square feet is
the smallest—compared with 132 feet on *Sovereign of the Seas*
and 190 feet on any of the eight Carnival *Fantasy*-class vessels.

Cabin Fever

Cabins were not very comfortable on early cruise liners. D. Keith
Mano, writing in the *National Review* in 1979, had this description
from his mother of a Cunard cruise liner's cabin she occupied:

> Deluxe this was. Each with an iron rail six inches high around,
> like we were in intensive care. You know my condition, I have
> to get up three or four times a night—what was I to do, pole-
> vault out in pitch blackness? So I call the steward and he asks,
> "Are you in an upper bunk?" That's deluxe, with undeluxe you
> also have to vault six feet to the floor. Not one place to sit, it
> was either on the intensive care rail or on the toilet. Worse, the
> air conditioning was so glacial, your body would keep until the

boat got back to Puerto Rico. No adjustment knob except, just where it was handiest, in the middle of the ceiling. Your poor sister had to make a staircase out of the bureau drawers and climb up to move it from COMFORT—COMFORT for popsicle—to OFF. Which should have read DEATH, because in five minutes the room was a floating can of Sterno.[2]

RCCL cabins in those days were decorated in what Peter Whelpton, Executive Vice President of Royal Caribbean Cruises, describes as "a plethora of bright warm Caribbean colors—vibrant orange, vivid yellow, and a green that would jump right off the wall at you." There were no pastels or other muted colors. Nor were there any television sets, although many cabins had radios on which the world news was broadcast twice a day—usually at nine and at six. One hot amenity of modern ships—balconies—were entirely absent in early mass-market ship designs.

Bruce Nierenberg, founder and former President of Premier Cruise Lines, and Executive Vice President of Sales and Marketing of NCL recalls a thin, elderly passenger who went missing one day on NCL's *Skyward*. Her traveling companion couldn't locate her and after some hours became concerned and notified the ship's staff. The staff searched thoroughly from bow to stern to no avail. Later that afternoon the woman was discovered by the cabin steward rolled up in a convertible sofa bed. Apparently the pull-down sofa back had somehow released, flipping her back behind the sofa bolster and putting her out of sight and because of the mattress, she was out of earshot as well. She was quite pleased to be found.

Capacity and Cabin Size

In deciding how many cabins to put on a modern vessel, and what size they should be, cruise lines take several factors into

---

[2]D. Keith Mano, *"My Mother Doesn't Go To Haiti."* Reprinted in *All In The Same Boat: The Humorists' Guide to the Ocean Cruise*, p. 196. Edited by Robert Wechler (Catbird Press, 44 North Sixth Avenue, Highland Park, NJ 08904). Reprinted with permission of National Review Inc., 150 East 35th St., New York, NY 10016. Copyright 1979.

consideration. Some lines have pursued a strategy of smaller cabins and therefore higher-density vessels—that is to say, more cabins for a given size ship than other lines that opt for fewer but larger cabins. Their rationale is that as long as the cabin is functional, size isn't important because so little time is spent there. Proponents of this strategy for many years included Royal Caribbean and Norwegian Cruise Line.

Disney Cruise Line has made a point of promoting what they claim to be the biggest staterooms in the mass-market segment of the industry. One reason, of course, is that they are focusing on the family market. Thus, most cabins must be of sufficient size to accommodate three, four, or even five persons. Disney is also designing significant numbers of interconnecting rooms to provide for larger families.

Jon Rusten, a naval architect who has designed ships for NCL, including the *Dreamward* and *Windward*, and is now with Disney Cruise Line, suggests that a cabin smaller than 150 square feet is perceived by consumers as "small" no matter whose ship it's on or how it is decorated. Maybe this is a leftover perception from the "Love Boat," where cabins were actually Hollywood sets and at least double the size of the real ones on board. Even today, photographers use wide-angle lenses in shooting brochures and commercials to make cabins appear as large as possible.

It makes more economic sense to have the cabins as small as possible, and early pioneers of mass-market cruising all followed this formula. The situation changed, however, when Carnival introduced the *Tropicale* in 1982, a ship that set a new mass-market standard (which was ignored for ten years) with inside cabins of 165 square feet and outside cabins of 180 square feet. The previous standard was between 125 and 135 square feet. Royal Caribbean and NCL continued to build ships through the early 1990s with smaller cabins, adhering to their philosophy that the size of the cabin is relatively unimportant.

Today however, RCCL's six new *Vision* ships, as well as Princess' new mega-ships (aimed at the mass market) all feature larger cabins, comparable in size to those of the Carnival fleet. Had Carnival decided to build small cabins—thus conforming to the then-industry norm—undoubtedly all of today's new mass-market ships would have small cabins. But they gambled that their high-cost, low-density approach would eventually pay off, and it did.

One can easily imagine that the same thing would happen in the airline industry if a major carrier decided to focus on consumer demand and increase the size of all seats on every flight in tourist class. In the airline industry, however, enormous cost pressures preclude accommodating the consumer to that extent. Moreover, if a major carrier did make the move to larger, more comfortable seating in tourist, its competitors would be forced to match the product upgrade to negate the competitive advantage. At the end of the day all the airlines would have a higher cost operation for which they could *not* increase price to recover the cost. Why? Because the domestic airline industry offers a commodity product with relatively low capacity utilization—in the mid 60 percent range. Therefore, suppliers cannot increase their prices to recover the cost of product enhancements that offer no competitive advantage. In fact today's airline industry has been methodically reducing costs even to the point of reducing consumer benefits such as hot meals and lowering the number of flight attendants, in an attempt to keep prices down to encourage more purchase. (Yes, Virginia, the law of price elasticity of demand does apply in the real world!)

Eating and Drinking

Aboard modern cruise ships, like their ocean liner ancestors, food has always been considered an important as well as a necessary component of the product. Some historians believe that one of the reasons the Pilgrims landed at Plymouth Rock, instead of continuing on to their original destination of Virginia, was that they were running out of food, especially beer.[3] On today's cruise it may have something to do with the sea air, the companionship and sociability fostered by a meal together, and the feeling of being taken care of by being offered three full meals a day served in style and featuring a choice of dishes that one would never find at home or even in the average restaurant.

---

[3]Marcel R. Escoffier, "Food Service Operations In the Cruise Industry," *FIU Hospitality Review*, Spring 1995.

The Old Days

Because of limited galley facilities, menus were limited on early cruises. In the early 1970s out of Miami, a typical dinner menu might have consisted of a fruit or shrimp cocktail, consommé, a choice of Filet of Sole or Beef Wellington, and Black Forest Cake or a tray of cheese and crackers and a fruit basket. On the whole, cruise passengers favored large portions of hearty, plain American food—beef and mashed potatoes were favorites, along with lobster.

Before dinner, passengers would converge in the main lounge for cocktails, during which Scotch & Soda, Seven & Sevens, Manhattans, and Martinis were consumed in large quantities. Dark whiskies were a much more important part of beverage sales then, and umbrella drinks (as today's Piña Coladas and Rum Punches are called in the trade) were not much in evidence. The conventional wisdom was that if you didn't eat and drink until you passed out (hopefully in the company of an attractive companion); you didn't have a successful cruise.

According to industry food and beverage veterans, wine lists on early ships were narrow by today's standards. California wine was unheard of, and early cruisers demanded European wines and Champagnes. Choices ran from *rouge ordinaire* to White Star nonvintage champagne and Dom Pérignon. Lancers, Mateus Rosé, and Blue Nun Liebfraumilch were other favorites of the time. Today's wine lists are significantly more extensive, with the notable addition of California, Australian, and Italian selections.

In the early days of cruising a good deal of provisions and water had to be carried aboard, since cruises were typically seven days or longer and there were no reliable provisioners in the Caribbean ports of call. Storage rooms and freezers were stuffed to the gills (like the passengers).

Sometimes this lack of storage space proved an embarrassment, as in a case of death at sea. Today's ships have morgues for deceased passengers, who can hardly be offloaded at the next port. But these facilities are relatively new. In the 1970s the custom was to wrap dead bodies and store them in the freezer. There is one story (true) about a butcher who removed a package of what he believed to be beef from the freezer. When he began to unwrap it a human foot appeared and the poor man ran screaming from the galley. He was so upset the ship's doctor finally had to sedate him.

Modern Galley Design and Organization

Today's food service is very different. To begin with, marine architects now work with chefs and marketing executives to determine what the target market for a new ship will be and thus the menu is specifically designed to please that market. Only once the food is selected are the galley size and the equipment needed determined—not before.

For instance, when Seabourn commissioned its two ships, its research showed that upscale travelers regarded the perceived quality of a line's cuisine as the single most important factor in the success or failure of the entire cruise. They recognized that all meals on this luxurious vessel would need to be true haute cuisine—or as they called it, "Nouvelle Classic." This style of food would be cooked to order—à la minute—and there would be many special orders that were not on the menu. Two more considerations at this point in the planning process were the amount of space that had been set aside for the galley and the number of crew available.

With this information factored in a menu plan was established. Each dinner menu would contain four appetizers (two hot, two cold), three soups (two hot, one cold), two salads, five entrées (one fish, one seafood, one roast, one grill, and one sauté), a cold seafood plate, and four desserts. Similar decisions were made for breakfast service (in-suite, restaurant, and verandah buffet), luncheon, 24-hour room service, tea service, and cocktail hour, and sample menus were then developed for each of these. It was further decided that for proper restaurant service the food would need to be plated in the kitchen to ensure quality and attractive presentation.

Once Seabourn executives knew what the galley had to produce, they were then in a position to design it. There were some immediate problems to overcome. One of these was the shape of the space that had been allocated for the galley; this was broken up into a *U* because of a large spiral staircase that descends through the center of the ship. Then there was placement of equipment; for example, the hot galley (where the hot dishes are cooked) needed to be placed as close as possible to the dining room so that passengers would receive their food hot. Plating the food in the kitchen also required special storage space for the silver cloches that would cover each plate while en route to the table. And, of course, all designs and equipment had to conform to the sanitation standards of the U.S. Public Health Service.[4]

Another design consideration is the kitchen organization, which on a ship may be very different from that in traditional land-based resorts. Dedrick Van Regemorter, Food and Beverage Director aboard the *Star Princess* and formerly with Marriott's Marco Island Resort, points out that in a typical land-based resort one might find a hot preparation area, a cold preparation area, a banquet kitchen, and an à la minute section. But the *Star Princess* galley is more traditional, with sauce, soup, and vegetable stations, as well as fry and grill stations.

The point here is that because people are different, menus are different and because menus are different, ships themselves have to be different. One of the mass-market cruise lines, in an effort to improve their food service, invited some culinary consultants on board for a month to make recommendations for improving the product. One of the recommendations seemed simple enough—plate the entrées in the kitchen so they could be decorated to give them that "nouvelle cuisine" look—for example, make the carrots look like butterflies and the tomatoes look like flowers, and add a few swirls of colorful sauces. To implement this simple solution would have required more chefs in the galley, but the crew quarters had been designed very carefully with room for only a fixed number of food and beverage personnel. That number could not be increased without reducing the number of cabin stewards, social staff, or other equally important personnel. As a result of this constraint, the program was never implemented.

---

[4]We wish to acknowledge the assistance of Larry Rapp, Vice President, Hotel Operations of Seabourn, in developing this material

Storage

Storage space for provisions is another constraint. The *QE2* carries 1,600 items in its food inventory on an average sailing—about three times as much as many full service hotels require to operate. A Carnival ship's provision list is almost as large at 1,500 items. Remember, if you run out of bananas at sea (which American Family Cruises—no longer in business—did on her inaugural voyage) you can't call up a vendor to send for more. Provisioning a ship poses unique problems. First, there is the matter of vendors. Cruise ships have a very short turnaround cycle—in the Port of Miami a ship arrives at 8 A.M., the waste is offloaded, and new provisions for the next cruise have to be on board by 4:00 P.M., when the ship is ready to sail. Since storage space is at a premium, virtually the whole ship must be restocked—even down to the ketchup and mustard used on the hamburgers and hot dogs, and that means suppliers have just a few hours to load. "Just-in-time" inventory control is now becoming popular in retail and manufacturing, but it has been a linchpin of the cruise industry for over twenty years.

Not only must provisions be delivered on time but there is no room for quality errors. There is no chance to replace a crate of spoiled tomatoes; if they are discovered at sea, it is too late. For quality reasons, ships cannot be provisioned at ports of call. Even when cruising the Mediterranean, lines regularly fly in beef and other foodstuffs from the States, because the cuts and quality available in Europe are different from those that satisfy the tastes of American passengers.

To supply the voracious appetite of cruise lines, many vendors have set up separate operations. City Sea Food, a Los Angeles-based food wholesaler, has an office and cold storage plant in Miami that employs 50 people and supplies Carnival, Kloster, and Princess ships. Vendors have even formed their own trade group, the Marine Hotel Catering and Duty Free Association, based in San Francisco. Estimated annual purchases of food and beverages by the cruise lines are more than $600 million.

Healthier Menus

Ships in the old days did not have or consult dieticians—they would have been run off the ship by the chefs. Today, however, cruise menus are not only much more varied than ever before . . . but also a good deal healthier. The change, just as with smoking, has to do with our new lifestyle, which calls for an increased emphasis on fitness and healthy diet. Restaurants were quick to respond to these new consumer demands for lighter and healthier foods. Salads gained popularity and pasta started appearing on more menus along with a larger selection of seafood and poultry dishes than in prior years.

Cruise lines were at first hesitant to follow this lead. In the minds of many passengers, quality equaled quantity and the kind of quantity people wanted was lots of prime roasts, 16-ounce New York strip steaks, and mounds of ice cream topping their enormous slices of fresh-baked apple pie. But as post-cruise comment cards started reflecting a real demand for lighter fare, lines began experimenting with healthier dishes and smaller portions. Curiously enough, it didn't come easily. Restaurants were universally applauded for responding to dietary concerns—indeed, some writers suggested it was unethical not to offer a wide variety of healthy dishes because it forced people eating out to eat foods with too many calories, too much fat, or an overload of sodium.

On the other hand, some travel agents (especially the more corpulent freeloaders) immediately complained that the cruise lines were trying to cut costs by serving lighter foods and smaller portions. *ASTA Agency Management* actually ran an article in February 1992 entitled "Cruise Cuisine: Cutting Costs or Cutting Calories?" In fact, healthier food is often more difficult to prepare and more expensive. Lendal Kotschevar and Marcel Escoffier, in their well-known text *Management by Menu*, point out that food costs increase when the variety of menu selections is expanded, which results in increased spoilage, and when a switch is made from cheaper items like ground beef to more expensive items like fish.

To ignore passengers' dietary concerns is not only insensitive but bad business. There has to be enough variety to satisfy every taste and health concern, and just about all of the North American cruise lines now recognize this. Holland America, for instance, besides having four regular dinner entrees, has a vegetarian entrée such as Vegetable Kebab and a "Light and Healthy Entree" that is prepared in accordance with the American Heart Association and is low in cholesterol and sodium. Even most of the regular entrées are available without sauce on request. Carnival labels certain appetizers, salads, entrees, and even desserts as "Nautica Spa Fare" on every menu, and all of these items are lower in calories, sodium, cholesterol, and fat. Salads are prepared with diet dressing and desserts are made with Sweet 'N Low or NutraSweet instead of sugar. Royal Caribbean has a similar system with their dinner menus that they call their "Shipshape" program. Princess also identifies dishes that are low in calories and can be served plain with no sauce. All of the lines invite passengers with special dietary needs to contact the maître d'.

Of course, for passengers who still like the old-style menus, there are Russian cruise ships plying the waters of the Caribbean (mostly patronized by well-endowed German tourists) that will heap your oversized plate with Beef Stroganoff smothered in a rich sour cream sauce!

Menu Planning

Cruise lines today have become more sophisticated in their menu planning. Both Princess and Holland America told us about changes they make every year when they reposition ships from Alaska to the Caribbean. Princess's experience is that Alaska passengers prefer food of a higher caloric content that is not highly spiced. It has to do with the climate, they have found. The closer their ships come to the equator the more spicy the food has to be to entice their passengers; it should also be a bit lighter. Holland America notes that in the Caribbean their passengers are younger then those on their Alaska cruises, which is not surprising considering that the air fare to Miami from most places is considerably less then the air fare to Vancouver or Anchorage. At any rate, younger passengers have larger appetites, and when on one cruise a table for 8 ordered 15 entrees the line realized they needed to increase the portion size.

Not everything has changed. César Ritz is gone but his nautical dining tradition lingers in Celebrity Cruise Lines use of famed French chef Michel Roux as a "cuisine consultant." Roux develops recipes and sails aboard Celebrity ships several times annually to assess quality, preparation, and presentation. He is also closely involved in wine selection. The truth is that while all lines strive for a higher quality of shipboard cuisine there is and will always be a limiting factor. True gourmet cuisine must be cooked à la minute, and when you are feeding 1,000 people at a time that is a virtual impossibility. However the cruise industry has in fact developed a widely held reputation for outstanding food and food service. Consider that a cruise ship can serve a thousand or more meals at a single sitting—at top restaurant quality, so it's no wonder that food is one of the significant factors that have helped the lines achieve the high satisfaction rates they enjoy. After all, think of what your dining experience would be like if you had to eat at a hotel with 1,000 fellow diners!

Cruise Ship Food Quality

Research supports these satisfaction ratings. In one independent study of travel agents, more than a dozen cruise lines, including all of the ones mentioned here, received a score of 9 or 10 (10 being the highest possible) for providing quality gourmet food. This is in sharp contrast to the hotel industry. Because 70 percent of the revenue and a larger percentage of the profit comes from the rooms division, food service in hotels is often regarded as a necessary evil—a convenience for the guest that must be provided. Thus, few hotels offer food beyond the commonplace. Moreover, because the typical hotel cannot count on a stable, predictable, controlled utilization of restaurant facilities, food quality and service suffer.

On a ship, dining room utilization and consumer demand are predictable and controlled even to the point of knowing exactly what percentage of the guests will opt for Veal Milanaise at the Captain's dinner or Escargot on French night. As a result, at any comparable price point, cruise ships can deliver a food product superior to that of their land-based competitors.

But it gets even better than that. Because of precise predictability, very high utilization of food (which translates into almost no spoilage), and very fresh foodstuffs, almost any cruise ship can offer a better dining experience at a much lower cost, thus contributing meaningfully to the value advantage of cruising as a vacation.

Food Costs

The cruise industry looks at food costs on a per-diem or per-passenger-day basis. In the ultra-luxury end of the market, it is not uncommon to spend $25 to $30 (per passenger per 24-hour day) for the raw food (exclusive of labor and overhead). In the premium segment, the cost is typically in the neighborhood of $8–$18, and for mass-market, costs run $8 to $11. Passengers can have (and some do have) one breakfast in the cabin, another one on deck, and a third in the dining room. And that's not all. They can eat lunch twice—on deck and in the dining room—and have an eight-course dinner! Of course, there are also mid-morning and mid-afternoon snacks to tide you over, as well as one or two late-night buffets. If that's not enough . . . if you're still hungry . . . there's twenty-four hour room service on most ships; and on many pizza parlors and ice cream bars are open much of the day. All of these dining opportunities are included in the price.

In contrast, the rule of thumb in the restaurant business is that food costs ought to run between 25 and 30 percent of the selling price. Compared to a mass-market cruise line with a food cost of $10 per day, any restaurant or hotel to be competitive, could only charge $33 to $40 per person for a comparable array of food. It's unlikely that any land-based food service operation could survive on such pricing!

In addition to predictability of usage, the cruise industry benefits from enormous economies of scale, which drive costs down further. Carnival Cruise Lines, for example, uses 24,500 dozen eggs every single week throughout the year. In addition, their passengers consume 29,800 pounds of tenderloin and prime rib, 47,000 pounds of chicken, and 4,970 cases of wine and champagne each week. Obviously, with these huge quantities, purveyors sharpen their pencils to offer terrific prices. Part of the cost savings results from inexpensive distribution, as less than a dozen ships account for this usage. Even when a large hotel chain negotiates a blanket food contract, the cost of distributing small amounts to hundreds of hotels around the country negates a good bit of the savings.

Remember, too, these economies are achieved by serving identical menus on all ships in the fleet (a strategy utilized by all of the profitable cruise lines—RCCL, Princess, and Holland

America). This is one reason that the major lines tend to build ships that have similar configuration and size although different interiors. These ships are often built simultaneously—side by side. Similar layout and size translate into similar menus. These allow for the economies that result in increased value for customers. For example, Carnival's eight *Fantasy*-class ships have the same size storerooms, kitchens, and dining rooms, and of course identical menus on the same itineraries. Royal Caribbean's trio of *Sovereign*-class vessels have been equally successful through uniform design.

Games People Play

On early cruises, activities, like dining, were constrained by space because there were only a few interior public rooms. The largest of these, besides the dining room, was the grand saloon, which was used for entertainment and dancing and showing movies (as many as three a day). Since there was little awareness of fitness concerns in the seventies, most activities were designed not to keep you healthy—just happy.

In good weather as many things as possible were scheduled on deck—table tennis, shuffleboard, and calisthenics were particularly popular, as were other kinds of fun and games. Humorist Richard Gordon tells of a cruise he took in 1967:

> The passengers on a cruise thus face the same situation as so inconvenienced the *Bounty* mutineers on Pitcairn Island. Any females available must be fought for, and the nicer they are the nastier the scrap. Blatant rough-and-tumbles on the boat deck being frowned on by authorities, the aggression becomes restricted to the ship's games. I once watched a pair of Tarzans playing the finals of a deck tennis competition, under a blazing sun and the eyes of the sexiest girl aboard, with a ferocity that ended the contest by putting one in the ship's hospital with a suspected fractured ankle, and the other with a suspected coronary occlusion. Table-tennis, the rowing machine, the gymnasium fixed bicycle, pillow fighting on the greasy pole, even bouncing on the trampoline are similarly abused as primeval exhibitions of masculine vigor. Even *Walking* is a

perilous activity at sea. The knowledge that five times around the promenade equals a mile seems to obsess overweight males who ashore wouldn't stroll out to post a letter.[5]

A Night's Entertainment

In the evening, entertainment consisted mostly of a vaudeville variety show and events in which the passengers participated. Dancing was very popular and usually necessitated carrying a large orchestra to replicate the sounds of Tommy Dorsey and Benny Goodman.

Joseph Meltzer of Fort Lauderdale, Florida, showed us his dance card and program for "Ladies Night" aboard Norwegian American Line's *Sagafjord* in the seventies. This kind of entertainment, often called "Sadie Hawkins Night" was universally popular in the early days.

Here are the rules for the evening's entertainment printed on the *Sagafjord's* card:

1. Only ladies are allowed to ask gentlemen for dances.
2. Ladies must not leave their dancing partners stranded on the dance floor, but must escort them back to their seats.
3. Ladies may buy gentlemen drinks, but no propositions allowed.
4. Ladies must light gentlemen's cigarettes or cigars.
5. Ladies must use discretion, and not try to dance with the same partners twice.
6. Ladies are cautioned against pinching gentlemen.
7. Ladies are requested not to use cheek-to-cheek tactics while dancing, and should face their partners at all times.
8. Ladies are not permitted to tempt men with offers of Vicuña coats and Cadillacs
9. Single girls are at liberty to ask bachelors for their hands.
10. Ladies should select gentlemen other than their own husbands.

---

[5]Richard Gordon, "Salt Water Hikers, Etc." Reprinted in *All In The Same Boat: The Humorists' Guide To The Ocean Cruise*, p. 62. Edited by Robert Wechler (Catbird Press, 44 North Sixth Avenue, Highland Park, NJ 08904). Copyright 1967, Richard Gordon, by permission of Curtis Brown.

There are spaces on the card for 12 dances, including Viennese waltz, fox trot, quick step, jive, and rumba, and a blank line next to each, to record the name of the gentleman scheduled as partner.

Other popular forms of entertainment included fifties and sixties nights and amateur night. Passengers who wished to sing, perform magic tricks, or even recite poetry could do so. For others who wished to participate but had no special talents, the cruise director would devise a skit that any couple could perform. One favorite was "Nothing To Declare" in which the husband was given a uniform and asked the play the role of a customs inspector and his wife was given a heavy wool coat. The dialogue went something like this:

INSPECTOR: What did you buy on this cruise?

WOMAN: I have nothing to declare.

INSPECTOR: You mean you didn't buy anything?

WOMAN: I have nothing to declare.

INSPECTOR: Why are you wearing that heavy coat?

WOMAN: I have to carry it off the ship.

INSPECTOR: Would you take it off please?

WOMAN: (Holding it tightly) I'm too cold.

Inspector reaches for coat and opens it over woman's protests revealing linings on both sides with knives, forks, watches, etc., sewed on.

Passengers also participated in a cruise version of the popular TV show "The Newlywed Game." The idea was to see how many intimate details spouses knew about each other, and prizes were awarded not only for the newlyweds on the ship but for those who had been married a long time. While one spouse was off stage the other was asked questions such as "What is the name of the girl who gave your husband his first kiss?" and "What size bra does your wife wear?" Spouses were then brought back on stage to guess their partners' answers, and the ones with the most matches won.

For the masquerade party, passengers who had not brought along costumes from home were given some basic materials like posterboard in various colors, pieces of fabric, safety pins, and crayons so that they could make their own outfits (with the help of a cruise staff member). On one Princess Cruise in the Caribbean the winner was a woman with an oversized behind who pinned clumps of navy blue fabric all over her rear and sang "I found my thrill on Blueberry Hill."

Show Business at Sea

Of course, there was some professional entertainment as well. Royal Caribbean Cruises' Pete Whelpton remembers offering "three-act, hour and a half, variety shows in those days two days a week on our 7-day cruises. Usually they were on the evenings when we held the Captain's Welcome Aboard Dinner and the Captain's Farewell Dinner, which were also our formal nights. The show opened with a vocalist. Then there was a stand up comedian and finally there was always what we called a sight or specialty act—a juggler, single-wheeled cyclist, magician, or even a harmonica player."

A popular comedian on early Royal Caribbean cruises was Joey Villa, who often opened for Frank Sinatra. Villa would come on stage dressed in his tux and singing "I'm gonna live till I die." People thought he was a crooner, but 45 seconds into his act he'd convulse, jump into the air, and fall down flat on the stage. He would then pick himself up and go into his comedy routine.

On some cruise lines the stand-up comedian was also the Cruise Director and acted as Master of Ceremonies. Jokes such as this one told to us by the *Star Princess'* Cruise Director, Mark Iannazzo were common:

> Just before sailing a new bride told her husband that she had left her birth control pills home and was worried about getting seasick. He told her not to worry—there was still time for him to get off the ship and go to a drugstore. When he got there he told the druggist " I need some birth control pills and some dramamine." The druggist looked at him and said. "Pardon me, but if it makes you sick, why do you do it?

Today, in the competition for passengers, entertainment quality has become a major strategic weapon and one in which the major players have spared no expense. Comedians that have been featured on *Saturday Night Live* and The Comedy Channel are commonplace, and even big box office names like Victor Borge and Steve Allen are often found on special cruises.

The Big Productions

More than anything, a trademark of the big mass-market ships and a focal point of every cruise has become the lavish Las Vegas–style "flesh and feathers" shows, which are produced twice nightly. These are huge productions with casts of as many as 30 performers, accompanied by a full orchestra, and performed in a show lounge typically seating 1,300 and using state-of-the-art equipment. John Maxtone-Graham recalls watching in awe as a huge video wall was installed in the Sound of Music Show Lounge on the *Monarch of the Seas*, which was being built at the Chantiers de l'Atlantique shipyard in France for Royal Caribbean Cruises in 1990. The screen, the first one afloat at that time, can be suspended in alternative flexible modes: either as two separate sections, each five screens by five screens square, or joined into one broad façade. Thus, it can hang to either side of the stage or be united to form a 50-screen effect as a backdrop for production shows.

These theaters are some of the most complicated parts of a ship to put together because they depend so much on special effects and computers. To begin with, there is the question of where to put them. They are huge—often two decks high for seating with space on a third deck for the sets to be raised and lowered. And they are noisy—on Carnival ships, for example, officers' cabins are located above and below show lounges and they must be well insulated since these personnel have rotating shifts and are often trying to sleep while the show is on. Finally, they require very complicated audio and lighting equipment, built especially for use at sea since land equipment is not designed to withstand the vibrations from machines and propellers. Moreover, because the equipment is being placed on a ship, the weight must be evenly distributed. You can't just put lights and speakers where they logically ought to go. If you do, it can affect the stability of the ship. Regulations, installation materials and methods, ceiling height, electrical systems—everything is different from working on land. Power consumption, a factor hardly ever considered in designing land-based theaters is crucial—more power means more cables, which can easily add a couple of tons to the ship's weight and thus reduce her speed.

Nevertheless, being able to mount a top-quality show is very important, and it depends in large part on the technical facilities. The *Carnival Destiny* will have a traditional-style orchestra pit that can be raised and lowered in front of a 58-foot-wide stage housing a 26-foot turntable, smoke ejectors, and substantial laser and scene projection equipment.

High-Tech Entertainment

The *Grand Princess*, debuting in 1997, will be the first ship to feature a motion-based virtual-reality theater and will also have a "blue screen" room that will give passengers who have a yearning to be in show business the chance to star in their own video production. The *Sun Princess*, introduced in December of 1995, features two main show lounges (both theater and cabaret style). Celebrity's new 1,740-passenger *Century* boasts a showroom designed to replicate an outdoor amphitheater. Designed for Broadway-scale productions it includes fly towers, telescoping wall, revolving stage, hydraulic orchestra pit, and interactive equipment, as well as sophisticated sound, lighting, and special effects.

The new technology isn't limited to new ships. Carnival's *Holiday*, launched in 1985, has a 9,000-square-foot entertainment complex called Blue Lagoon containing two virtual-reality machines. Players compete in mock combat scenarios while their movements are tracked by video headsets that change the scenery and the action. Even the venerable *Rotterdam* installed a special ice skating rink for a "Celebration on Ice" revue for her 1995 world cruise.

Showtime at Sea

Once you have the equipment you still need the shows. These are often provided by theatrical production firms that specialize in cruise-line entertainment. One such company is Jean Anne Ryan Productions in Ft. Lauderdale, Florida, which provides the entertainment for Norwegian Cruise Line ships; another is Ellis Island Entertainment in New York, which produces the Holland America shows. Again, there are differences that require special consideration. Costumes need to be lighter than in the theater;

dance routines need to be choreographed so they can be performed easily even if there is some motion aboard the ship; and since different itineraries attract audiences of different age groups and cultural backgrounds music has to be adapted to audience tastes.

Everything, of course, is not better than it used to be. A few niceties have disappeared—some because of the large number of passengers on today's ships, and some because of our contemporary lifestyle. For instance, all of the old Home Line ships featured reserved teak deck chairs. Usually before or immediately after sailing, passengers could go to the sun deck and pick a chair, which would have their name inserted in a holder indicating it was reserved for them exclusively for the duration of the cruise. Home Lines also published a passenger list by the third day out so people could check off the names of people they met and so remember them. Today, people value their privacy more and probably wouldn't want a passenger list published (although lines like Seabourn still provide them). As for reserved deck chairs, the informal lifestyle of a ship today would make them an anachronism.

There's No Business Like Fat Business

Picture the gymnasium of a cruise ship sailing out of the Port of Miami in the early seventies. The room was 10 feet by 12 feet, and one wall was mirrored floor to ceiling with a dance barre bisecting it. Typically, the room was located in the bowels of the vessel in an out-of-the-way location. (Presumably, those few people who wished to exercise would be sufficiently motivated to find the damn place!)

The equipment in this room consisted of a vinyl-jacketed exercise mat, a manual rowing machine and that funny-looking machine with the big strap that went around your fanny. When you flipped the switch, the strap would simultaneously undulate and vibrate, and as you stood up and leaned back, theoretically your caboose would get loose and the pounds would melt away. No respectable cruise ship would be without this gizmo.

As you can imagine, the fat-consuming, cholesterol-unconscious passenger complement had little interest in shedding their recently garnered tonnage. Today . . . my, how times have changed!

Today's passengers expect modern mega-liners to have thousands of square feet of exercise and spa area. The rowing machine has been replaced by electronic rowers with computerized graphics, stairmasters, treadmills, and exercise bicycles. But that's not all: There are free weights, progressive resistance exercise stations, steam baths, saunas, massage rooms, herbal wrap rooms, mud baths, and more. The small gym of 25 years ago may have cost $1,000 or so to equip. Today, cruise ships spend three or four times that amount on just one machine. A well equipped spa now occupies more than 8,000 square feet, has a staff of roughly 20 professional trainers, aerobic instructors, masseuses, and spa technicians, and can cost in excess of $500,000.

Ports-of-Call

Ports-of-call in the Caribbean in the seventies were the same ones that are popular today, but they often lacked the infrastructure to handle the number of passengers that even a small ship brought in at one time. There were few buses available, so tours were most often sightseeing rather than experience oriented. Given the age of the cruisers there was little interest in participative sports such as snorkeling, golf, or horseback riding on the beach. Mainly you climbed in a taxi and the driver showed you the Governor's Home, a sugar or banana plantation, the marketplace, and the rain forest. Then you returned to the ship.

The most popular Caribbean tours by far were the night club shows in Puerto Rico and the Bahamas. Few cruisers had ever seen a "flesh and feathers" production unless they had visited Las Vegas or Paris, and the ones in San Juan featured name entertainers like Sophie Tucker, Sammy Davis, Jr., and even Jack Benny (who owned a piece of the Condado Beach Hotel and played there every year). There were also casinos in the Puerto Rican hotels and none on the cruise ships (except for slot machines). Casinos were introduced slowly into cruising because operators were fearful of getting involved with organized crime.

Royal Caribbean didn't have them until the late seventies because their Norwegian owners were opposed to the idea.

Ship Personnel

When the cruise industry was just a fledgling, shipboard personnel on the whole were not well trained, and the experience of being on a cruise ship was as new for them as it was for their guests. There is the story of a Haitian cabin steward who, while cleaning a passenger's cabin, shook out a pillow so vigorously that it burst open and the feathers went flying around the room. He believed that chicken feathers were an evil voodoo charm, and the very sight of them sent him fleeing from the cabin and right off the side of the ship, never to be heard from or seen again!

Stories like this remind us of a joke still used today by Mark Iannazzo, a Princess Cruise Director, about a passenger who was locked in her room all day. Finally she called the Purser's office and explained her dilemma. "There are no doors leading out of my cabin," she said. "Madam," answered the Purser, "there are at least two doors in your room." "I know," she replied, "one is to the bathroom, the other one has a sign on the handle saying "Do Not Disturb!"

As the industry evolved so did the recruiting and training of onboard personnel. Today, all of the major lines have elaborate training facilities to orient their staff, most of whom have never been to sea before and have not had training in either the practical or social skills required to serve passengers. Holland America has a school in Indonesia, and Princess has one in the Phillipines. Carnival operates its own Carnival College at sea and ashore, which stresses team building and motivational techniques at all levels. Royal Caribbean has similar programs.

An important aspect of recruiting and training is making certain that all employees speak fluent English. On the whole, it is a requirement on most North American ships, but the different lines have had varying degrees of success in achieving this. Even though they are supposed to be screened on shore, Princess requires that all new shipboard personnel, from the Captain to the deckhand and dishwasher, take a recorded oral test in English administered by a third party. They are required to answer questions like "What is the appropriate fire extinguisher for this fire and where is it located?" and "Where can I find the Purser's office?" These tapes are sent to Princess headquarters in Los Angeles for evaluation. Crew members who do not pass are supplied with tape recorders and recorded English lessons to study in their spare time.

Of course, it is possible to find Europeans and Americans with sufficient training for dining and cabin service. Even today the luxury lines hire such staff; but their ships are small and their staff needs are small. On mass market ships the executive maître chefs and some other key personnel are Europeans, as are the food and beverage managers, but the larger fleets have found that these jobs are more enthusiastically filled by people from the Far East, the Caribbean, and South America, where the wages paid are very high by the standards at home. These employees are willing and capable of learning, and they enjoy the lifestyle and economic opportunities a cruise ship offers.

The cruise industry has grown tenfold between 1970 and today. In the early years, with smaller numbers of folks and smaller ships, the passengers were older empty-nesters, with relatively simple tastes. Today's cruise vacationer is everyman. Consequently, the ship's product delivery, whether food, entertainment, or ports of call, of necessity is more diverse and complex.

3

Life on the Ocean Wave

Living and working aboard modern cruise ships

Whose Country Are We in, Anyway?— Flags of Convenience

Every commercial ship is registered to a flag state (that is, country) under whose rules and authority the ship operates. The choice of country depends on many factors, including, perhaps, the financing of the vessel, the cost of operation, and/or the routes the vessel sails. The flag-of-convenience tradition dates back to the early days of naval warfare when merchant ships, to avoid being attacked, carried the flag of a neutral nation, thus protecting their passengers and cargo from the ravages of war.

Staffing considerations play a big part in the decision about a ship's flag state. Many countries, including the United States, Norway, and Britain, have strict regulations concerning unionized labor which severely constrain the ability of a ship to staff with an optimal crew mix, and almost invariably create a higher labor cost than a free-market environment. So-called *flag-of-*

convenience countries, do not have these constraints. Panama and Liberia, which together amount to 30 percent of the world shipping tonnage, are the most popular; others include Monrovia, Bermuda, the Bahamas, and the Netherlands Antilles.

International Crews

Today, cruise liners as well as freighters continue to use flags of these and other nations rather than their own countries for convenience. Ships roam all over the world, and it is thus both convenient and practical for them to hire crew from ports everywhere without concern for nationality. If a chief engineer becomes ill in Istanbul, it makes sense to recruit a new engineer from Turkey if one is available. However, with its strict labor policies, a U.S. flagged vessel would not have that option. British, Italians, Norwegians, and Greeks are all renowned for their nautical skills, rigorous training, and strict licensing standards, and just about every major cruise line recruits their captains from one of those countries. Likewise, the French, Germans, and Austrians, who often manage the world's finest dining rooms and kitchens, are recruited for ship food service. In short, on a ship an international crew is often the most desirable as well as the most practical to staff.

International Labor Policies

The problem is that most countries have labor unions and regulations that severely restrict the ability of a ship to staff itself with what may clearly be the optimal crew mix. These laws are designed to protect the jobs of each country's citizens, but they are both impractical and costly in some instances. The United States, for example, requires that all ships registered in the USA use only licensed American officers and that three-quarters of the unlicensed crew be U.S. citizens. Other countries have similarly restrictive regulations.

The Advantages of an International Crew

When a ship carrying an international crew is registered in Liberia or Panama, it is not subject to union and other restrictive crewing policies. This means that owners are in a better position to negotiate fair and equitable compensation packages in a global, free-market environment. Of course, ships registered in these flag-of-convenience nations pay lower wages and taxes on an aggregate basis than those registered in the United States (or Norway or Italy for that matter). But that makes it possible for them to offer cruises at a much lower cost than if their ships were registered in countries with restrictive hiring policies. And that's one reason why American-headquartered cruise lines such as Royal Caribbean and Carnival choose not to operate under American flags.

Another reason, frankly, is that it is more difficult to find Americans who have a flair for service hospitality. The egalitarian nature and heritage of Americans tend to work against their ability to be motivated to serve others. Moreover, citizens of highly developed countries like the United States who work on these ships generally make about the same as they would at home, whereas citizens of underdeveloped countries like Costa Rica and the Philippines make considerably more on board ship than they can make in these countries—if they can find a job at all when unemployment may be as high as 30 percent. The plain fact is that Americans won't kill to get a job at sea because there are so many comparably compensated positions shoreside (remember, the unemployment rate in the United States generally hovers between 5 and 8 percent). And when they do work at sea, they're not as motivated to excel. Third-world citizens hold these jobs in high esteem because they are both employed (which is not a given at home) and rich by native standards.

All things considered from the standpoint of a global economy, flag-of-convenience cruise ships, operating in a free market, provide more value to the worldwide labor pool, with significantly less cost to its operators, and therefore lower prices to its consumers.

The Perceived Threat of International Crews

Despite these factors, there have been a number of attempts by some members of Congress over the years to gain more control over foreign-flagged tonnage and thus gain a foothold for American labor and shipping interests. For example, Congressman

William Clay, a Democrat from Missouri, has proposed a series of bills (none of which has passed) to extend U.S. labor laws to foreign-flagged vessels despite the fact that the State Department has insisted for years that any such legislation would violate long-standing international law and comity. Kirk Lanterman, President of Holland America, points out some of the problems of this type of legislation: "It could create a situation where when we leave Miami we are under U.S. labor laws, but when we dock in the Bahamas, we are subject to a different set of local laws. It would be so onerous as to push cruise lines offshore." Holland America already adheres to labor laws of Holland and Indonesia, countries whose natives form the majority of its crew.

Other cruise lines have similar arrangements when large portions of the crew come from a single country. Seabourn and Royal Caribbean, for example, operate ships under a special Norwegian flag that incorporates more flexible labor laws in recognition of the international nature of the cruise business.

It's amusing to watch attempts by Congress over the years to legislate the world marketplace. It is ironic that a country built on the principle of open-market competition has created a situation where its maritime industry is puny by global standards and its cruise industry practically nonexistent.

Long-standing American cabotage laws in the cruise industry have cost our nation billions of dollars and ten of thousands of jobs. If the United States truly wants to capture a fair share of cruise line jobs and other economic benefits, it should exempt the cruise industry from the Passenger Shipping Act of 1896, which precludes foreign-flagged vessels from operating between U.S. ports when there is no U.S. flag competitor. Virtually all of the lucrative Alaska cruise business is now home-ported in Vancouver, British Columbia, because of this legislation. Consequently, over a billion dollars annually is lost by the Seattle, Washington, economy to its neighbor to the north. Seattle would be the natural home port for Alaskan cruises because of its superior airline infrastructure. Indeed, all lines offering cruises to Alaska fly a significant number of their passengers to Seattle and then bus them 150 miles to the port of Vancouver. However, as there are no deep-water U.S.-flagged cruise ships operating to Alaska, there is simply no U.S. flagged cruise business to protect! Only one deep-water U.S.-flagged cruise ship, the *Independence*, built in 1951, operates in the world today. She operates only in Hawaiian waters for American Hawaii Cruise Lines, a division of Delta Queen Steamboat Company.

U.S. jobs, ranging from longshoreman to teamster to port agent, to pilot, to provisioner, are lost in the name of protecting a nonexistent U.S. cruise industry.

Other U.S. Policies and the Cruise Industry

The absence of any U.S. flagged cruise lines to speak of is also the result of other forms of long-standing protectionist policy. U.S. flagging requires that the ship be built in the United States as well as operated by a predominantly American crew. But the shipbuilding industry here has for years been entirely focused on lucrative, cost-plus naval contracts, because of which it is inherently highly subsidized. If there is a cost overrun (remember the stories of the $1,350 hammer?) it is added to the bill plus the normal shipyard markup. For the record, no self-respecting cruise line would ever sign a ship-building contract without a firm price guarantee. The U.S. Navy, however, apparently can operate in a more cavalier manner—stockholders are always harder to please than taxpayers.

The Captain and the Crew

In Chapter 2 we described what is generally called "the front of the house" in most hospitality enterprises. The term has its roots in the theater where the front of the house is what the audience sees—the lobby, the ornate boxes, chandeliers, and seats, and of course the stage. Framed by the proscenium and behind the curtain is the set on which the action takes place. This is front stage, where illusion turns actors into characters and painted backdrops into city streets or country gardens. Backstage, behind the scenes and out of view of the audience, are the stage hands, the wardrobe and makeup artists, the lighting and set designers, and of course the producer, director, and choreographer.

Cruise ships, like hotels and restaurants, also have a front and a back of the house. One reason the term is appropriate in all of these enterprises is that many service businesses recognize that part of their service is a "performance" in which the customers are the audience and the staff are like actors playing roles. The Disney organization calls all of its park employees "members of the cast," and whether they are sweeping Main Street or boarding guests onto the Space Mountain Roller Coaster, they play the parts they have been assigned when they are "on stage"—that is, anywhere in the park they can be seen. Hotels, too, have always called their lobbies the front of the house and their kitchens and laundries the back.

So it is with cruise ships. A vessel such as the *Star Princess*, which carries 1,494 passengers (basis two), also carries a crew of 563. Carnival's *Fantasy*-class ships, which carry approximately 2,040 passengers, typically carry a crew of 920. The *Seabourn Spirit* carries 202 passengers along with a crew of 140. On all such ships, waiters and pursers are seen by the ship's guests regularly when they are in the front of the house; others, such as engineers may never be seen. Nevertheless, all of them live their personal lives aboard the ship and are under the command of the ship's Captain.

Three senior officers report directly to the Captain: the Staff Captain, the Chief Engineer, and the Hotel Manager (or Chief Purser, as he or she is called aboard British ships). Everyone else reports to a department under the supervision of one of these three officers.

The Captain

Passengers are frequently curious as to what the Captain does all day. Put simply, he is the ultimate authority on board, charged with carrying out company policies and rules and complying with all applicable national and international laws and regulations. The Captain has legal authority to enforce these laws—it is granted to him by the government of the flag state—the country in which the ship is registered.

And since many cruise lines operate ships which are registered in more than one flag state, their captains must be familiar with the laws of all of them. Royal Caribbean ships, for example, operate under Bahamian and Liberian flags and a special Norwegian flag of convenience. In truth, however, most flag-of-convenience countries have few laws governing ship operations, so the ship operates under its company's policies and procedures.

Local Laws and Regulations

Vessels also have to comply with the laws of the ports they sail to and from. The U.S. Coast Guard inspects all ships sailing from the United States four times a year, in three quarterly drills and one annual drill. During the quarterly drills the Coast Guard observes the crew in a full-fledged fire drill and abandon-ship drill. Crew members climb into lifeboats, which they then lower. In the annual inspection the focus is also on all of the equipment used. The Coast Guard checks that it is all in its proper place and that all escape routes are clear (not converted to storage space, for example). It then issues a certificate showing that the ship has passed inspection. Most lines don't wait for the Coast Guard, but perform these inspections weekly for their own training and inspection purposes.

The U.S. Public Health Service Centers for Disease Control and Prevention (CDC) inspects galleys and other food-handling and storage areas and awards scores to ships for their sanitation.[1]

Insurance

Ships carry a good many insurance policies, covering equipment such as the hull and machinery as well as liability. All of these policies have conditions attached that the captain must enforce. The insuring organization, such as U.S. Bureau of Shipping, Lloyds, and Norske Veritas, inspects each vessel to make sure it is "in class." If a ship isn't in class, it is deemed uninsurable and it cannot operate until the deficiencies are corrected.

---

[1]Copies of these scores are issued monthly; interested consumers may receive them by writing to: Chief, Vessel Sanitation Program, National Center for Environmental Health, 1015 N. America Way, Room 107, Miami, FL 33132. Results are also published in *Consumer Reports Travel Letter*.

Crew and Passenger Safety

Everything else aside, the Captain's primary responsibility is to ensure the care and safety of everyone on board and, with that in mind, to make sure that the ship is seaworthy and that proper navigation and operating procedures are carried out. He is responsible for the navigation of the vessel: its speed, direction, bearings (location), and port maneuvering; and for its itinerary and schedule. Captains are on duty all of the time and must be called when safety problems of any sort are spotted. One veteran captain recalls that he was summoned one evening when a fire alarm went off in one of the cabins. The Captain personally responded to the alarm, only to discover that it had been triggered by the heat from a honeymoon couple's candlelight dinner.

The Captain's Job Description and Credentials

Norwegian Cruise Line's job description for their captains lists these tasks among others:

1. Ensuring the ship's officers, staff, and crew carry out their assigned duties in a seamanship manner at all times.
2. Maintaining a high standard of discipline on board using any lawful methods deemed necessary as the situation demands and ensuring the Department Heads instruct the crew members in all applicable rules, regulations, and company policies. (He is ultimately responsible for the discipline of the crew using the Staff Captain and other Department Heads to carry out this responsibility.)
3. Promoting the welfare and well being of the crew, being attentive to their environment and ensuring each enjoys the privileges to which they are entitled. He shall use periodic inspection rounds as an opportunity to strengthen the personal contact between himself and the crew.
4. To maintain a world class standard of service to the passengers.
5. To take actions as necessary to prevent or mitigate circumstances which place the ship, passengers, or crew in danger.
6. The Captain shall have a thorough knowledge of the ship, including the construction, safety equipment, stability char-

acteristics, ship handling procedures, and emergency procedures. He shall ensure that his officers have the same knowledge in their areas of responsibility. He shall ensure the
ship's maintenance program meets or exceeds that required
by the Company and the authorities.

7. The Captain shall determine the extent of participation by
the officers and staff in social activity with passengers and
the applicable dress code, ensuring the regulations of the
Company are observed.

It is worth noting here the emphasis and use of words in this
job description (which is typical for all of the cruise lines), such
as "assigned duties," "seamanship manner," "standard of discipline," "privileges," "prevent or mitigate circumstances," and
"regulations of the company." A ship is a paramilitary organization, in which officers wear uniforms, and regulations, laws,
rank, and discipline play a prominent role in the way things get
done. This is both an advantage and a disadvantage in a service
industry whose success depends heavily on customer satisfaction. It is a disadvantage because motivation is somewhat inhib-
ited by the nature of the organization. The officers and crew
have an assigned rank and specific duties, and they cannot over-
step established boundaries. If they do not perform their duties
in a prescribed manner, they are subject to discipline. On board
a vessel run in a paramilitary manner, sound service management theory, which emphasizes empowerment and shared responsibility, can have only a limited role. This is a business
where you earn your stripes by obeying orders and following
regulations and by demonstrating your mastery of them as you
work your way up the ladder.

Captains often begin their careers as deck hands when they
first go to sea and then attend navigation school to receive a
Masters license. From there they usually move up the ladder,
from Cadet to Third Officer, Second Officer, First Officer, and finally to Captain. Most navigating officers on cruise ships do hold
a Captain's license. On the *Queen Elizabeth 2* nine officers hold
Master Mariner's Certificates, which means that they are qualified to command any British ocean-going ship. On Carnival
ships, all deck officers have Master's licenses.

On-Board Discipline

The Captain is the ship's chief executive officer, and in that capacity he organizes and maintains a staff of officers to carry out all duties necessary to operate the vessel. Though he has an office (usually in the living room of his suite), he also works from the bridge. He is the ship's ultimate disciplinarian, and while at sea he acts as both the judge and jury in any dispute that cannot be resolved at a lower level.

On a day-to-day basis, the Staff Captain handles the routine disciplinary issues. Guidelines on the kinds of actions subject to discipline are usually found in the "Masters Rules and Regulations," which are the universally accepted code of ship operations, and which crew members are required to sign when they begin service. Typical Masters rules and regulations include the following:

- No drunkenness will be tolerated.
- No crew member shall have illegal drugs or offensive weapons in his or her possession.
- No indecent language will be used on board.
- No crew member is to be involved in a fight.
- Crew members off duty, below a specified rank, must not be seen in passenger accommodations or public rooms.
- Respect must be given at all times to all officers.
- Respect and a courteous manner must at all times be given to passengers.
- All crew members will attend boat drill.
- All crew members must report punctually for duty.
- Crew members will not miss the ship.
- Gambling is prohibited for all crew members.[2]

Management Style

Some Captains focus all of their attention on administrative matters and have little time for or interest in meeting or interacting with passengers. Others enjoy socializing and often dine

---

[2]Every ship has its own Masters Rules and Regulations. These are extracted from a pamphlet entitled "Shipboard Hotel Personnel Information Booklet" published for its employees by Royal Caribbean Cruises Ltd.

with passengers and invite them to the bridge. As with other CEOs, their behavior has much to do with their individual personalities. Some are customer-oriented—outgoing and gregarious—and act as real ambassadors for their companies. These individuals are frequently seen by the passengers throughout the ship at all hours of the day and night. Some like to be photographed as often as possible, some quietly observe the activities and entertainment to ensure quality control, and others are just on the prowl.

In fact, we have observed that some captains, because of their social and sexual prowess, have contributed meaningfully to the revenue occupancy of the vessel. Clearly, there are passengers who are drawn to the Captain's insignia and crisp white uniform. Imagine being entertained in the Captain's quarters (often a two- or three-room spacious suite furnished with leather sofas, a library, and a stereo) with a polite wait staff pouring Dom Pérignon and serving Beluga caviar!

The Staff Captain

The Staff Captain, the Captain's righthand man, is officially the Captain's deputy and second in command of the ship. When the Captain is not on board the vessel, even in port, he must be there to ensure that someone is in charge at all times. Moreover, he is responsible for all maintenance, radio communications, security, medical services, and normal ship's discipline. For example, the Staff Captain's job description on NCL ships states: "The Staff Captain shall receive all reports of misconduct and take appropriate action or make recommendations to the Captain in accordance with the procedures established by the Captain. He shall maintain a log of such actions as required by the Flag State."

Safety is the Staff Captain's top concern although more often of passengers than of equipment. Staff Captains ensure that the lifeboats work, that fire precautions are all in place, and that the crew is well trained and has frequent practice in all emergency procedures. Royal Caribbean, a typical example, requires every member of the hotel staff who has been on board less then three years to complete a 16-hour course in first aid, CPR, firefighting, and lifeboat handling.

Staff Captain Tom Strom, second in command of the *Nordic Empress*, talked with us about his job and career.

Tom Strom:

I started as a deck boy, working on freighters and tankers. I lived in accommodations you wouldn't think of offering to any crew member today—my quarters today are the same as Second Class passengers used to get on transatlantic crossings.

I am in charge of all the navigators (people on the bridge), security officers, safety officers, and the doctor. That's security as in sheriff and safety as in lifesaving. Our chief officer is a navigation officer—he has the four A.M. to eight A.M. watch on the bridge and assists me with the maintenance outside. The outside maintenance work is supervised by the Boatswain—he's like a sergeant and all the ablebodied seamen, the ordinary seamen, and the deck boys—report to him.

Of course, I worry most about fire. We had a fire in the seventies on the *Skyward* and had to evacuate all of the passengers, but no one was hurt and the ship was back in service in a week.

Security wasn't a problem until the hijacking of the *Achille Lauro* in the eighties. That was an eye opener for us—we realized that ships were no safer than other places from possible terrorist activities, so we have to be prepared for them.

Of course, we have no way of knowing if passengers bring weapons on board. So we X-ray luggage on a selective basis depending on the threat that is most evident at any given time. For example, we're influenced by whether there is peace or war, our itinerary, and the nationality of our guests. Any of those can trigger security concerns, which we address.

Among the crew we have occasional friction. So we have set up rather strict rules and go over them when they join the ship. Fighting or being late for work repeatedly are serious infractions. We have weekly attitude adjustment meetings for people who seem to have a problem dealing with their supervisors. We go through the issue at hand. If they feel they have been treated unfairly, we look into that as well. But the idea is to correct the situation so that it doesn't happen again.

Sexual harassment and gay rights are not a problem aboard our ships. We have heterosexuals and homosexuals, and they all get along. I've never encountered a sexual harassment problem, although we do have a policy against it.

You know, the people who work on ships are a special kind. We all live off the same hallway, and we share cabins. It's much more intimate than an office, where you see each other from nine to five. Maybe that's why we don't have as many problems. If you are a single person without family ties, it's a good place to be. There's a sense of belonging. When people do fight it's usually because they are trying to do the same job and bump into each other accidentally. They almost never fight for personal reasons.

Passengers sometimes confuse the Staff Captain with the Captain. Both are addressed as "Captain" and both may perform the duties generally associated with a ship's captain. The two uniforms have different stripes, however, which makes it easy to tell them apart.

The Ship's Doctor, and Shipboard Health Care

The medical facilities, under the direction of the ship's doctor (who reports to the Staff Captain), can be quite extensive, although they are designed only to take care of minor problems or to stabilize passengers until they can be safely evacuated to a shoreside hospital. Medical professionals would characterize them as infirmaries.

Carnival estimates that roughly 1 in 20,000 of their guests suffers a medical crisis serious enough to require evacuation. Other cruise lines may have a different experience perhaps because of an older passenger base or a longer itinerary, which would predictably result in a higher incidence of medical emergencies.

Cruise ships need to be prepared for the unexpected, which can and does happen while at sea and in foreign ports. For example in 1994— an exceptionally difficult year—there was an outbreak of Legionnaire's disease on the *Horizon*, a death from alcohol poisoning on the *Majesty of the Seas*, and an intestinal illness aboard the *Viking Serenade*. Sometimes passengers develop stomach infections while on shore excursions, as was the case with some of the *Fantasy's* guests in the Bahamas in 1995.

The 1994 incidents generated the most negative press the cruise industry has received in 30 years, but while the incidents were unfortunate, cast against the background of 4.5 million guests annually, the industry overall has an excellent health and safety record—far better in the last 30 years than that of the airline, hotel, and restaurant sectors of the travel and tourism industry.

Legally there are no American or international requirements concerning the level of cruise-ship medicine. However, since lines are in the hospitality business, it makes eminent sense to provide necessary and adequate medical care. *Condé Nast Traveler* examined the medical facilities of 12 major lines and reported the results in their February 1994 issue. One of their key findings was that the quality of care depended in part on the ship's itinerary—the further away it went from ports where passengers could be evacuated, the higher the level of preparedness. Another variable was the average age of the guests. Beyond that, facilities and credentials of doctors varied widely. Some ship doctors came from such countries as Denmark, the United Kingdom, the United States, and Canada. Others came from Colombia and Mexico. Some had been trained in primary- and emergency-care medicine and cardiology while others were specialists in dermatology, gynecology, and radiology. Some of the ships had X-ray machines and said they could and would perform operations such as appendectomies if necessary; others preferred to send the patient to the nearest hospital.

Ship's doctors are hired by a medical director ashore. Often they are semi-retired and enjoy traveling. Their work (for which they are paid directly by the passengers) frequently consists of treatment of minor ailments like a flu that passengers have brought down from the North and develop on the second or third day of the cruise. Another problem is medicine left at home, which ships make every effort to obtain for passengers (although obviously they cannot carry a well-stocked pharmacy nor do they try to).

The bottom line, as with other shipboard services, is that cruise lines make judgment calls based on their perception of the needs of their guests and a cost/benefit analysis. All well-run lines realize that their guests' health is critically important and pay a great deal of management attention to this complex issue.

The Physical Plant and the Chief Engineer

A ship is a very large and sophisticated complex of machinery. Its power plant consists of diesel engines and electrical generators, a heating plant that produces steam for water heating, an air-conditioning plant, a desalinization plant to produce water, a sewage disposal plant, intricate plumbing and electrical systems, fire and safety systems, a closed-circuit TV system, and a host of computers for equipment monitoring, regulating, and operation.

Maintenance

Everything on a ship can and does break down, frequently when the ship is at sea. Modern ships thus have a variety of redundant systems so that they may operate uninterruptedly in case of a system failure. When things do break down it is critical that the ship have the technical competencies as well as material to repair or replace them. Sometimes it's as simple as a clogged toilet in a passenger's cabin, but it can be as complicated as the malfunctioning of the main generator, which supplies all of the ship's electrical power. In any case, in the middle of the ocean there are no outside repair persons to call, so everything must be able to be fixed or replaced immediately for the comfort and safety of those on board.

Erik Bakken, Chief Engineer on Norwegian Cruise Lines' *Seaward*, is responsible for power, waste management, lights, telephones, air conditioning, and refrigeration on his ship, with the assistance of a staff of 30. The heart of his operation (which passengers never see) is a control room in the bowels of the ship filled with gauges, dials, and computer displays, where engineers work four-hour shifts.

Bakken (who reports to the Captain), says that the key to taking care of any emergency on board is to carry sufficient spare parts. Thus, the *Seaward* carries 11,000 items worth over $3 million dollars—everything from light bulbs and TV sets to major machinery components and even a spare sauna heater. Ninety percent of these are tracked in one of Bakken's computer databases and replaced as needed.

Waste Treatment and Disposal

The waste-disposal plant on a modern cruise ship is a good example of the high-tech machinery operated by the engineering department. It shows how the modern art of shipbuilding and operation has had to adapt to changing societal needs and a changing business environment. Historically, waste disposal was never a concern in the cruise or shipping business—after all, it's a big ocean. So disposing of the waste from ships—bottles, paper plates, newspapers, human excrement, and bilge water—was considered to have so little impact as to be without any significance.

Our growing awareness of our environment and our effect on it and our quality of life have changed that thinking forever. It didn't begin with cruise lines, of course. Automobile emissions have been an issue for more then three decades now, railroads no longer discharge waste onto their tracks, and fast-food restaurants have for the most part abandoned styrofoam packaging. But because cruise lines sail out of sight of land for much of the time, no one really cared what they did with their waste. As we stopped believing that the oceans were virtually indestructible and came to understand that they are a critical part of our environment, international agreements were negotiated to safeguard the seas. The London-based International Maritime Organization (part of the United Nations), for example, set a policy of zero tolerance of the discharge of any plastics into the sea, and that policy has the force of the laws of 140 member nations behind it. Even the equipment for trapshooting, a popular activity off the sterns of cruise ships, and golf balls had to be redesigned because shotgun ammunition and golf balls contained plastic!

It was a rude awakening for many operators. They certainly agreed in principle with keeping the oceans clean and were willing to comply, but their equipment simply wasn't adequate for the job. Space, as we have pointed out, is at a premium on a ship, and a modern vessel carrying 2,700 passengers and a crew of 900 can easily generate a ton of garbage as well as other kinds of waste daily. There was no place to put all those empty cans, plastic and paper cups, discarded wrapping from shopping expeditions, and old bingo cards until the ship completed its cruise. Even if there was space for ordinary garbage, the ships had no holding tanks for toilet discharge—this had always been dumped at sea and was believed to be good for the fish.

It turned out that ship waste wasn't good for the fish, and soon it was clear that there were only a few viable options. The first, of course, was to reduce whatever waste you could—for one, by replacing paper napkins and disposable plates and cups with cloth and dishwasher-proof plastic where possible. The problem then became the additional space needed for dishwashers, to say nothing of the fresh water that the ship had either to carry or make on board to do the extra washing. And that produced dirty water, which itself had to be recycled before it could be discharged.

Of course, you could stick with paper and incinerate it instead of throwing it overboard, but that, too, would require a good deal of space for an incinerator that would be both safe (remember, fires of any sort are highly undesirable on ships) and smokeless (passengers don't like soot on their bathing suits). A third alternative was to offload garbage in various ports of call, but not all ports had the infrastructure to handle it.

The problem was exacerbated by a sense of urgency. New rules were being set all the time, and ships that could not adapt would have to be withdrawn from service. In the future, virtually all waste would have to be processed on board to a point where it could be disposed of without environmental impact, or brought back home.

Today's newest cruise ships incorporate complete waste-disposal systems that are more efficient than those found in most towns. They easily cost $10 million or more and can be up to three decks high. The purpose of these systems is to grind, incinerate, shred, compact, and treat every form of waste so that it can be either converted into an acceptable form for incineration or discharge or stored compactly until the ship returns to home port, where it can be recycled or transported to landfills. On a large cruise ship there may be as many as five crew members for whom waste disposal is a full-time job.

Passengers, too, now do their part. It usually starts with announcements and posted notices requesting them not to throw anything overboard. Royal Caribbean, for example, has a highly visible "Save Our Seas" program, which includes a film shown on board and buttons worn by crew members. On most ships of all major lines, separate trash cans for plastic, glass, and metal are clearly marked to assist in the sorting process, and cabin stewards are asked to sort waste into metal, glass, and burnables. For recyling, metals such as the aluminum from beer and soda cans are shredded into small pieces and compacted into large blocks; plastic and styrofoam materials are treated similarly (although plastics generally have been eliminated as much as possible; some lines no longer offer small bottles of shampoo, and others package cabin ammenities in cardboard); however, paper and cardboard are incinerated after shredding.

Leftover food is placed in cold storage until it can be processed in a pulper/grinder, which squeezes the pulp and extracts the water. A sewage-treatment plant breaks the waste down into water and purified waste, which can be discharged after treatment in specified areas. Even bilge water has its oil separated out and recycled before the residue is discharged. Princess' President, Peter Ratcliffe, points out that the company's newest ship, the *Sun Princess*, was designed to implement their new "Planet Princess" program, which completely eliminates all discharge into the ocean. In addition, on all Princess ships plastic drink stirrers have been replaced with wooden ones so that they can be incinerated, and vendors have been instructed to deliver all provisions with plastic wrappings removed.

Virtually all major cruise lines have instructed their crews that throwing *anything* overboard is cause for immediate dismissal. Signs to that effect are posted in crew quarters, as gentle reminders.

The Hotel Manager

The third senior officer reporting directly to the Captain is the Hotel Manager. He has the largest staff on the ship since his crew are the people directly responsible for creating the vacation experience that the line offers. One of the key people in the Hotel

Manager's department is the Chief Purser, who is the ship's banker, information officer, and complaint handler, and who is also responsible for clearing the ship though foreign ports.

As we pointed out earlier, on British lines such as Princess, the Chief Purser *is* the Hotel Manager. Indeed the very title "Hotel Manager" is relatively new on cruise ships—in earlier times, the Chief Purser on most lines managed many of the hotel functions. Even Carnival made this transition only a few years ago to reflect the new functional responsibility that encompasses food and beverage management, hotel operations, entertainment, and the casino.

The Food and Beverage Manager, who runs the dining room and bars, reports to the Hotel Manager on most lines (although not all), as does the Executive Chef. Finally there is the Cruise Director and his or her staff. On a large ship, this may number as many as 70 people including the entertainers, musicians, port lecturers, children's counselors, and aerobic instructors.

Responsibilities

The Hotel Manager is often responsible for other services such as photography, the beauty salon, and the gift shops. On some ships many or all of these services are provided by outside concessionaires; on others they are directly owned and managed by the cruise company. For instance, Royal Caribbean uses a concessionaire to handle its onboard photography (a highly profitable venture), but runs its own gift shops, whereas Carnival handles its own photography, but subcontracts its gift shops. Both lines operate their own casinos, and both use the same concessionaire, London-based Steiner-Transocean, to run their beauty salons and spas. Steiner-Transocean has this concession on a majority of the North American cruise lines.

Carnival, Norwegian, and Royal Caribbean run their own food and beverage operations; however, many lines, such as Premier, use concessionaires to provide these services (often referred to as ship's chandlers). Some subcontract everything, including entertainment. In these companies, the Hotel Manager is only in charge of housekeeping and social activities.

Credentials and Experience

Many Hotel Managers on today's ships come from the hotel industry, although that is a recent development. Most of them have spent their careers at sea, working their way up through the purser's, food and beverage, or stewards departments.

Gunnar Mikkelsen, whom we met on Norwegian Cruise Line's *Seaward*, had been with NCL for 18 years and before that with RCCL as Chief Steward. He spends four months on board followed by two months off—a schedule typical for a ship's Hotel Manager and other senior officers—and like many others, he is married and has children; his family makes their home in Florida. In contrast, Johannes Moser, Hotel Manager of the *Seabourn Spirit*, is an Austrian with a food and beverage background who grew up in the hotel business. His Irish wife is the Housekeeper on board (a position equivalent to Chief Steward on other lines). Her family owns a hotel in Dublin. Similarly, Jacques Bourguignon, a Royal Caribbean Hotel Manager, has a degree in hotel and restaurant administration from Jean Drouant School in Paris. His credentials include the Ritz in Paris, the French Novatel Hotel Chain, and Westin Hotel and Resorts.

In recent years, as capacity has expanded, more and more hotel people have been attracted to the cruise business, and many lines now have Hotel Managers who were trained at hotels—either in the rooms or food and beverage divisions.

Functions of the Hotel Manager's Department

Typically, the Hotel Manager's job is to orchestrate the vacation experience that the cruise line has promised its passengers. To do this requires coordination of all passenger services and ensuring that the line's standards are maintained. Everything that has to do with guest satisfaction is the Manager's bailiwick. If any vessel has a low guest satisfaction rate, he or she is held accountable long before the Captain unless problems are due to mechanical failures or marine operations.

Control of onboard revenues and expenses is the Hotel Manager's second major function (more about that later). He is also responsible for the human resources functions of all of the departments that report to him, including everything from scheduling work (or approving schedules) to communication and morale. Finally, the Hotel Manager must submit a number of reports to shoreside management after each voyage to make them aware of performance and any problems.

The Hotel Departments

Managers, by definition, accomplish their jobs through other people, so perhaps the best way to describe how the Hotel Manager gets his job done is to observe each of his departments and see what it does. While these departments function similarly to their hotel counterparts, there are some profound differences at sea.

The Purser's Office

The Purser's job doesn't exist in a traditional hotel, although in some ways it is similar to the front office or rooms division (except that ship passengers do not check in or check out). The Purser's staff operates the reception desk found in the ship's central area. It is the place passengers go to ask for information, register complaints, and deal with money matters.

In the absence of the Hotel Manager, the Purser is also the chief financial and administrative officer on board. His or her primary duty is to take care of accounting—that is, keep track of what is spent by each passenger as well as the revenues taken in by every department. The purser holds all of the money on board, usually in a large safe located in the office. Passengers come here to convert travelers checks and to get cash for the casino, for duty-free shopping, and for other activities such as bingo. In addition, the crew is typically paid in cash on board twice a month, and funds are needed in port to buy supplies, pay tour operators, and so on. The amount of cash a large ship carries can be substantial (more than $500,000 for a week's cruise is not unusual).

Most cruise ships today use a credit system to handle guest accounts, which minimizes the handling of cash by crew members. If passengers don't have credit cards, they may be required to deposit cash with the purser at the start of the voyage for purchases on board; when that deposit is used up credit is cut off. The Purser's office is responsible for establishing individual passenger credit at the beginning of the cruise and settling accounts before debarkation when the cruise is over.

The Purser's office, like a hotel's front desk, is where guest go for help and information. They may decide to upgrade their accommodations from an inside to an outside cabin ("ocean view" as they say at Carnival). Or there may be a mechanical or plumbing problem or lost luggage. (Usually it's found, but sometimes the airlines failed to deliver it; then it has to be located and arrangements made to retrieve it at the next port of call). The Purser's desk also functions as the lost and found department as well as the focal point for passenger questions such as "What time is the midnight buffet?" (Frequently asked, honestly) and "Which elevator do I take to the front of the boat?"

A major task handled by the Purser is customs and immigration. All passengers and employees must pass through U.S. Customs and Immigrations before leaving a cruise ship. Moreover, every time the ship pulls into a foreign country there is specific paperwork to be done before local authorities will clear the ship for passengers and crew to disembark.

Purser's Staff

On the major lines, the Purser's staff are often Americans because these jobs appeal to them and aren't regarded as servile. Each shares a cabin with another employee and is allowed the privilege of being in specified public areas when off duty, provided the ship's rules and regulations are followed.

Food and Beverages

All of the preparation and service of food and beverages on the ship is under the direction of the Food and Beverage Manager. Since food is considered one of the most important components of the cruise experience (the most important to some folks), delivering a high-quality product to more than 2,000 passengers is a monumental job. Passengers are more likely to comment on and remember details about food service than any other part of their cruise.

The miracle of the whole cruise dining experience is that guests are made to feel that they are eating "gourmet" food presented with very personal service in an elegant restaurant, when in fact they are being fed "banquet style," large numbers at a time. It is an enormously complicated process that works.

The key, of course, is that whereas at a banquet ashore guests have no choice in the food selection, on a contemporary ship like one of Carnival's, they can choose from three soups, two salads, a pasta, seven entrees, and six desserts. Being able to offer an extensive choice to so many people given the constraints of time and space is only possible because of a very precise and accurate forecasting system. If it's Italian Night on the *Ecstasy*, Carnival's management know precisely how many of the 2,400 passengers on board will order the Steak Genoa, the Veal Parmigiania, the Pollo Novello Alla Diavola, the Poached Filet of Sole, and the other three entrees, and they have baked exactly the right number of Cappuccino Pies and Amaretto Cakes. Thus, their store rooms carry just what they need because there is no room for any extra.

The preparation of the food is usually under the supervision of an Executive Chef, who has a set of recipes developed on shore that must be followed exactly. Often the recipes are accompanied by an album of photographs showing the specific presentation of each menu item.

The Galley

Because of safety, sanitation, and health requirements, the galley is one of the most disciplined areas of the ship. Everything must be done by the book with no room for exceptions. The dishes are timed to be cooked just before they are served, so that if the first sitting is at 6:30 P.M., the servers will have the orders in to the galley by 6:45 P.M. and begin serving the appetizers. The first of the main entrées will start coming off the line at 6:55. By 7:30 the first dirty dishes will be coming in (to be immediately washed and reused for the second sitting) and desserts and coffee will be coming out. By 8 P.M. people will begin to leave (they have to if they want to catch the first show—a graceful way to empty the dining room)! This leaves time for the servers to reset the tables with clean linen and table ware for the second sitting at 8:30.

Servers are well trained and highly motivated. Their salaries are very low, but their tips can be substantial—staff on the three major lines average around $24,000 a year tax free, and since all of their meals, accommodations, and medical expenses are provided that's money they can take home. Top servers make $30,000 or more—a small fortune in countries like the Philippines and Nicaragua.

Employee Dining

The Food and Beverage department is also responsible for feeding the employees, who may number 900 or more on larger ships. This is no small task in itself, particularly since unlike the passengers, who are a homogeneous group, the crew can come from 50 to 70 different countries. They do not all eat at the same time, and they do not like the same food. Also, they use different dining rooms depending on their rank (three is average: one for the officers, one for the staff, and one for the crew). There is always a separate galley to feed employees and a choice of dishes to satisfy the cultural diversity.

Food and Beverage—A First-Hand Account

Perhaps the best way to capture the problems and solutions of living and working aboard a cruise ship, and feeding a shipload of passengers with high expectations, is a firsthand account. Dedrick Van Regemorter is the Food and Beverage Manager onboard the *Star Princess*. Dedrick comes from a hotel background—before joining Princess he had spent fifteen years with Marriott working in properties all over the world from Amsterdam to Marco Island, Florida. He decided to move to a cruise line when the hotel business slowed down and with it the opportunities for further promotion.

Dedrick Van Regemorter:

There is a tremendous difference between Food and Beverage service on land and on board a ship. The ship is a very closed environment. You work with the people you have to live with, and you live with the people you have to work with. Therefore, it's extremely important to develop good interpersonal skills. Because you have to live with your people, it's not like a land-based job where you go to work in the morning and if an employee is not doing his job or if things go wrong, you can get upset or take disciplinary action. You know that in the evening you can go home and leave all that behind, and the person you got upset with also goes home, and in the morning all is forgotten. You see everyone all of the time so you have to be very positive, but at the same time you have to keep their respect, and you have to keep very strict discipline. One of the things I noticed coming from the outside is that the number of stripes you carry on your shoulders is very important. It makes a big difference in the amount of attention you get from others on the ship.

Aside from the living conditions, the responsibilities of my job are very different from when I worked in a hotel. While I do all of the ordering for our ship as far as items and quantity, I don't have to get involved with the financial details as I did on land. When I worked in a hotel, there was tremendous pressure on me as well as all managers to control wages, overtime, and other costs, as well as to generate income. I do have a consumption budget I need to watch and some other expenditure guidelines, but that's all. I don't worry about food costs—I don't even know what it costs to feed a passenger. Ninety-five percent of my energy and all of my staff's energy goes to making our passengers happy.

When it comes to the differences in the way we do our job, we have to remember to view a ship, from the customer's point of view, as entirely different from a hotel. On a ship the primary reason for being there is to have a good time. There are no business meetings, faxes, or phone calls—there is nothing to remind you of home. When you walk across that gang plank the ship sets off a psychological switch that allows you to escape into another world—a world where there are no worries and where everything will be taken care of.

Those of us who work on a ship are in a different world as well. When you work at a hotel the influence from outside never leaves you. You might worry about your baby who is sick at home, for instance. But we never leave the ship so we tend to have fewer distractions. Our transmission didn't break down on the way to work, the landlord isn't threatening to kick us out. The atmosphere is very positive. Moreover, a lot of our employees come from countries where the hospitality business is highly respected, where being a waiter can be an important job, so they like their work. Since we're an incentive-based industry the majority want to keep their jobs, and they realize that the better they are at doing them the more money they will make. Finally, everyone has made a commitment for a certain period of time, six months or a year, so they feel they might as well make the best of it. If they are poor performers because of lack of experience, we try to help them. In the dining room, we might put together a smaller station for a week or two, supervised by a headwaiter, or assign them to work with a more experienced waiter until we can bring them up to the same level as our regular staff. But if they have a lousy attitude, then we simply suggest they go home and find something else to do.

Serving tables on a cruise is very different than in a hotel. The group being served stays the same for a whole week. This enables the waiter to develop a relationship with the guests so that he can improve his service to them. For example, after the first night when your servers ask you whether you prefer coffee or tea, they should not have to ask you again. The experienced ones remember whether you want a single or double espresso, or decaffeinated coffee with cream, or regular coffee with sugar. A hotel waiter doesn't have that opportunity and so doesn't even focus on it. The only people at the hotel who remember preferences are bartenders because they try to develop a regular clientele. On a ship remembering details, developing a relationship with passengers, and having a real "service" attitude become the most important thing.

In a hotel, waiters have other concerns that they don't have on a ship to distract them. They have to worry about the handling of cash, they have to worry about how many people they have to serve at one time—sometimes they have their hands full, other times they have nothing at all to do. Here our waiters know exactly how many people are going to be coming to dinner and what time they're going to arrive. So everything is planned and organized; there's no idle time. It is hard work—our waiters may work as many as 12 hours in a 16- or 18-hour period. Because it's in shifts, they get an hour or two off in between. But we all adapt to the routine—we wake up at the same time, we take the same time off, we eat at the same time—the structure of the routine removes some of the stress from our life.

Another difference from a hotel is in the way we do our cooking. The majority of our galley crew is European. They are all trained cooks. The levels and positions are different. To be a first cook, which means to be responsible for a station in the galley like the fish station, takes quite a few years. It is more than on land because we still use the traditional French culinary setup. We do everything from scratch, while in hotels the move to convenience and prepared foods is accelerating. For instance, on land many kitchens use powders to make their stocks. We make our stocks from bones. Nothing goes to waste. On land we often bought our meat preportioned and vacuum-packed. On a ship you buy a whole hindquarter and cut it down.

We use a lot more labor, and that is what accounts in part for the high quality of our food. We even make our own bread. In many hotels we would buy fresh, brown-and-serve, or frozen bread. Here I buy five thousand pounds of flour, add yeast and water, and put a baker to work. He will produce twelve thousand fresh rolls.

That brings up another interesting point. In hotels you might use leftovers to make a new dish the next day. You won't find that on a ship. We don't have leftovers. We have limited storage capacity and a strong tradition of no waste. Remember, there are no trucks to come by daily and take away what we don't use. In a hotel, they forecast how many people are going to show up, order a certain item, and if the people don't show up there are some things left over. We know exactly how many people are coming and exactly what they are going to order. That's because even though we have a lot of choices, we serve the same menu on every cruise, and while we can't forecast individual demands, human being are creatures of habit and we're dealing with a large group of them. Sometimes we have an odd week or two where it's possible to run out of an item. Sometimes produce and fruit like strawberries, at certain times of the year or under certain weather conditions, can spoil faster than anticipated. If that happens, I can't pick up the telephone and ask someone to send over some more. But if we should have a problem like that, and it hasn't happened to me yet, I would talk to the printer, who would change the menu on the computer and could get the press rolling to turn out a thousand new menus in 20 minutes. We are self-sufficient and we must be able to react.

Our passengers expect quite a bit when it comes to food. They do not expect to eat the same foods they would have at home or even in an ordinary restaurant. I like to compare the food we have to serve daily to the food you might order when you go to that one extraordinary restaurant for special occasions every four months. That's why lunch consists of four or five courses, and dinner is a six- or seven-course event. Moreover, the stress of what to order is relieved because price is no consideration—you've already paid for it. At home your eyes go immediately to the right side of the menu before you order that lobster or rack of lamb, but on a cruise there is no right side at all.

Part of that quality dining experience is of course service, and on land it is not possible to give 800 people a really first-class dining experience in an hour and 40 minutes. When I was at Marriott we thought, "wouldn't it be great if we could go to a meeting planner and offer a menu that gave the guests a choice of four entrees? But there was no way to pull it off in a hotel banquet kitchen, which has only a few people and a small space because everything is prepared earlier in the main kitchen and most of the work and manpower is focused on the restaurants. On a ship everything we do is different. I have 107 people in our galley and they don't have to worry about what people are going to order or when to prepare it. All they have to worry about is taking orders from 108 waiters and assistant waiters and cooking them individually. Our food goes right from the oven to the plate to the passenger. You know, having a ship that's consistently full removes a lot of uncertainty and allows us to produce really fine food and serve it with style.

The Steward's Department

The Steward's department (on some lines called the Housekeeping department) is charged with the cleaning and general maintenance of all cabins and interior public areas on a ship. They are also responsible, in most cases, for cabin food service and passenger laundry and dry cleaning, as well as the cleaning of all of the crew's uniforms and all linens, sheets, and towels for the dining rooms and cabins. We spoke with George Drummond, the Chief Steward on NCL's *Seaward*.

George Drummond:

I've been at sea 29 years. My job is to see that we have a clean ship; our passengers are entitled to spotless cabins. I'm also in charge of getting the luggage into and out of cabins. On three- and four-day cruises, passengers may bring as many as three pieces of luggage on board—multiply that by 1,600 and you can see I have my hands full every time we embark and disembark the ship.

It takes three to four hours to get everyone's luggage on board and delivered on a ship this size. We can unload it in thirty to forty minutes because we collect it the night before and stack it on pallets.

I enjoy making the passengers happy. The pool attendants are in my department, and we send them around to spray the passengers with water to cool them off, which they really appreciate when they're lying in the sun. I expect my cabin stewards to give their passengers service, not just make up their rooms twice a day. They need to tell them to have a nice day, ask them if they need anything, and get it if they do. I also expect them to offer to press their clothes for the Captain's party and to make sure the passengers know them by name.

It takes a lot of training. Many of my people come from places where the word "clean" doesn't mean the same to them as it does to me. I have to show them, and I personally go around with every new steward to show him what I expect.

The Cruise Director and Staff

Cruise Director is another title that doesn't exist in a traditional land-based resort. Many resorts have social directors, but theirs is an entirely different function from that of the Cruise Director on board ship. Unlike social directors, who typically work alone, a ship's Cruise Director has a good sized staff to manage: entertainers, musicians, shore excursion managers, youth activity directors, aerobic instructors, a newsletter editor, and, on some ships, a print shop and television studio. On Royal Caribbean's *Sovereign of the Seas* the cruise staff numbers 70.

Like the Food and Beverage department, the cruise staff can

and does make a huge difference in how people feel about their cruise. Remember, the product that customers are buying is a vacation experience, and the persons responsible for all of the activities on board and ashore hold the keys to making that experience memorable and satisfying.

The Daily Activities Schedule

The most visible product of the Cruise Director's work is the daily schedule of activities—usually placed in the passenger's stateroom the night before. If the ship is going to be in port the next day, the schedule lists the tours that are available and when they will be leaving. If there's going to be a port lecture, a dance lesson, a bingo game, or a tour of the bridge, it's in the schedule and will be run by one of the cruise staff. Youth activities are listed here as well as parties for singles and grandmothers. The idea is to have something for everyone and to see that every activity starts and finishes on time and is run consistently with the line's standards.

At port, after the shore excursions have departed (which the cruise staff are also responsible for selling), the cruise director may visit the shops that are part of the ship's program to see the merchandise (and collect the promotional fees). She checks out possible new shore excursions and monitors old ones; and she may arrange for a local group to provide entertainment on board before the ship leaves—for instance, a Mexican mariachi group with folk dancers, in Acapulco.

Entertainment

At night, the cruise director is all over the ship, checking on the two big shows presented in the show lounge (which she may introduce), the pianist at the piano bar, the DJ in the disco, the comedian in another lounge, and the teen party in the club room. In fact, she may be the star of a show or two herself.

The cruise director may be the first person up in the morning and the last to go to bed. It is a grueling job—seeing that 2,400 people make new friends and have fun for as many of the 24 hours in a day they can handle in three, four, or seven days, and then starting all over again with a new group on the same day the old group departs. Cruise Directors come from a variety of nationalities and backgrounds. While many started as entertainers, others come from the ranks of pursers and from managerial posts ashore. They like people and get along with them, and they're adept at handling temperamental artists. Good ones are hard to find, but can make all the difference in how passengers remember their vacation.

Putting It All Together

The problem a cruise line must solve is that its vacation experience has a significant number of components (some of them, such as entertainment, quite complicated), which need to be assembled, packaged, and coordinated effectively to satisfy the guests. The solution lies in the ship itself, which is a controlled and confined atmosphere, a cocoon if you will, in which a well-trained staff following a pretested and standardized routine can deliver superior service with very little opportunity for error. It takes the team work of a number of specialists, from chefs to captains, supported by a strong infrastructure to pull it off, but the results justify the efforts.

4

Home on the Rolling Deep

Case studies in backstage management

It is not within our scope to give the reader an in-depth feel for the cruise product offered by the major industry players (several of the guide books on cruising, such as *Berlitz* and *Fielding*, do an excellent job of this). However, we thought it might be interesting to dissect some of the elements of managing the cruise experience on board. We chose two examples to show differences and similarities—a smaller, luxury ship and one of the major, mass-market vessels.

Our choice for the smaller vessel was the *Seabourn Spirit* during a 14-day cruise from Istanbul to Venice in July of 1994. While Seabourn has only one other ship, the *Seabourn Pride*, the line has been consistently ranked by travel agents, journalists, and consumers as the world's best cruise line. Among others, the readers of *Condé Nast Traveler* have awarded Seabourn that title for three consecutive years.

Cruising with Seabourn

Seabourn was founded by a young Norwegian industrialist and entrepreneur named Atle Brynestad, a self-made man who started his first business at 16, knitting and marketing his own line of Norwegian sweaters. From sweaters, Brynestad took an interest in real estate, hotels, and department-store glassware (he acquired Norway's oldest company, the Hadeland Glassworks, which today creates some of the world's finest crystal). Sensing that there was a growing market for cruises and that Norwegians seemed to have a knack for running them well (both Royal Caribbean Cruise Lines and Kloster Cruise Lines, which operates Norwegian Cruise Lines, are Norwegian owned), Brynestad decided to develop a new cruising concept. He was attracted to the luxury end of the market because of his personal lifestyle and experience.

Luxury Cruising

By the mid 1980s, there were several concepts of luxury cruising in the market. Cunard's *Queen Elizabeth* 2, was a 66,000-ton dual-purpose ship built for both transatlantic crossings and cruising. The first purely premium line, however, was Norwegian American, which operated the *Sagafjord* and the *Vistafjord*. Built for long-range cruising and to resemble elegant European hotels, these smaller, 24,000-ton, ships carried between 600 and 700 passengers.

Royal Viking, another luxury cruise line of the time, was founded in 1970 also by Norwegian interests. Warren Titus, its first president, felt that the line could successfully differentiate their product by providing a larger number of deluxe cabins and suites and using a new, modular prefabrication system that allowed for greater freedom of design and considerable cost savings. The line had three 20,000-ton, 500-passenger ships by 1974, the *Royal Viking Star, Sky*, and *Sea*.

At the opposite end of the size scale was another Norwegian company, Sea Goddess Cruises, with two ships launched in 1984. These ships were designed to have the ambiance of large luxury yachts. At 4,253 tons each, they had a passenger capacity of only 116.

The Seabourn Philosophy

In 1987 Brynestad recruited Titus from Royal Viking, and the two men, along with a group of associates (most of whom are still with the company), set out to design a cruise line that would be both better than and clearly different from the available luxury offerings. They reasoned that while Royal Viking's facilities and service were undoubtedly the finest afloat, its ships were too large (they had been stretched to accommodate 700 passengers) to provide the kind of intimate and exclusive quality of service that the men felt luxury-minded clientele would demand. And while Sea Goddess was for the most part able to satisfy this expectation, its two ships were so small that they lacked many of the amenities the market also expected (such as a full-sized spa) and they didn't behave as well as a larger ship in choppy waters.

Brynestad and Titus' solution was to design a new kind of ship—10,000 tons in size—that would accommodate 204 people, all of them in 106 suites of 277–575 square feet each. By contrast, on Royal Viking ships some cabins were as small as 138 square feet, while Sea Goddess suites ranged from 205 to 475 square feet. The men believed the new Seabourn design would offer both the intimacy of a small yacht and the amenities and spaciousness of a larger ship. Another important consideration was that a ship of this size could accommodate a galley large enough to prepare all meals à la minute rather than banquet style. Also, the greater size would enable a large enough crew for the highest crew/passenger ratio in the industry (two for every three passengers), thus ensuring top-notch service.

Seabourn's first ship, the *Seabourn Pride*, made her maiden voyage in November 1988. Her sister ship, the *Seabourn Spirit*, was launched a year later. In 1989 *Travel & Leisure* magazine, in a lengthy cover story on Seabourn described it as "the one to beat."

Seabourn's Pricing Strategy

From the beginning, Brynestad recognized that he was not selling a cruise but, in his own words, "a unique vacation experience"—one that, because Seabourn would carry only 200 passengers on a ship (other cruise lines carried 400 or more passengers) and because of the very high crew/passenger ratio, would have to be priced at the very top of the market. Thus, Seabourn's Mediterranean cruises today cost a minimum of $878 to $933 per day per person and most cruises are 14 days long, although they can be purchased in shorter, 7-day segments. There are, of course, other itineraries (the two ships sail all over the world, including China and the Amazon) and shorter and longer cruises, some with more modest prices. Given virtually any itinerary, however, Seabourn is the most expensive cruise product there is.

With such a high price tag come extremely high expectations. Market studies show that the average household income of Seabourn clientele is $200,000. According to Brynestad, "our clientele doesn't need to save up their money to go on one of our cruises. Further, they are not determined to have a good time, no matter what happens or how they are treated. To satisfy them we need to *win their hearts*." Indeed "heart" is a very important part of Seabourn's corporate culture. We heard the word used several times not just by Brynestad but by other Seabourn executives and employees. After every voyage, each Seabourn client receives a tangible expression of Seabourn's heart—a dozen roses in one of Brynestad's Norwegian crystal vases delivered to their home.

The Cruise

When passengers arrive in Istanbul for this particular cruise, they are transferred to the Ciragan Palace Kempinski, certainly one of the world's most beautiful and unique hotels. Located directly on the Bosphorus, the Ciragan is a nineteenth-century sultan's palace modernized and converted to a 322-room luxury hotel.

Seabourn provides a hospitality desk in the lobby for two days prior to sailing staffed by two local agents whose sole duties are to act as personal concierges for Seabourn guests. Accordingly, they may help organize private tours of Istanbul, shopping excursions, or even recommend and negotiate rug sales in the bazaar. When it is time to board the ship, Seabourn representatives pick up guests' luggage directly from the hotel and take it to the cabins of embarking passengers. All embarkation procedures are completed in the hotel before guests' departure for the ship so that when they arrive, they are handed a complimentary glass of high-quality French champagne (such as Piper Heidsieck non-vintage Brut), greeted by name by the hotel manager and his white-gloved staff, and escorted to their suites. There is no waiting, no lines, and no formalities. A complimentary bottle of properly iced champagne is waiting in every suite along with the luggage. Within a few minutes a cabin stewardess appears, introduces herself and orients the guests to their suite.

Accommodations

Unlike a hotel room or even an ordinary cruise-line cabin, Seabourn accommodations do require some orientation. Their standard 277-square-foot suite seems more like a small studio apartment. The decor is muted pastels set against a five-foot picture window with electric window shades. There is a convertible dining/coffee table with a sofa and two chairs next to the window, a queen-sized bed, a desk with personalized monogrammed stationary, and a large walk-in closet with a combination safe, TV, VCR, a bar and refrigerator (stocked with guests' favorite alcoholic beverages and soft drinks determined by a special questionnaire sent to all passengers several weeks before), and Hadeland crystal glassware. The marble bathroom has two sinks, a shower, his and hers towels, terry cloth robes, and more.

Next to the VCR is a tape entitled "Welcome to Your Suite," which points out all of the special features and how to use them. For example, room service is provided 24 hours a day (including all the caviar you desire at no charge). During meal hours, complete dinners from the dining room menu are served in the suite one course at a time by regular waiters for those who want a romantic candlelight dinner or who simply don't want to dress up and dine in the restaurant. Unlike many other cruise ships where important announcements are automatically piped into cabins, on Seabourn, announcements are only broadcast on one of the four channels, and it remains silent most of the time.

Dining

The ship is spacious but small by usual cruise ship standards, so it does not take long to tour the public areas. The large main dining room is open from 8 to 10 for breakfast, 12:30 to 2 for lunch, and 7 to 10 for dinner. Seating is open, so passengers can come in any time without reservations and sit wherever and with whomever they wish. There are plenty of tables for two for couples who wish to dine alone as well as larger tables for groups of four to twelve who wish to dine together. No one ever sits alone unless the individual so chooses—single passengers are invited to join other guests or dine at tables with officers and senior hotel staff members.

Menus feature classic and Nouvelle Cuisine but are finished in a more contemporary, lower-calorie manner. Everything is prepared à la minute, and all dishes are plated on specially designed china to achieve a stunning presentation. Favorite dishes, according to the company, include Sautéed Thai Prawns, Ahi Tuna with Aioli and Olive Tapanade, Marinated Breast of Capon with Polenta and Cranberries, Caribbean Fresh Conch Chowder, Rack of Lamb Pre Sale with Mint and Garlic, and Ginger-Marinated Cornish Game Hen, to name a few. In our opinion, Seabourn's restaurants would merit at least one and probably two stars by *Guide Michelin*.

In addition to the main dining room, the ship offers a Veranda Café with indoor and outdoor seating. This cafe is open for breakfast and lunch and some special casual dinners. While it is buffet style, waiters stand by to carry plates to the table or serve passengers as well as to handle special orders.

Entertainment

The ship has three public lounges, where entertainment consists of a small musical group with one or two soloists and one or two other cabaret-style entertainers. Typical of the entertainment staff is Paul Balfour, a pianist and soloist who performed at White House teas and other official functions while he was in the U.S. Army Band. The intimate casino features slot machines, roulette, and two black jack tables. There is also an enrichment lecturer who is usually either a college professor or an expert on the area the ship is cruising. For a D-Day memorial cruise to Normandy earlier that year, the lecturer was Walter Cronkite. On the Istanbul-Venice Seabourn voyage the enrichment lecturer was Dr. James Bill, Director of the Center for International Studies at the College of William and Mary and an expert on Middle Eastern affairs.

Amenities

Shipboard amenities include a spacious gymnasium complete with treadmills, stair-climbing machines, bikes, rowing machines, a separate aerobics room, sauna and steam baths, beauty salon. There are three whirlpools and a swimming pool, a jogging track that circles the vessel (15 times around equals one mile), a gift shop, and a library stocked with over 200 videotapes and a broad selection of recently published and classical fiction and nonfiction. There is even a self-service laundromat for guests who don't wish to use the ship's regular service.

The Atmosphere

More than most lines, Seabourn recognizes that in the hospitality business, the passengers are part of the physical product. Guests expect each other to behave and dress in a certain way, so both vessels have very strict dress codes, casual, informal, and formal. The ship's daily program lists the acceptable dress in public areas each evening after six. Passengers understand that this is not a matter of personal choice since those who do not wish to dress are able to dine in their cabin and watch a movie or read. On formal nights, it is rare to see a male passenger without a tuxedo or evening jacket. Indeed, on our cruise we heard one passenger complain to the Hotel Manager when a guest at another table removed his dinner jacket during the meal. The headwaiter politely asked him to put it back on!

Human Resource Philosophy

Seabourn's philosophy of superior service is based on two main tenets. First, you have to take care of your internal guests (your employees) before you can expect them to take care of your external guests (the passengers). Second, the guests are Seabourn's most important asset, and it is the staff's job to find out quickly what each individual expects and to make sure that it is delivered in spades so that the guest will clearly be able to differentiate Seabourn cruises from the ordinary and articulate that difference to others.

   The company doesn't just pay lip service to these concepts—they constantly reinforce them with a passion. Vice President of

Hotel Operations Larry Rapp believes that this level of service starts with human resource management. "In order to provide superior service," he says "each employee must feel absolutely secure in his or her position. He or she has to feel, from a psychological standpoint, free to take whatever decision needs to be taken to satisfy our guests without constraint from a company system, a budget plan, or an organization plan. The crew member who is speaking to a guest has to have the power to provide satisfaction—no hierarchy should get in the way of that." The "Twelve Points of Seabourn Hospitality" a document that every employee has and that is posted in the Hotel Manager's office, contains several points aimed directly at encouraging this behavior:

- Any crew member who receives a guest complaint "owns" that complaint. He/she is responsible for ensuring guest satisfaction.
- Always remember the importance of teamwork and service to co-workers.
- Communicate guest problems to fellow employees and management.
- Take responsibility for your own behavior.
- Do not be afraid to make a mistake as long as your efforts are sincerely intended to do your job in a better way.

Supervisor Responsibilities

To ensure that there is no misunderstanding of what is expected, the Seabourn *Hotel Operations Manual* specifically states that every Seabourn supervisor is to receive, *before* signing on the ship, a document called "Supervision of Hotel Employees" with his or her employment contract. The document is very specific and states that performance evaluations will be based on the ability of supervisors to accomplish these tasks. Here are some relevant excerpts:

> It is the duty of each supervisor to find a way to motivate his or her team to:
>
>> Find out what each guest wants.
>> Give it to them.
>
> Supervisors have the responsibility to encourage open communication by creating in their employees:

Self confidence
Empathy
Respect

And here is an outline of the "management style" Seabourn Cruise Line expects of it's supervisors:

I will support frontline employees, not try to control them.

I believe that EVERY employee wants to do the best job he or she can.

I fully realize that my employees' attitudes and feelings affect their performance, and that my supervision can affect those attitudes and feelings.

I will give positive feedback to my colleagues as often as sensible.

When I need to give negative feedback I will only refer to facts, NOT people. I will say "The ashtray needs cleaning." I will not say "You don't take proper care of the ashtrays," or worse "You are a sloppy person."

I will listen to the ideas of my employees and give them full credit when they contribute to a success.

I will give each of my colleagues all the respect that is their right as a human being. This means treating them as they want to be treated.

Staff Meetings

Every week there is a waiters' meeting after the dining room closes at 11 P.M., during which guest comment cards from the previous week's cruise are reviewed. In attendance one evening were Hotel Manager Johannes Moser, Maître d' Herald Lange (who chaired the meeting), Chef Jurg Inniger, and all 17 servers from 10 countries.

The meeting began with Chef Inniger reading aloud the negative comments from the previous week concerning the food. He stated first that these comments were not negative but constructive. "We want to maintain our reputation for the best food," he told the group. The first comment was that the "pasta was not done correctly." A waiter pointed out that this comment was from an Italian family, and Italians are very particular about their pasta. But the same card went on to say that "the food improved the second week." The waiter added, "By the second week we knew this family. They liked spicy food and we gave it to them." Lange complimented the waiter for being on his toes. Another comment stated that "the pastry needs improvement." A member of the group said that he had tasted the croissants that morning and they were horrible. The chef agreed and noted that the baker had become ill in Istanbul and left the ship—a new one was due the next day. The only other negative food comment was that "the menu was too Americanized." Chef Inniger told the waiters he needed more feedback from them as to what their European and Asian clientele liked.

Next some of the positive comments were reviewed. They included "Great selection." "Superb meals," "Good cuisine and variety—better than before," "My kind of food," "I blame you for the weight I gained," and "All our special requests were handled with no problem." Overall the score on cuisine was 9.81 out of a possible 10. Inniger noted that 87.3 percent of the responses gave the cuisine a perfect 10, and no one gave it below an 8.

Maître d' Lange then reviewed the comments on the servers' service, out of which there were only three negatives. The first dealt with slow dinner service on the veranda. Lange recommended that waiters concentrate more on their stations. Another guest mentioned that their wine glasses had been removed before the end of the meal and said this was not a good idea for there was always the possibility that someone would want more. Everyone thought this was a good comment. "From now on we won't do it," said one of the servers. Finally, a guest wanted to know why they couldn't order full room service by the pool but had to return to their suite to get it. Lange noted that they didn't have enough manpower on board to offer this. "But" he added, "people paying $35,000 ought to be able to get it." Several servers contributed ideas, and it was decided that the full room service menu would be offered from one of the bars on deck and that trays of sandwiches would be passed around at lunch time so that guests would not feel the need to order room service. Lange then turned to the positive comments they had received: "You have given a new meaning to class and superb service," "We are used to traveling on a private yacht, but we like this cruise so much we're spending an extra $25,000 to stay another week," and "All your waiters are as adorable as my two sons." Several waiters were mentioned by name, and the others applauded or cheered whenever one of these comments was read.

The meeting ended with a review of the known likes and dislikes of the guests boarding in Athens in a couple of days. One liked certain cheeses and a note was made to check with the provision master to be sure they would be on board. Another liked bran cereal and skim milk for breakfast every day. One was known to like fresh fruit juice brought to him while exercising on the treadmill—this turned out to be one of us. (And, yes, I did receive my juice each day.) Everyone made notes so they would remember.

The meeting was highly participative. After every negative comment there were several suggestions as to how to improve things. No one was criticized directly and there were no recriminations. A similar meeting took place the following morning in the housekeeping department. Every negative comment was reviewed and the tone of the meeting was always "How can we solve this problem?" never "People don't understand that we can't do this."

As a result of this continuing process, Seabourn is constantly refining and fine-tuning its service. "The whole secret is getting everyone involved in producing the product," says Johannes Moser, the Hotel Manager, who was one of the original developers of the Seabourn concept and their first Food and Beverage Manager. "Then it becomes theirs and they own it and are proud of it. I not only solicit their ideas, I try them out when I can. If they work, I adopt them." When I asked how he could do this with such a demanding clientele, where mistakes can be fatal, his answer was "We hire good people we can trust and then we train them. (God is in the details, said Frank Lloyd Wright.)"

Training
Training goes on continually at all levels. Hotel managers have been supplied with a series of management tapes used in business schools and training seminars. These are regularly shown and discussed on a voluntary basis. The company also offers all supervisors the opportunity to attend courses at any hotel school of their choice when they are off the ship on vacation. The wine

steward gives monthly tastings and lectures on wines and the regions they come from, and the chef briefs the wait staff every night before dinner, not only presenting the dishes that are on the menu that evening but giving a short lecture on the recipes and how they are prepared. Servers are regularly quizzed in writing to improve their knowledge of food and wine. Questions include "What do you know about sabayon?" "What ocean or sea does the turbot come from?" and "Name three types of caviar." In keeping with Seabourn's nonthreatening, nurturing atmosphere, the quiz, along with the answers, is posted a week in advance so everyone has a chance to study the answers.

Motivation and Compensation

Moser doesn't see the *Seabourn Spirit* as a cruise ship at all. "We're a small hotel that floats." We heard the same sentiment later in the voyage from another crew member. "I would never work on a cruise ship," he said scornfully. In truth, as we pointed out earlier, we believe that cruise ships are not floating hotels but floating vacation experiences. Nevertheless, it serves Seabourn's purpose from a recruiting, training, and motivational standpoint to encourage that kind of thinking.

Compensation aboard Seabourn ships for service personnel is unique. There is no tipping permitted. The hotel staff is paid by salary plus a revenue-sharing plan, which is based on the number of guests on board each cruise. The theory, says Moser, is that "If we do a good job, people will take more cruises and tell their friends. If they do that, the company makes more money, and so the people responsible for creating that experience should share in it."

Crew and Guests

Seabourn's method of crew involvement in the product, combined with its eclectic itineraries in which different ports are visited every week (unlike mass-market ships, Seabourn cruises do not go back and forth between the same destinations on a regular schedule), offers some unique opportunities as well as problems. The most important opportunity is the chance to forge a lasting personal relationship between the customers and the company. The morning after the *Seabourn Spirit* departed from Istanbul with 90 new passengers joining those already on board, the dining room servers met to study pictures of all of the new folks and memorize their names. In the lounges and dining room, whenever a crew member recognizes a person, he or she repeats their name aloud so that other crew members can hear it and so also greet the guest by name. The payoff is most obvious in the dining room: Even if you sit at a different table each night with a different server, you are greeted in a personal way.

Cuisine

Rapp points out another opportunity for a unique experience, Seabourn's cuisine. Their policy is to buy fresh regional products at ports where they are available. Chef Inniger, on our voyage, had purchased fresh strawberries in Odessa, fish in Istanbul, and goose liver in France. During one stop in the Greek Islands, he headed off to the local fish market to buy some of that day's catch, which appeared on the menu that evening.

Freshness is an obsession on board. The orange juice is squeezed daily—yesterday's fresh juice is consumed by the crew. Even the wine steward and head bartender buy many of the wines used on the ship in their countries of origin. "Because I am involved in the wine selection I can explain the wines and sell them enthusiastically," Head Bartender Norbert Fuchs says.

Shore Excursions

Any problems are most likely to occur on shore excursions. Unlike a 7-day Caribbean cruise on which the ship visits the same port every week, a Seabourn ship may visit some ports only a few times a year. That means that they have to work harder to ensure the availability of the best equipment and tour guides for their excursions, since the infrastructure in some areas is dominated by the larger vessels that call more regularly. Moreover, things change often—some museums and other sites close for renovations, new ones open, and the recommended shopping and dining venues can chance. Guests expect and want superior and unique excursions, and these can be hard to come by especially if the tour manager hasn't been there for six months.

But the real problem is that ships cannot run their own shore excursions—that is reserved for operations in the local community virtually everywhere. Thus, the guests are off the vessel and interacting with people who are not company employees, although the tours, like the airline flights, are perceived as part of the Seabourn experience. Seabourn's method of dealing with this is to set their offerings apart, as much as possible, from the run-of-the-mill. Thus, buses that hold 49 passengers are only half filled, and every bus gets not only a local guide but a member of Seabourn's travel staff. Bottles of water and soft drinks are carried on board and a complimentary refreshment stop is included. The company tries hard to audition the guides who will be used and specifically requests the best ones whenever possible. Detailed written contracts are given to all tour operators that specify, among other things, that all admissions are to be included; that there will be no tipping either solicited or permitted; the hours at which the buses will arrive and depart at each stop; and any other special requirements, such as "After lunch the guide will be stationed by the bell tower on the square to answer questions."

At some destinations it is possible to offer tours not available at all on other ships. These are usually quite expensive and are offered only when enough passengers sign up well in advance (and they often do). An example might be a balloon trip over vineyards in France. Or it might be "an unforgettable evening in 18th century Venice" for guests willing to pay $390, consisting of a five-course dinner in a restored Venetian palazzo. The feast includes period Venetian dishes served after a "Degustation of Wine," and entertainment was provided by a trio of musicians in period costumes playing ancient instruments as well as a group of actors from La Commedia Dell 'Arte. There is also a private tour of the Guggenheim Museum for $85 hosted by one of its curators after closing hours, with wine served.

Again, these tours are often the unique creations of the ship's travel office, which gives the staff a feeling of ownership and thus a mandate to see that they succeed.

The Secret to Seabourn's Success

Seabourn's success can be attributed to a complex and carefully orchestrated corporate culture based on values shared among the management, employees, and guests. President Larry Pimentel, a former travel agent himself, tells agents in sales seminars that they should "sell what counts, not discounts," which is for Seabourn a key point. Everyone who works for the company understands what counts. The passengers who are paying more than $800 per diem know they are buying a unique and personal experience, and that's what counts for them. They expect uniqueness and customized service; indeed, they demand it. The company shares the same value. "It is those very qualities that makes the difference," says Pimentel.

"It doesn't matter what you want—the company will get it for you" is a reality in Seabourn's service-delivery system. Guests frequently bring their own recipes on board, which the chef gladly prepares. It gives the company a chance to further customize and thereby differentiate their product. In some cases, special ingredients are flown to the ship to fulfill these requests. Pimentel points out that Seabourn is not simply an expensive cruise but an entirely different experience: "Buying a Seabourn cruise is a lifestyle decision." And to provide that experience the company relies on highly trained and motivated people—motivated not by money (although they are well paid) but rather by a genuine pride in what they do. That pride is reinforced regularly. When Seabourn won the Condé Nast Award the first time Atle Brynestad sent every crew member a piece of his crystal. After a spectacular party on our cruise the following memo was sent to every manager on the ship and posted in the crew quarters:

> To Everyone Involved In the 4th of July BBQ yesterday, thank you all for the effort you have put in to make this special day a SUCCESS. Many guests commented, how much they appreciate your hard and professional work. *Some people dream of worthy accomplishments, while you stay awake and do them.* Congratulations, Johannes Moser, Hotel Manager.
>
> Another key is Atle Brynestad's "heart." The company shows genuine respect and empathy in dealing with its employees on every level. The easiest way to lose your job at Seabourn may be to lack that empathy for fellow employees and guests. If the company had a song it would be that old vaudeville number "You Gotta Have Heart." Heart translates into a recognition that everyone on the ship is literally in the same boat, and that it is a special boat where dreams come true for guests and employees.

Seabourn and Carnival

As a result of an investment in 1992, Seabourn is now a joint venture with the Carnival Corporation, which owns 25 percent of the stock and has an option to buy another 25 percent. In 1994, Seabourn posted its first profit—the first that any line has made in the high end of the luxury cruise market. "It shows you that these [small luxury ships] cannot make money on their own," says Carnival's Chairman and CEO Micky Arison. "However, by being linked to the Carnival family, they have the opportunity to use our purchasing power and sales force, which have been instrumental in turning them around."

When all is said and done, what drives Seabourn is that it is a creation of the people on the front line who interact with the guests and together shape the experiences for the benefit of all parties. According to Larry Rapp, "Everybody in this industry talks about moments of truth. There is no place on earth where a company has more moments of truth than on a cruise ship. When they wake up in the morning they meet their stewardesses. They go to breakfast and see our waiters. From there they go to a lecture on the next port of call or to an aerobics class. Every time they turn around they encounter a member of our staff. There are hundreds of moments of truth every day. And obviously every one of those has to be positive or we lose."

We believe that the techniques that have won Seabourn its top ranking as a service experience are equally applicable to other segments of the hospitality and travel business such as hotels and restaurants. They are simple to enumerate but difficult to accomplish:

1. Affluent guests don't buy rooms or food or seats. They buy experiences. The more personal the experience you provide, and the more unique it is, the more customers are willing to pay for it. Value is not merely function of dollars. Satisfaction is an equally important dimension.
2. Treat your employees with the same kind of respect you expect to receive. It goes without saying that managers need to understand what respect means.
3. Involve your employees in shaping your product and empower them to deliver it, so that they share in the pride and

rewards that comes with accomplishment. Give them constant feedback so they can see how they are doing. People want to work in an organization because they want to accomplish more than they can alone. Companies that can mesh the personal goals of employees with an organization's overall goals will succeed and prosper.

Cruising on Carnival

Cruising on a Carnival "Fun Ship" is a very different experience from a Seabourn cruise, yet as we will see, there are many points of similarity. If Seabourn is delivering an expensive and exclusive vacation for the affluent, Carnival is offering a scaled down experience for the mass market. Carnival's average price point is $150 a day, a fraction of Seabourn's $800 plus, and its target market is adults between 25 and 54 with minimum household incomes of $30,000. Also, whereas Seabourn targets 1 percent of the population of the United States and Canada (ignoring its truly global affluent market for the moment), Carnival aims at 40 percent—40 times the target market of Seabourn! In short, as truly remarkable as the Seabourn product is (both of us would do anything to sail on Seabourn again and again), the reality is that most people not only can't afford it but also would not appreciate (or may not even like) it. Perhaps that's why Carnival owns a chunk of Seabourn, not the other way around.

As a mass-market vacation provider, Carnival is challenged to find about 1,350,000 customers in 1996, and that number will grow to at least 1,750,000 vacationers by 1999, as three additional "Fun Ships" come on line, creating a 14-ship fleet. Of course, it's not enough to spend billions to provide a fleet of sparkling white ships. As many other travel providers have sadly realized, investing in capacity doesn't always mean that that capacity will be utilized. As with Seabourn, it's the software that has made Carnival so uniquely successful.

Embarkation

But the hardware does contribute. After being electronically processed at Miami Seaport Terminal 8 or 9—the cruise capital of the world—guests are greeted at the gangway by cruise-staff members and stewards, who direct them to their staterooms. Their first impression is typically one of awe at the soaring 7-story neon-outlined atrium. It's fun to watch people react. There's excitement in the air as they realize that this will be no ordinary vacation.

Once in their staterooms, guests can see that their accommodations are spacious by cruise ship standards. In fact, Carnival's standard stateroom is larger than those on the other Miami-based lines. The inside cabins measure 165 square feet, and the ocean-view cabins are 190 square feet. Both are equipped with individual twin beds that convert to one king-size bed (and stay that way even under battlefield conditions), as well as telephones, televisions, wall safes, ample closet and drawer space, and a vanity table. The bathrooms feature a large shower and are roomy enough to move around in comfortably. Also, the ocean-view cabins have large picture windows, not the small, round port holes of yesteryear.

Many staterooms have one or two fold-down upper berths, and some provide space for a rollaway bed, thus expanding the accommodations to up to five people.

Departure and Luggage
Embarkation hours in Miami are 12:30 to 3:30 with the ship sailing at 4:00. Eager vacationers begin to arrive before noon, and embarkation generally starts earlier to accommodate them. Luggage is delivered to the stateroom by 6 o'clock, but most bags arrive an hour or so after the guests check in.

After locating their stateroom and meeting their cabin steward, most passengers consult the *Carnival Capers* daily shipboard schedule and either head for the Lido restaurant for the embarkation lunch or explore the vessel. Some, of course, immediately take to the open decks and begin working on their tans.

The Lido lunch, by the way, is an informal buffet with a full salad bar, pasta stations, hamburgers, hot dogs, barbeque chicken, and the like. Upgraded in 1995, Lido service now features more extensive menu choices and servers circulate to take beverage orders and assist guests with their trays. During the week, different food stations are set up at breakfast and lunch to offer greater variety. Choices include customized omelets and frittatas at breakfast, and grilled chicken or shrimp with fresh tossed Caesar salad or fresh pasta at lunch.

Guest Credit

At embarkation, guests receive a sail-and-sign card with a magnetic strip enabling them to make purchases or board without cash. This is very convenient for them and probably contributes to a slightly higher level of on-board purchase. The card also acts as the guest I.D. and includes the dining-room table assignment.

Dining

Fantasy-class vessels like the *Sensation* feature two comparably appointed restaurants seating about 650 each. The center section of each restaurant is elevated so that all guests have sea views through a wall of windows on both sides of the vessel. Tables range in size from four to twelve and are reserved for the length of the cruise. There are two sittings, early and late, with start times of 7:30, noon, and 6:00, and 9:00, 1:30, and 8:15 for breakfast, lunch, and dinner, respectively. Typically, senior citizens and families with small children prefer the early sitting; most of the rest tend to gravitate to the late sitting. Additionally, there's a continental breakfast service in the stateroom each day including cereals, the aforementioned Lido for breakfast and lunch, and complimentary 24-hour room service featuring a selection of sandwiches, fruit plates, and the like.

A new feature, 24-hour pizzerias, are now offered on the *Holiday*, *Imagination*, and *Inspiration* and are being extended to the rest of the fleet because of their great popularity. The pizzeria offers eight kinds of pizza and calzone, including exotica such as goat cheese with sun-dried tomatoes.

Dining each night presents a myriad of choices for appetizers, soups, pasta, at least six entrées (including two vegetarian selections), cheeses and fruit, and a variety of desserts. Lunch and dinner menus also feature the Nautica Spa cuisine, which offers low-calorie, low-fat, low-salt, and low-cholesterol choices, including sweets.

While obviously not à la minute, the food is invariably better on a Carnival ship than anywhere in Orlando or Las Vegas at all but the highest-priced restaurants. In at least one, probably biased, author's view, it's equal to or better than all other lines out of Miami.

Guest Suitability

Because of the "Fun Ship" positioning, vacationers come on board expecting a good time, however they choose to define it. It's something of a serendipitous, self-fulfilling prophecy: they expect to have a good time, so they do. In fact, the Carnival sales force tells agents *not* to send certain type clients on Carnival. Let's face it, there are people who seem to be happiest when sour or carping about everything. These are the kind who seem to perpetually wear overstarched underwear. And if one of them is assigned to an otherwise affable, convivial table of six or eight, how pleasant will that be for the majority? It's not a luxury for Carnival to tell agents whom not to send but a necessity. Perfection is in the details—including obtaining the appropriate clientele and winnowing out those who won't fit in. (While on this somewhat delicate but critical subject, Carnival also instructs agents not to send folks who wish a truly gourmet, à la minute dining experience as well as those few who would be most pleased to travel with others as long as they're just like them.)

The crew is oriented to refer to the passengers as "guests" through Carnival's training programs (offered under the banner of "Carnival College"). The whole idea, of course, is to emphasize treating them as guests in their shipboard home . . . with the full gamut of hospitality implications that the term implies.

Guests' Expectations and Their Delivery

The shipboard staff as well as all shoreside employees understand that purchasers of Carnival vacations have made a highly discretionary decision to spend their time and money experiencing the Carnival product. Guests therefore have a reasonable expectation regarding the food, service ambience, entertainment, and activity choices that the product offers, and they anticipate an enjoyable, hassle-free vacation that will provide lifelong memories. Individually they may anticipate meeting new friends, rekindling romance, finding romance, quiet and solitude or pretty much nonstop partying—and every possibility in between.

The core of this product delivery is summed up in Carnival's vision statement: "To consistently provide quality cruise vacations that exceed the expectations of our guests." All employees know this vision statement and are motivated to execute it.

Training

Interestingly, this vision statement wasn't defined and articulated until 1994, which was the first year that fleetwide and shoreside hospitality training was instituted. Prior to that time, there was a very extensive shipboard program, for several years. The problem was that so few crew members were trained that when the trainees went back into the shipboard environment they were outnumbered by the vast majority of crew who didn't have this training and so who could not relate to the "new" concepts and ideas practiced by the recently trained minority. Without an environment that positively reinforced the newly learned attitudes and behaviors, there was, if not total atrophy, a propensity for these new skills never to reach full fruition.

Even so, the success Carnival achieved prior to fleet-wide training is mind-boggling. It suggests that the natural corporate culture was sufficiently focused to ensure reasonable levels of passenger satisfaction—a kind of street-smart but effective mentality.

Carnival management waxes enthusiastic over its future product-delivery potential. The new training has been seeded, has taken root, and has already shown very encouraging results. Guest satisfaction has greatly increased and, perhaps even more important, the crew and even many of the guests are acknowledging the process. It's one thing to experience good service and warm, caring hospitality. It's even more powerful if you become consciously appreciative of the service as it is being performed. This leads both to enhanced enjoyment (somewhat analogous to savoring a wine rather than simply drinking it) at the moment of truth (as Carnival refers to it) and to the possibility of enthusiastically telling others about it. Remember, positive word of mouth from returning cruise passengers is the industry's most powerful tool of market expansion.

The Carnival Approach

Carnival's strategy is to enhance the product experience, to deliver a *better* food, service, and entertainment product than other cruise lines at higher price points and at the same time maintain and fine-tune its unique fun-ship ambience. The enormous economies of scale that accrue to Carnival as it grows ever larger combine with its powerful economic strength to secure the lowest capital costs in the industry. In this way Carnival achieves ever increasing nonproduct cost savings and growing profit margins (already twice as profitable as the next closest cruise line, with a 1995 profit margin in excess of 20 percent).

The strategy also calls for a continual reinvestment of a portion of these cost savings in increased on board product cost—funding a stream of product enhancements. This approach is contrary to the industry's tendency in the last few years of taking cost out of the cruise product to partially offset the adverse profit effect of declining yields and occupancies.

The next chapters will draw attention to what we believe is a further threat to the cruise product of many lines: The contracted ship capacity coming on line by 1999, coupled with insufficient growth in first-time cruiser demand, will cause unprecedented yield erosion for most if not all of the so-called "premium" lines. These are the lines priced just above Carnival—the very ones that Carnival is targeting to surpass in product delivery.

The last piece of Carnival's strategy is to implement its objectives with virtually no fanfare, in this way not raising the expectations of its guests beyond the minimum threshold required for purchase. This creates the highest probability of ensuring the implementation of its vision statement.

Employee Empowerment

Like Seabourn, Carnival promotes the image of employees as internal guests, which allows each member of the crew and shoreside staff to view his or her work as important in itself and integral to the success of the team. The theory is that if employees can understand what the company is all about and view themselves as contributions to a successful organization, they'll take more pride in and derive more personal satisfaction from their day-to-day jobs. Add empowerment, which permits staff to deal with problems and situations on the spot, and latitude to deal with unique situations, and you have a formula for exceeding guests' expectations. Servers are trained to ask guests how their food is and to offer a different selection if necessary. The Purser's desk personnel strive to resolve whatever may "go bump in the night" quickly and in a caring manner. How they would like to be treated, if the roles were reversed, is an important litmus test. The Golden Rule truly has universal applications.

Promotion

Because of the dramatic growth of Carnival from one ship in 1975 to ten in 1995, and Carnival's belief in promoting from within, virtually all shipboard managers have come from within the ranks—a fact that certainly contributes to a happy, motivated crew. Crew members realize that its not enough to do a good job to reap your benefits, but understand that to do a great job, above and beyond the norm, they must demonstrate sound team building, communications, and conflict resolution skills. Carnival not only puts its best foot forward with promotions, attendant compensation, and prestige benefits, but they see the ever growing number of positions that will need to be filled. With five new ships coming in the next three years, staff should not (and do not) consider themselves in dead end jobs! Sustained growth and home-grown promotions also aid Carnival's never-ending quest for new crew. The obvious Carnival advantage in career opportunities acts as a huge magnet attracting people from around the globe. A not insignificant percentage of these have worked on other ships but were motivated (on an unsolicited basis) to switch because of perceived better career possibilities. At last count, 64 countries were represented in Carnival's crew manifest.

Choices for Guests

A big part of the Carnival "Fun Ship" experience is choice. Like its successful land-based competitors in Orlando and Las Vegas, Carnival strives to offer activity and entertainment choices

broad enough to satisfy just about everybody. Here is a short list
of activities offered to show the diversity:

Couples & Lovers Party

Captain's Gala Cocktail
    Reception

Grandparents Party

Honeymooners Party

Mature Singles Party

Singles Party

Welcome Aboard Reception

Wine Tasting Party

Wine & Cheese Party

Bar Mixology

Cooking Lessons

Fruit Carving

Health, Beauty, & Fitness
    Demonstrations

Ice Carving Demonstration

Napkin Folding Demonstration

Dance Contest

Golf Putting Contest

Hairy Chest Contests

Knobby Knees Contest

Limbo Contests

Pillow Fight Contests

Art Lecture

Cellulite & Inch Loss Seminar

De-Stress Seminar

Naturalist Lecture

Nautical Knot-Tying Seminar

Perfume Seminar

Aerobics

Art Auction

Bingo

Blackjack Tournament

Bridge Tournament

Bridge Tour

Adult Comedy Entertainment

Country Line Dance Class

Dr. Ruth's Love, Sex, &
    Romance Quiz

Facials

Fashion Shows

Galley Tours

Gambling

Hair Workshop

Horse Racing

Jogging

Karaoke

Las Vegas/Broadway Style
    Revues

Lottery

Massages

Ping Pong Tournament

Shuffleboard

Shopping

Shore Excursions

Slots Tournaments

Swimming

Talent Show

Trivia Quizs

Volleyball Tournaments

The following table shows some of the Camp Carnival activities. With the exception of the *Tropicale* which doesn't offer a program for two- to four-year-olds because of port-intensive itineraries, all other ships offer activities geared to kids ages two to four, five to eight, nine to twelve and teen:

Intermediates (Ages 8–12)—4 Day Cruise

Sunday

8:00–9:00 p.m.	Come and meet some new friends and play Some Crazy Games!
9:00–9:30 p.m.	Pizza Pig Out
10:00 p.m.	Slumber Party begins (Please sign up by 5:00 p.m. at the Purser's Desk)

Monday

7:00 a.m.	Arrival in Freeport. (Formal Night)
8:00 a.m.–10:00 p.m.	Open Playroom. Please sign up the day before.
2:00–3:00 p.m.	Treasure Trail
3:00–3:30 p.m.	Volleyball
5:30–6:00 p.m.	First "Formal Coketail Party"
7:00–8:00 p.m.	Second "Formal Coketail Party"
8:00–9:15 p.m.	Movie Time
10:00 p.m.	Slumber Party begins (Please sign up by 5:00 p.m. at the Purser's Desk)

Tuesday

8:00 a.m.	Arrival in Nassau
8:00 a.m.–10:00 p.m.	Open Playroom
9:30–10:30 a.m.	Scavenger Hunt
10:30–11:30 a.m.	Crazy Card Games & Other Fun Activities
7:00–8:00 p.m.	Special Arts & Crafts
8:00–9:00 p.m.	Indoor Beach Party/Limbo & Hula Hoop. Please come in beach wear.
9:00–9:30 p.m.	Graphic Art Poster & Late Nite Munchies
10:00 p.m.	Slumber Party begins (Please sign up by 5:00 p.m. at the Purser's Desk)

Wednesday

	A Fun and Crazy Day at Sea
9:30–10:00 a.m.	Breakfast with Your Happy Youth Staff!
10:15 a.m.	Bridge WalkThru (weather permitting)
10:30–12:00 noon	Ship Drawing Contest, Bingo & Games
2:00–3:00 p.m.	Autograph Hunt
3:00–3:40 p.m.	Face Painting Fun
3:45–4:00 p.m.	Ice Cream Party
7:30–8:30 p.m.	Farewell Party (All prizes won during the cruise will be given out here.)
10:00 p.m.–1:30 a.m.	Slumber Party begins

Without question, fitness is a huge and growing aspect of today's life-style, and Carnival's Nautica Spas provide the exercise and training options people are looking for. At 12,000 square feet on *Fantasy*-class vessels (and proportionally smaller on the rest of the fleet) these spas are the largest afloat. They are equipped with 6 treadmills, 2 stair-machines, 4 bicycles, 2 rowing machines, free weights and benches, and 16 different gas-operated progressive-resistant exercise stations. Also offered are separate high- and low-impact aerobic areas, saunas, steam, whirlpools, and a cushioned outdoor jogging track. The spa offers a complete array of treatments: mud packs, aroma therapy, and so forth. The facilities and treatments are fully comparable with the finest on land.

Adult Entertainment

Entertainment options are also many and varied. Each 7-day cruise, for example, includes two lavish original production shows. One might feature be-bop, with fast-paced singing and dancing to the music of the fifties and sixties. The other might feature the best of Broadway, reprising tunes from Broadway shows like *Miss Saigon* and *Phantom of the Opera*. Other nights feature cruise staff performing with audience participation, stand-up acts such as singers, comedians, musicians, jugglers, acrobats, and dancers, and the invariably popular guest talent night. (When you have 1,100 to 2,600 people on board, chances are excellent that you'll have a terrific pool of talent to draw from.) These shows take place in the main lounge, but there's another lounge on every vessel that features a dance band with one or more singers and late-night cabaret entertainment. There's also a state-of-the-art disco that pulses with the latest sound but also fulfill requests for blues, country and western, and golden oldies.

A dance band also performs each night in a highly visual themed lounge—another expression of Carnival's entertainment-architecture format. The theme may be based on the movie "Passage to India," or evoke memories of an "Endless Summer" or conjure up the exotic Orient with "Chinatown." Similarly, the library, a quiet retreat, may be patterned after Tara in *Gone With the Wind* or a retired senior officer's study or an exclusive London club. Sing-along piano bars are also themed, ranging from ancient Egypt to Rick's Café Americain with its sultry Moroccan setting.

The casinos on Carnival ships are the largest afloat, featuring blackjack, craps, roulette, wheel of fortune, and Caribbean stud poker. On *Fantasy*-class vessels they offer 235 slot machines, ranging from nickel to progressive mega cash which has paid out a jackpot of over $1 million to lucky guests from Alaska.

The Extra Touches

The Carnival crew is trained to provide extra little touches and unexpected surprises. A room steward may arrange night clothes in the shape of a different animal each night or a waiter may offer magic or napkin tricks to kids of all ages and show interested guests how it's done. At several dinners throughout the cruise, the wait staff may sing and parade through the dining room. A Carnival Caribbean favorite is Buster Poindexter's song "Hot! Hot! Hot!" which is practically guaranteed to get a sizable number of the guests weaving through the dining room along with the staff. Waiters with trays of drinks balanced on their heads lead the parade while performing amazing limbo contortions.

The contrast to hotel or restaurant dining is vivid. The electricity of folks laughing and enjoying themselves is no part of the often somber, library-like atmosphere on land. Part of the difference is the "Fun Ship" crew, who truly enjoy making guests happy; part is the guests' expectations of having fun and good times, and part is the unique shipboard opportunity (certainly not limited to Carnival) for people to dine together and make new friends. Let's face it, in the land environment of a resort restaurant most folks tend to stick to themselves and have little meaningful interaction with others. Couples may nod or exchange pleasantries in a hallway or elevator, but the typical hotel experience is one of social isolation. We believe folks today, more socially isolated than their parents or grandparents, welcome the opportunity to meet others. Friendships and romances formed on ship can be most gratifying and frequently last a lifetime. In fact, we think this is one of the key reasons that cruise vacations enjoy higher levels of customer satisfaction than do their land-based counterparts.

5

Getting Underway
The public discovers
cruising vacations

We might as well call the period from 1970 through 1993 the "halcyon days" of cruising. This was when the industry truly got under way. Consumer interests in trying out this new kind of vacation was pushing ahead of the supply, and there was a dramatic growth of new passengers. In fact, in 1970 only half a million people had ever taken a cruise—two-tenths of 1 percent of the American public.

Growth was slow at first because capacity was limited and ports of embarkation were few and remote. But the pace accelerated as new cruise lines and cruise ships were launched. By 1979, the figure had doubled to 1 million—it reached 2 million in 1985 and 3 million in 1988. Between 1970 and 1993 business increased ninefold to 4.5 million making cruising the fastest-growing segment of the travel business.

The explosive growth was the result of the cruise industry redefining itself from a narrowly focused niche product to a broader-based, mass-market vacation experience. New cruise lines that docked for the first time in Miami and other ports around the world included, Carnival, Monarch, American Hawaii, Chandris Fantasy, Sea Goddess, Seabourn, Pearl, Renaissance, Premier, and Celebrity. There were few barriers to entry—almost anyone with a modest amount of capital or credit could start a line. And the low cost structure was appealing. New operators could lease or buy from a selection of "previously owned" ships retired from transatlantic or other service and laid up; they could build new ones for a relatively small investment— a ship like the *Skyward* could be leased for as little as $2,500 a day or built new for $11 to $12 million. Profits were pretty well assured because of the small capacity of the industry at that time and high consumer demand, on whose tide all ships rose.

As with other oligopolies with a small number of suppliers and large number of consumers, with this dramatic expansion, not surprisingly, many lines were forced to close (including some of the newer ones). Among the brand names that lowered their flags in this period, by selling their ships, merging, or just going out of business, were Monarch, Swedish American, Norwegian American, Greek Line, Italian Line, French Line, Exploration Cruises, Pearl, Home Lines, and Sitmar.

In truth, the business was so small it *had* to grow; its embryonic state ensured its growth, especially considering the unusually high rate of consumer satisfaction cruising was generating. The product was simply so good compared with land vacations, that growth continued despite spates of mismanagement and inept marketing. Moreover, for the rising middle class, which was anxiously collecting every new status symbol it could lay its hands on, the cost efficiencies of cruising created a real vacation value, compared with land alternatives, that was (and still is) difficult to match.

The Target Audience

The demographics and psychographics of the target audience for cruises in those early days were very different from those of today's. While cruises cost less than they do now in current dollars, they were still far above the means of the average household where Mom stayed home and took care of the kids while Dad worked as a bank teller or even the head buyer in the shoe department of a large department store. Then too, most cruises were 7 and 14 days long, so if you were going to go on one you needed to wait until the kids were old enough to be left with a sympathetic maiden aunt or grandparents who could control them. In fact, most cruisers in those days were themselves grandparents! A cruise was not a place to take young children—the facilities for them, if any, were basically babysitting and were offered only when school was out—mid-June to Labor Day. Moreover, the majority of passengers considered other people's children an intrusion on their golden years' vacation, because most cruisers had long since shed themselves of their child-rearing responsibilities.

The only ones who had the time and the money to take a cruise were over 55, and that age group set the tone and ambiance of the experience. They were the country-club set who were at least 55 in 1975, born in 1920 or earlier. Many were World War II veterans, folks who "had made it," who represented a new generation of American wealth that did not come through inheritance. They still liked to Charleston and dance to tunes like "Sentimental Journey" and hits from "Your Hit Parade," such as "Don't Fence Me In" and "Slow Boat to China."

Of course, there were a few younger cruisers—lawyers, doctors, and top managers—but they could not help noticing that most of the other passengers were older than they were. If they did bring their children, the kids were bored at sea; only in port, where there were old forts to explore and beaches for snorkeling, were the activities suitable for the whole family.

Not only were there few families, there were fewer honeymooners. Back then cruises were more appropriate for silver and golden anniversaries. Many cruisers were either living in Florida or "snowbirds"—visitors who regularly came south. The ships could easily be seen dominating the Port of Miami and thus provided some degree of consumer awareness. In the trade, these passengers were called "condo commandos" or "condo dragons."

Early Marketing Maneuvers

Royal Caribbean had 13 or 14 air gateways to Miami in the seventies (compared to 155 today), and Rod McLeod, their Executive Vice President of Sales, Marketing and Passenger Traffic, recalls that 35 to 40 percent of their passengers were from California, linked to Florida with special air charters. California was considered a ripe market because many people there had taken cruises, principally to Mexico from Los Angeles. They hadn't been to the Caribbean and wanted to go, but it was too expensive.

McLeod remembers the exact date of RCCL's first California departure. It was January 1, 1971, at 1 A.M.—New Year's Day. The plane was a Boeing 707 stretch, 180-seater, and it was completely sold out. "We were reaching out for a new market," McLeod tells us, "and offering round-trip air from Los Angeles, a B-deck outside stateroom with two lower berths on the *Song of Norway* to Nassau, San Juan, and St. Thomas. Our price, including all port charges, transfers, and a quick sightseeing tour of Miami and lunch on Key Biscayne before boarding the ship, was only $368! Since this price was only $50 or $60 higher than RCCL's brochure-cruise-price, it was a tremendous bargain by any standards.

In contrast, Carnival relied heavily on the local senior market and tour operators during its early years, 1972 to 1974. This was logical because the local market was cheaper from an advertising standpoint (remember, Carnival started on less then a shoe string) and Carnival's owner at the time was AITS, a large nationally recognized tour operator. It wasn't until 1975 that the line adopted the marketing strategy that would ultimately result in its unparalleled growth.

There were two problems with Carnival's first strategy. First, the local South Florida market was subject to frequent price dumping as lines tried to pick up last-minute business. The fact that the elderly were close by and largely retired meant that they could react to a favorable price offer with only a few days' notice. Indeed, it was not unusual to see septuagenarians milling about the embarkation area, bags in tow, hoping to take advantage of a standby rate or a last-minute cancellation.

In the early to mid-70's, last minute rates were *very* negotiable. You could hear rumors that a 7-day cruise regularly selling for $225 could be "had" for $75 to $100 per person at the pier! In some instances the embarkation supervisor and/or purser pocketed "gratuities" in exchange for the cabin gratis or for a favorable rate.

There was a great deal of entrepreneurship on the vessels in those early days. It wasn't universal, but many cruise directors, pursers, maître d's, staff, and waiters had their own deals going. These could range from a "per head" payment for passengers delivered to shore-tour operators, to a percentage of the revenue from an island store. Additionally, anybody who handled the ship's money had the potential to become a "partner," the term used in the cruise industry to describe someone who was diverting corporate funds to his or her pocket. These abuses are largely absent today, thanks to on board computers and credit card purchases. With current stringent cost controls, every penny is accounted for, making partnering a thing of the past for most lines.

Carnival's Early Marketing Approach

The problem with the tour-operator sourcing strategy for Carnival was that the company could not control the tour operator. For example, if an operator took a block of 85 cabins for a week on a year-round basis, it didn't mean that he had to sell them but only that he would try. Consequently, if the operator could only sell half the cabins, Carnival was stuck with the remainder— usually with only 15 to 30 days' notice prior to sailing. This situation used to drive Bob Dickinson, Carnival's then Vice President of Sales and Marketing, bananas, especially when you consider that he was dealing with as many as eight different tour operators at a time. Some days he faced an inventory of 200 unsold cabins two weeks prior to sailing on the *Mardi Gras*, which only had 457 cabins to begin with!

Where were the tour operators getting those passengers? Dickinson asked himself. Obviously, from travel agents. Thus, the solution was patently clear—Carnival would have to deal with those travel agents directly and that way would at least know which cabins were really truly booked with customer names and deposits and which ones represented wishful thinking. Carnival became in effect its own tour operator by packaging round-trip air fares, transfers between the airport and pier, overnight or day hotel rooms, as necessary, with the cruise. The program began in 1975 with 10 gateway cities operated in conjunction with Delta Airlines and the now defunct National Airlines. This allowed Carnival to deal directly with travel agents though its field sales force, which at the time consisted of just eleven people. Today Carnival operates from 190 cities throughout the United States and Canada, covered by a field sales force numbering 100.

Relationships with Travel Agents

Dealing directly with the travel agents was an improvement over the tour operator system, but one more hurdle had to be overcome. Twenty years ago, the strong winter and summer seasonality of the vacation business was such that tour operators, cruise lines , hotels, and airlines maintained a "love-hate" relationship with travel agents. They loved the agents in the shoulder season (soft periods such as the fall and spring), and they would break, not just bend, their own rules and wheedle, cajole, pamper, feed, and entertain them in an unabashed attempt to get business. On the other hand, in the winter and summer when there was a strong demand for vacations, these same companies typically became extraordinarily inflexible: No rules were bent, let alone broken, and travel-agent commissions were paid with great reluctance because the vendors reasoned that they would have gotten the business anyhow. It hardly made sense to them to pay a travel agent what amounted to a windfall for consumer demand that the hotels, airlines, and cruise lines themselves, not the travel agent, had generated.

It was obvious that this supplier/agent relationship was fragile at best and certainly dysfunctional, with rancor, suspicion, and duplicity on both sides. Depending on the time of year, agents and suppliers talked out of both sides of their mouth. Dickinson saw that if Carnival was to break through the clutter of thousands of travel suppliers and win the hearts and minds of travel agents, it would have to both act differently and make sure that agents knew and could see the change. The logical course of action would be not only to rely completely on the travel agent community but to treat them with respect, cordiality, and candor at *all* times. "After all," says Bob, "we were selling an intangible product that only 1 percent of the U.S. and Canadian population had any experience with. Clearly we needed travel agents (and still do) to explain the cruise experience to a largely unfamiliar audience. Our challenge then was to tell the agents that we were a different sort of supplier and to back up those words with action. It was a high-risk game, because if we failed to follow through, the agents would never have forgiven us."

Bob remembers many travel agent speeches in which he reminded agents that "suppliers bend over backwards for you in the fall and don't know you from a 'Hot Rock' in the winter." This level of candor was uncommon at the time but it did get agents' attention. No doubt some lines were angry that a colleague would point out this flawed relationship, but they couldn't and didn't dispute the veracity of the claim.

In the short run it undoubtedly cost Carnival money to become a reasonable partner to travel agents on a year-round basis, but that turned out to be money well spent because long-term agent loyalty and support were virtually priceless.

"The Good Ole Days"

By 1979, almost all cruise lines were operating at 100 percent of their revenue capacity. There were few if any berths being offered on a complimentary basis or at reduced rates to travel agents to stimulate business or even as incentives or perks for company employees. In those days, it was so difficult to get aboard a ship without significant advance planning that Sitmar was running newspaper ads with pictures of the *Fairsea* and *Fairwind* in Alaska and the Caribbean headlined: "If you want to be in this picture next year, see your travel agent today."

In many circumstances this kind of advertising appeal works because it plays on peoples' desire for status by possessing or experiencing something unique and presumably scarce. But it can also produce exactly the opposite effect—consumers may think to themselves "if it's so hard to get, I can do without it." And that's exactly what frequently happened in this case. While going on a cruise was a status symbol, it was also to most people an unknown and untested experience, one they could easily forego if it wasn't easy to acquire. Travel agents felt the same way. Why try to sell your customers something you couldn't book for them, even after you made the sale? (Talk about frustration!) The result was what the trade called the "sold-out-syndrome" in both consumers' and travel agents' minds. There was no way you could book a cruise for next month or even the following one on impulse as there were so few cabins available.

Consumers who were sufficiently motivated to try anyway visited their travel agents, who dutifully called for reservations and were told, as they had anticipated, that there was no space available. Their reaction was natural. When other clients suggested a cruise, unless it was for the following season, agents discouraged them. Far from even trying to book, they would tell prospects, "Don't even bother to think about it for now—there isn't any space."

The Problem of Canceled Bookings

After a while, when enough agents had begun to develop this mindset, an unanticipated problem arose. Five to 10 percent of the long-term bookings that had been made many months or even a year ahead were canceled because of normal attrition (personal tragedies, illness, business conflicts, etc.). Berths that were not previously available went back on the market, but the second time around they were not as readily sold because of the widespread perception of being sold out already. For years, industry marketing executives like Bob Dickinson and Rod McLeod gave interviews to the trade press and speeches to travel agents decrying the sold-out syndrome and reminding agents that berths were indeed available for last minute sailings.

The Decline of the Nineties

As the cruise industry continued to expand, the inevitable happened. Berth supply began to catch up with consumer demand. Take a look at Table 5.1.

The dramatic increase is clear in the number of cruise passengers. Yet 1994 represents the first year since 1970 that North American passenger volume actually declined from the prior year. Though minor (only 32,000 passengers), this decline was significant because at the same time industry capacity increased by 1 percent. This atypically poor performance resulted in the lowest capacity utilization rate in 20 years: 84 percent.

Table 5.1
Cruise Passengers Marketed/Sold from North America and Industry Occupancy

Year	Passenger Count	Estimated Occupancy Rate
1970	500,000	90.0%
1975	690,000	95.0%
1980	1,431,000	96.0%
1985	2,152,000	93.0%
1990	3,640,000	88.9%
1991	3,979,000	87.0%
1992	4,136,000	87.6%
1993	4,480,000	88.0%
1994	4,448,000	84.3%
1995	4,378,000	79.6%

Source: CLIA for passenger counts, the authors for estimated occupancy rate

Unsold Cabins

Just when the industry is poised for its largest capacity increment, occupancy rates are in an ominous decline. For the period 1994 to 1998, the contracted industry capacity increase is 44 percent, the largest building spree in cruising history. The newest, most innovative, most luxurious, and most expensive cruise ships ever built are coming on stream as consumer demand is shrinking or, at best, slowing dramatically. In other words, at a time when the industry will be putting its best foot forward, consumers may be likely to show their poorest response to the product. If one trends out the 1994–1998 capacity increase of 43.8 percent and assumes a comparable rate of occupancy falloff as occurred between 1990 and 1994, when the fleet increased by 23.7 percent, the 1998 cruise fleet occupancy will be an unprecedented 76 percent! This is clearly illustrated in Table 5.2:

Table 5.2
Cruise Industry Actual/Projected Growth

	Actual		Projected	1998 Better/(Worse) 1994	
	1990	1994	1998	Amount	%
Passengers (000)	3,640	4,448	5,781	1,333	30%
Capacity (berths)	83,491	103,296	148,540	45,244	43.8%
Capacity utilization	88.9%	84.3%	76.2%	(8.1 pts)	(9.6%)

The financial impact of reduced capacity utilization is awesome. In the 1990–1994 period, the reduced capacity of 4.6 percentage points (88.9% to 84.3%) cost the industry 204,600 passengers in 1994 (and progressively smaller numbers back through 1991). When a passenger is "lost" to the industry, the financial effect on the bottom line is the net total revenue less variable cost—economic profit.

A composite industry average unit economic profit is estimated in Table 5.3.

As the table illustrates, we might assume that a passenger buys a cruise for which the brochure price (similar to the rack rate in the hotel business) is $2,200, including round-trip air fare from point of origination. Cruise berths, like hotel rooms and airline seats, are perishable commodities—if they are unsold today they are worth nothing tomorrow. The problem is exacerbated in the cruise business, where an unsold cabin stays unsold not for a few hours or one day but for the entire length of the trip.

Discounting
Therefore, to give consumers an added incentive to buy, most cruise lines offer "permanent discounts" off the brochure rates. Carnival brochures point to savings that can be achieved through their Super Saver programs, telling readers to "See your travel agent for details." Princess puts a card in its brochure

Table 5.3
1994 Estimated Average Industry Economic Profit
per Passenger

Gross ticket revenue	$2200.00
Discounts	−660.00
Less commission (13%)	−200.00
Air cost	−320.00
Transfers	−17.00
Credit card fees	−16.00
Plus on board revenue	+250.00
Less on board cost	−100.00
Less other variable cost:	
Reservation/documentation	−40.00
Food	−97.00
Economic profit/passenger	$1,000.00

advising consumers that Love Boat Savers may be available; Royal Caribbean calls such discounts Breakthrough Rates. Special group and other promotions by either travel agents and/or cruise lines may reduce fares even further on some sailings or in some specific cabin categories.

For our example, we've assumed that the discounts on our cruise amount to $660, bringing the net rate paid to $1,540. From this the cruise line deducts a series of expenses, starting with travel agent commissions. These vary, but we're assuming 13 percent, or $200. Next is the cost of the air fare, which the line must pay, in this case $320, and transfer fees (getting the passengers from the airport to the ship and back), which are $17. About 50 percent of passengers pay for their cruises with credit cards today so we need to allow $16 to cover the credit card fees. Once the passenger sails, however, he or she spends money on board—buying drinks and souvenirs, gambling, shore excursions, massages, and more. We call that on-board revenue and peg it on this hypothetical cruise at $250. Of course, there are costs involved in on-board revenue, so we deduct $100 to cover those. Then there are other variable costs—those involved with reservations and ticketing, which are $40, and the cost of food, which for this 7-day cruise we're calling $97. This works out to an economic profit per passenger of $1,000.

Lost Profit
The economic profit per passenger is in fact the marginal net profit because all other costs, shipboard and shoreside, are fixed in the short run. The industry's lost profit in 1994 was therefore $204.6 million ($1,000/passenger times 204,600 "lost" passengers).

Using the data in Table 5.2, we calculate the lost profit for 1998 alone (ignoring the intervening years) at $963.5 million, conservatively assuming no increase in economic profit. This appears to be a very safe assumption given the environment of the industry in 1998 with a projected 76 percent load factor. Make no mistake about it, 1994 was not an aberration. CLIA data for March year-to-date 1995 versus the comparable period in 1994 show a consistent pattern of sales deterioration in the face of expanding industry capacity. As shown in Table 5.4, Industry sales volume declined in the face of a capacity increase of 3.5%.

If we were to project 1998 capacity utilization by trending our 1995–1990 data rather than our 1994–1990, as shown in

Table 5.4
1995 QI vs. 1994 QI

	Actual		1995 Better/(Worse)	1994
	1995	1994	Amount	%
Passengers (000)	1,096	1,140	(44)	(3.9)
Capacity (berths)	103,296	99,846	3,450	3.5%
Capacity utilization	79.6%	84.2%	(4.6) points	(5.5%)

Table 5.5
Cruise Industry Actual/Projected Growth (Worst-Case Scenario)

	Actual		Projected	1998 B/(W) vs. 1995	
	1990	*1995**	*1998*	*Amount*	*%*
Passengers (000)	3,640	4,378	4,950	542	131
Capacity berths	83,491	103,296	148,540	45,244	42.8
Capacity utilization	88.9%	79.6%	62.4%	(17.2 pts)	(21.6)

*Annualized 1st quarter data

Table 5.2, the deterioration appears even more serious, as Table 5.5 shows.

Let's face it, if the worst-case scenario shown in Table 5.5 occurs, and the industry faces unused capacity of 37.6% by 1998, either most cruise line executives will have been fired by then or their owners will be members in good standing of the International Society of Masochists!

Airlines—Cruising's Future?
One could make a case that as the cruise industry's capacity utilization approaches that of the airline industry (66–70%), it will become more like the airline industry in terms of pricing, decreasing product differentiation, and financial losses. When the level of capacity utilization is in that range (or lower), there's a marked disparity between supply and demand. Pricing becomes extremely volatile as anxious suppliers chase after hesitant buyers. The relatively perishable aspect of an airline seat or a cruise berth simply won't tolerate "take it or leave it" pricing. Unused hotel rooms are also perishable, but a room unsold at 6 P.M. may still sell by 10 P.M. even on Tuesday, but at the hour a cruise ship sails, her unsold berths remain unsold for three, four, or seven

days! The fixed costs are spent, *any* revenue is found revenue, and practically all the revenue is profit.

How volatile can pricing be? Remember Peanut Fares? Half-Price Sales? Penny Fares? The airline industry has shown a great deal of imagination in setting prices for its products. Because their situation is similar to cruising; when the plane goes, it's gone!

In fact, airline pricing has become so confusing since deregulation in 1978 that consumers have been driven to order their airline tickets from travel agencies in the hope of finding the lowest fares. In 1978, only 59 percent of tickets were purchased through travel agents, but by 1994 that figure had become 89 percent—an increase of 51 percent!

Price Instability

More important than the shift in purchasing patterns, however, is the unseen, negative marketing force that price instability generates. People don't want to make poor purchase decisions, especially with discretionary purchases such as leisure and VFR (visiting friends and relatives) travel. They don't want to appear foolish, and they don't want to be ripped off. Unstable pricing, with consumers seeing a myriad of pricing schemes, acts as a drag or deterrent to discretionary purchase decisions. The perception is that someone else will be offered the same thing for a lower price tomorrow.

Business travel is largely unaffected by ever-changing pricing, because it is usually not viewed as discretionary but necessary. Moreover, it is not the traveler who normally pays for it but the company. Leisure and VFR travel are adversely affected by price instability because people can opt out of the purchase decision—and in fact many do rather than run the real or perceived risk of paying too much.

Commoditization

Unused capacity, perishable capacity, inevitably and inexorably drives pricing lower in an effort to attract discretionary purchasers. Pricing has an elastic effect on demand, especially in travel and tourism. Typically, the lower the price the greater the demand. When downward price pressure has become institutionalized in an industry—because of overcapacity over a long period of time—product costs get squeezed, leading to commoditization. In other words, products are seen as interchangeable commodities, which blurs their differences.

This is certainly evident in the airline industry. A coach seat between New York and Los Angeles is purchased on the basis of price, not the perceived differences in the products. This has led Bob Crandall, President of American Airlines, to suggest on more than one occasion that American's pricing is dictated by the cheapest operator in the market. While in fact there are product differences between American and, for example, TWA, the differences aren't significant enough to override even a few dollars difference in the purchase price. The perception then, at the consumer level, is that an airseat is an airseat. And with brand differentiation meaning little or nothing, the industry can only jockey price and availability (convenience). For that matter, they can't push convenience too far because many people will greatly inconvenience themselves—change aircraft, fly at inconvenient times, or forego a meal, for a few dollars savings.

The domestic airline industry "can't afford" to be truly dazzling, creative, innovative, and exciting. These things cost money and, with severe, long-term overcapacity, consumers are simply unwilling to pay that cost. Stripped down, utilitarian commodities inevitably win out over uniquely differentiated style and class when it comes to mass transportation.

How the mighty have fallen! Just imagine what the cruise industry will be like if it follows the airline industry model of prolonged overcapacity. Volatile pricing, commoditization, and financial loss will indelibly change the face of cruising forever. This specter is enough to make at least one of us consider early retirement to the Home for the Bewildered!

Missing First-Time Passengers—the Culprit in the Decline

How did this happen? Why is consumer demand growth slowing? The principal reason, in our view, is attributed to the diminishing number of first-time cruisers as a percentage of total berths occupied. Throughout the seventies and eighties when industry growth was at its peak, some 65 to 75 percent of cruise-industry passengers were first-timers. Since 1990, however, that percentage has been declining. CLIA estimates that no more than 40 percent of cruisers in 1994 were first-timers. In other words, as many as 1.5 million additional folks should have tried cruising that year but did not. If they had, there wouldn't have been enough capacity to carry all of them.

There are a number of reasons for the decline in first-timers. First of all, as more and more people cruise for the first time and come back satisfied, they book additional cruises, which of course raises the number of repeaters. On a recent *Sun Princess* cruise to Alaska, for example, there were 500 members of the Captains Circle (repeaters) out of 1,600 passengers on board.

Many cruise lines offer incentives to repeat passengers in the form of lower prices and cabin upgrades. Seabourn, for instance, has a series of cruises that are offered to Seabourn Club members (repeat passengers) at a 10-percent discount. And any guests they bring who occupy a suite on the same sailing, receive a 5-percent discount. Club members are also entitled to substantial fare reductions for accumulated days sailing. After 28 days aboard a Seabourn ship they're entitled to a 25-percent discount on their next 14-day cruise, and after 70 days the discount goes to 50 percent.

Royal Caribbean's Crown and Anchor Club members receive savings of as much as 50 percent on some cruises as well as a quarterly magazine that often contains savings certificates and early booking information about upcoming cruises. Norwegian Cruise Line's Latitudes Club members get as much as 50 percent off on their next cruise plus certificates for on-board savings. Just about all of the lines have special on-board recognition events hosted by the Captain for repeaters.

As you can see, cruise lines have been effectively wooing these passengers, so you would expect their numbers to rise.

Other Options, Fewer Dollars

Moreover, many cruise line executives feel that it is becoming progressively more difficult to attract new cruisers as the market matures and vacation options increase. Rod McLeod puts it this way: "Our greatest opportunity was to take people out of hotels within our destination areas. And if we could empty out some Miami Beach hotels, some Puerto Rican hotels, some in Jamaica—all the better. We were so small [years ago] that we needed relatively few new passengers every year compared to the overall size of the travel market in our destination areas."

Then there is the question of sluggish economic growth. Says McLeod, "It is not a market share battle—it's an economic battle. For the first 20 years when we were growing, we really didn't feel the economic downturns. We might have felt the economic upturn because the demand strengthened and the prices went up, but not the downturns. We were dealing with people who as a percentage of total population had higher levels of household income. Today we're in a discretionary-income battle. We're competing with land-based resorts; we're even competing with the automobile industry!"

Marketing Strategy and the Loss of First-Time Cruisers

While all of these reasons are valid, we believe that the problem can be more directly attributed to marketing and advertising maneuvers within the industry itself. McLeod is right. There is an economic battle going on for discretionary dollars. The price of a 7-day air/sea cruise today is about the same as a new home computer, complete with a CD ROM, a laser printer, the latest, most enticing software, and access to the Internet. And there is a substantial segment of the market that, when forced to choose, would rather have the computer than take any vacation. Nevertheless, there *is* also a market share battle going on and, as we will see, it is having devastating consequences.

Upscaling
In the last few years, several leading cruise lines have redirected their advertising from first-time vacationers to repeaters. In a marked turnaround, after years of effectively wooing the first-timers, the lines have unintentionally but effectively turned their backs on them. To position themselves as upscale, companies have relied on Alice-in-Wonderland advertising to justify high prices, and inadvertently, they have reduced the industry's appeal to first-timers, who are thus lost as customers. In fact, with the exception of Carnival, no cruise line seems to want to even appear mass-market any more. There seems to be far more interest in selling "image" to the relatively few past cruisers than in

selling "substance" to the much larger universe of potential new customers.

There are several motivations for this upscaling:

- By setting significantly higher pricing for its product, a cruise line's projected profit, budgets, and business plans look more appealing, at least on paper. This has great appeal for the new executive trying to justify bigger budgets as well as for the tenured executive trying to cover up past sins.
- It is undeniably easier to market a cruise product to known past passengers than to identify unknown vacation customers and then persuade them to become first-timers.
- Cruisers typically have found their first cruise vacation to be highly satisfying and therefore want to cruise again; that's the vast majority of previous cruisers because of cruising's high satisfaction levels.

The irony of upscaling is that while the "image" lines have raised brochure prices and glorified their advertising, they have not materially changed their products. The actual on-board experience for the Miami-based lines, for example, is still largely the tried-and-true formula: casual dress, unstuffy atmosphere, an abundance of activities, and lots of good food. While it's true that the contemporary cruise experience has evolved and improved over the last 20 years (with more sophisticated menus, larger vessels, more activities and entertainment options, and more elaborate spas), the personality and atmosphere of the contemporary lines is still dramatically different from that of a truly upscale, traditional line such as Crystal or Holland America.

Cruising's Mass-Market Roots

There are, conservatively, at least 100 million people in the United States and Canada who have the wherewithal to take a cruise vacation but who have yet to try it. Only 19 million have cruised (and are still alive). In fact, it's even worse: cruising captures only 2 percent of the hotel/cruise vacation market each year. Clearly, the industry's greatest opportunity to expand is in mining the deep, rich vein of potential cruisers; it must begin retargeting them as a higher priority than repeaters. After all, look how well the industry flourished when lines positioned themselves as mass-market and addressed their advertising and brochures primarily to first-timers. Cruising grew sixfold between 1970 and 1988, adding 2.5 million passengers annually by 1988, 18 years from the start of this period of growth. In sharp contrast, the cruise industry is adding capacity that requires an additional 2.4 million passengers in just four years, by 1998, to fully utilize the incremental capacity. Now more than ever, we believe, these cruise lines need to go back to their mass-vacation market roots. Right now, frankly, it's lonely for the cruise industry in the middle, that is, the contemporary or mass-market.

You see, the vacation industry is like the pyramid illustrated in Table 5.6. The broadest number of buyers are at the base, where the lowest prices are. As you move up in price, fewer people can afford the experience, and by the time you reach the highest prices, (the top of the pyramid) there are but a handful of purchasers.

The cruise line categorization shown below the pyramid is based on price point, product positioning, or both. Note that in the contemporary market, with the exception of Carnival, everyone is either positioning themselves as upscale (premium) or seasonal, or as a niche operator. Premier, for example, positions itself as the family cruise line; and this narrower focus and small capacity prevent it from being a truly mass-market player. Majesty, with just one ship, and American Hawaii, with a ship solely dedicated to Hawaii, can't be considered truly mass-market either, also because of capacity limitations. Royal Caribbean and NCL were unabashedly mass-market products from their beginnings in the sixties and early seventies, respectively, but today they are both trying to position their products as upscale—straddling the top end of contemporary and the bottom of premium.

What many industry executives don't seem to realize is that the entire cruise industry already resides within the *upper half* of the overall vacation pyramid. (see Table 5.7).

This includes the so-called mass-market cruise lines. Consider the myriad of budget-oriented accommodations and eating places available to land-based travelers: Days Inn, Holiday Inn, the no-tell motel, Denny's, Burger King, McDonalds, and the like. There are thousand of hotel rooms in the United States priced at $40 a night or less on every highway and rooms priced below $85 a night at some fine beach front resorts.

Table 5.6
Positioning in the Cruise Industry

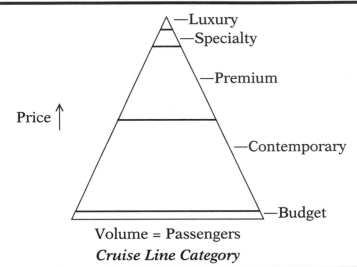

Price ↑

—Luxury
—Specialty
—Premium
—Contemporary
—Budget

Volume = Passengers

Cruise Line Category

Budget	Contemporary	Premium	Specialty	Luxury
Commodore	Carnival	Princess	Windstar	Sea
Fantasy	Premier***	Holland	Club Med	Goddess
Seawind	Royal	America	Pearl	Seabourn
	Caribbean*	Celebrity	Orient	Cunard-
Dolphin	NCL*	Crystal**		NAC
Regal	Costa****	Delta		Silversea
	Majesty***	Queen***		
	American			
	Hawaii***			

*   Straddling premium
**   Straddling luxury
***   Narrow-niche operator
****   Seasonal operator

Budget cruise lines, the so-called bottom feeders of the in-dustry, start at about $80 a night per person. That's $160 a night per couple. If you "comparably equip" a budget land vacation and a budget cruise, you see that a hotel room in the price range of $85 a night equates to the entry level of cruising, as shown in Table 5.8.

Table 5.7
Overall Vacation Positioning

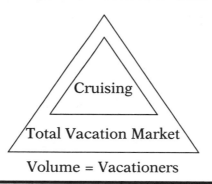

Volume = Vacationers

Table 5.8
Budget Cruise/Land Comparability
(Per diem per couple data)

	Cruise	*Land*	*Comments*
Transportation	N/A	N/A	Presumed comparable
Room	$160	$85	
Port charges/taxes	$28	$11	
Breakfast	Included	$10	⎧ Well we
Lunch	Included	$16	⎨ did say
Dinner	Included	$32	⎩ Budget!
Drinks	$6	$10	Duty-free on cruise
Tips	$10	$5	
Snacks	Included	$6	
Activities	Included	$17	Putt-putt golf, Wax Museum etc.
Entertainment	Included	$12	Movies
TOTAL	$204	$204	

To see where cruising sits in the vacation pyramid, figure that the land-based hotel rooms priced at $85/night or less are occupied 65 percent of the time (the industry average). Also, figure that the average length of stay is 4.5 nights, which is reasonable for a budget vacation.

- 200,000 hotel rooms × 65% occupancy = 130,000 fully utilized room equivalents.
- 130,000 fully utilized rooms × 365 days a year = 47,450,000 room nights.
- 47,450,000 room nights ÷ 4.5 nights (average stay) = 10,544,000 leisure trips × 2.2 persons/trip = 21,088,000 annual vacationers.

The budget end of the cruise industry amounts to roughly 1 million passengers a year. Therefore, the land-based hotel vacation market that forms the base of the cruise/hotel-based pyramid, below entry level cruising, is 21 times larger! This supports the claim that cruising, even at the budget end, is well into the middle or upper middle of the overall vacation pyramid.

Moreover, cruising is purchased in discrete increments: three, four, seven, or ten days. This, in effect, makes cruising more expensive because of the absence of, for example, one-, two-, five-day, and six-day possibilities (on rare occasions, cruises of these odd lengths are offered, but in negligible quantities). In other words, a whole spectrum of land-based vacations are less expensive than cruising, not just on a per-diem basis but on an absolute basis because of their shorter duration trip possibilities.

Too Much Capacity at Too High a Price

As cruise lines attempt to shift their fleet capacities to even higher price points, they are, effectively, attempting to defy the economic law of price elasticity of demand. As the pyramid shows, there are fewer, not more, purchasers as prices increase. In other words, while vacation demand looks like a normal pyramid, cruise capacity is beginning to look like an inverted pyramid, rather like the top of the Transamerica Building. This situation can't sustain itself. Like the law of gravity, price elasticity can't be permanently suspended. To the extent that there's too much capacity at a higher price point as a result of the combined effects of the following:

- Traditional, premium lines adding too much capacity (Princess, Holland America)
- New lines in the premium market (Celebrity, Crystal)
- The huge expansion of those new lines
- Repositioning of contemporary lines into premium-priced products (Royal Caribbean, NCL)

Some (or all) of those lines will have to lower prices to stimulate the demand necessary to fill ships.

Failure to lower prices means that either a line has such a unique product positioning that it is impervious to growing over-capacity or the line is going out of business. There is no middle ground: there is only success or failure.

Traditional premium lines like Princess are confident that they will continue to fill their new capacity because of their own brand awareness and base of loyal customers. "We made $150 million in profit in 1994, and were up 12 percent by the first half of 1995." Princess Chairman Tim Harris told us. "We intend to keep building on our strength. As one of the few brands with a profitable success record we'd have to be brain-dead not to continue to invest in our future."

Market Share versus Market Expansion

Cruise-line marketing strategies aimed at the repeat passenger are, by definition, market-share strategies that do absolutely nothing to expand the cruise market. With a *market share* strategy, a cruise line is saying, "My cruise line is better than your cruise line." With a *market expansion* strategy, a cruise line is saying, "My cruise vacation is better than your land vacation." A market expansion strategy is definitely more difficult to execute. It forces the line to explain its cruise product as a unique and desirable vacation experience to someone who has not experienced it, may have difficulty grasping the concept, and who very likely has misconceptions and/or concerns about cruising.

Market share strategies have none of these challenges. When the audience is made up of highly satisfied past cruisers, the cruise line is "singing to the choir" or "preaching to the converted." This audience knows how terrific a cruise vacation is from personal experience. No, the challenge of market share is easier and more focused: the line just has to say it's "better" in a fashion that will convince sufficient numbers of past cruisers to purchase *its* product because, after all, they are going to purchase some cruise product. Past cruisers do repeat, with growing frequency. CLIA data suggests that the majority of first-time cruisers plan to take another cruise within the next two years: The majority of frequent cruisers plan to cruise again within the next year.

How can such a strategy possibly keep pace with dramatically growing cruise capacity? It can't, unless the industry can induce repeaters to cruise more often. In fact, Al Wallack, the former Senior Vice President of Celebrity Cruises and 1994/1995 Chairman of CLIA, suggested at a Sea Trade industry conference in Miami in March 1995 that the industry must find ways to get experienced cruisers to cruise more often. Of course, given the low cruise prices generated by lack of broader (need we say first-time) cruise demand, some of these folks can save money by cruising more— it's almost becoming less expensive than staying home!

The problem is that individual lines, if they so choose, can certainly justify a market share strategy, especially if they're trying to justify high brochure rates. Rates in cruise brochures these days don't bear much resemblance to the reality of the marketplace. Any way you slice it, two-for-one pricing says that the brochure tariff is twice what the company is really offering to the public. Taken collectively, however, the individual efforts of three dozen lines, each acting independently, demonstrate that the industry is simply thrashing around and setting a course that leads nowhere. Not only does the primary message of the advertising focus on repeat passengers, ignoring the needs and concerns of first-timers, but we argue that the messages are actually de-motivating a large number of those first-timers.

Advertising in the Nineties

Current cruise-line advertising and brochures show Calvin Klein–style, sexily clad models, with about 4 percent body fat, lounging on the decks, dancing in the disco, or watching the sunset. How intimidating is that to the average American who may consider him- or herself overweight? And, how about the clothes? One ad for a line shows six folks in an idyllic scene waiting at a small Caribbean-island dock for the return of the ship's tender. Typically average middle Americans, they're dressed in white linens, white wide-brimmed straw hats, and immaculate white yachting shoes. They look like they graduated from expensive prep schools and have names like Muffy and Biff. And just where would you find such a cozy little scene in the first place? After all, this line features some of the largest mega-ships in the industry, routinely carrying 2,300 folks or more. Only six people on the dock? They must have missed the ship!

The Image Problem

Now think of the brand names of many cruise lines and their vessels. We may be biased, but let's take a look at what the industry is saying about its offerings to people who have no idea what a cruise is, by their names. There's Cunard Crown Cruises, Majesty Cruise Lines, Princess Cruises, and Royal Caribbean Cruise Line. To consumers who know nothing about them (and remember 93 percent don't) such names suggest experiences akin to spending a week at Buckingham Palace. That impression is reinforced by the names of the ships sailing today. The *Crown Dynasty, Majesty of the Seas, Norwegian Crown, Nordic Prince, Queen Elizabeth 2*—all sound like they might well be the Queen's royal yacht.

Contemporary cruisers are for the most part North Americans who not only don't relate to monarchies but whose forefathers fled Europe two hundred years ago to escape them! There are those who do seek this kind of social validation—they are the same ones who purchase heraldic seals from London mail-order companies that advertise in the *New Yorker*.

Sure, the names of the lines and ships suggest royal treatment, and many want that. There's an implied promise that you'll be on a floating palace, a special place where you'll be treated like a king or queen for the length of the cruise. We're not knocking the promise—that *is* the experience everyone is selling. But the royal analogy is much less suited to today's lifestyle than it was 20 years ago—it's too formal. Take a look at modern homes and those our parents or grandparents built. The formal living room (which those who still have one seldom use) has been replaced by the informal family room. Developers aren't stupid. If their research showed that people wanted formal rooms they'd be building them, but most people want a more relaxed, unpretentious style. The same is true with contemporary furniture. Our mothers had reproductions of Chippendale chairs if they could afford them. Go into any popular furniture store at any price range and try and find one of those today. Bloomingdale's has a few, but they're not the hot sellers. How many homes in any issue of *Architectural Digest* look like royal palaces either inside or out. We couldn't find any in recent issues.

This may seem like a small matter to some, but marketing history is full of products whose names may well have contributed to their downfall. Sapolio and Lava, with their medicinal-sounding names, were at one time the most popular soaps in America until Ivory came along. Eastern Air Lines had a hell of a time getting consumers to remember that it also flew west, and Pan American World Airways was rarely the first choice on the majority of its domestic routes. What your name is says a lot about who you are, especially if little else is known about you. If you doubt that, try introducing yourself to strangers as a Rockefeller, Rothschild, DuPont, or Vanderbilt, and watch their reaction, even today.

This image of exclusivity and formality is strengthened when you look closely at the photographs and words used by many lines in their marketing communications. All of the major lines (including Carnival) boast of their expensive art or antique collections. Brochures refer to luxurious staterooms, elegant dining rooms, five-star service, and gourmet food served on Wedgewood and Rosenthal china accompanied by polished silver and crystal goblets, and everyone's executive chef is a member of the prestigious, internationally recognized "Confrerie de la Chaine des Rotisseurs" (which ensures that your soup at dinner is more likely to be Crême Perigourdine with Truffles than Chicken Soup with Noodles). Female models in advertisements wear fashions by Theirry Mugler, carry purses by Gucci, and wear three-karat diamond rings. Males are dressed casually by Ralph Lauren or Versace or wear the latest styles in formal dinner jackets.

Are these symbols valid, real? Some of the time, yes, but some evidence suggests that they are not. Sociologist John Brooks in *Showing off in America* (1981) points out:

> The most effective status seeking style is mockery of status seeking . . . thus the well-to-do wear blue jeans, even worn and threadbare, to proclaim that one is socially secure enough to dress like an underpaid ranch hand.[1]

We need to ask whether these symbolic representations are what the majority of prospective cruisers look for. More importantly, is this what the average vacationer is looking for in a vacation? We think not.

Most past cruisers, with their first-hand experience, can penetrate the hype and fanciful advertising. They know that liberties are being taken. Liberties? There must be a stronger way to say that! But what about those inexperienced folks who don't have that advantage? How can they possibly interpret these elitist symbols and make sense out of all of it?

What Do Vacationers Want?
Before we tackle that question, let's consider for a moment what folks seem to want when they take vacations. The two most popular vacation destinations in the United States are Orlando and Las Vegas. Some 28 million visitors each year go to Las Vegas, and the Orlando area attracts around 40 million. For the most part, the hotels, restaurants, resorts, and attractions in these areas are anything but luxurious. No, they are very acceptable but unpretentious in every way. Operators try to provide good food and service in a comfortable, inviting, and imaginative settings.

Do people plan a trip to Disney or Circus-Circus with a great deal of concern about wardrobe? About whom they'll be with? What social situations they'll encounter? If there is any concern

---

[1]Cited by Richard P. Coleman in his article "The Continuing Significance of Social Class to Marketing" in *Perspectives in Consumer Behavior* (4th ed.) by Harold H. Kassarjian and Thomas S. Robertson (Englewood Cliffs, NJ: Prentice Hall, 1991).

at all, it's focused on the weather: What if it's hot? What if it rains? These typical land-based vacationers simply aren't concerned about fancy clothes. They've more than likely been to similar destinations and resorts elsewhere and therefore have a good idea what to expect—and it's not formality.

"The Love Boat"—the Image that Won't Go Away

Because the vast majority of vacationers have not been on a cruise, they don't know what to expect from one. Instead, they form their opinions from other people's views, old movies, "The Love Boat," and cruise-line advertising. Only 7 percent of the population has cruised, so chances are that other people's cruise experiences don't play a part in the noncruiser's idea of cruising. But what do you think the influence of movies has been? Probably nothing good. Old, late-night movies show glamorous people in white tie and tails prancing about in first-class suites and grand public areas on magnificent pre-war ocean liners. Nor are more recent movies like the "Poseidon Adventure" or "Stealing the Queen" examples of the most positive of experiences. Along with the disaster scenarios, the passengers themselves are depicted as society types, not the common man.

How about "The Love Boat?" A television staple for ten years, this show did much to publicize modern-day cruising. Most industry watchers agree that this program, an iteration of "Love, American Style," helped create top-of-mind awareness of this new vacation alternative, but not without a price. Talk about the beautiful people! Everyone on the show was gorgeous, handsome, or famous, and certainly glamorous. The few characters who weren't monied were either buffoons or crooks or gigolos, preying on the swells.

The show presented cruising in a way that, at least subliminally, had to have alarmed the average, middle-class American. After all, why would anyone want to spend his vacation worrying about "fitting in"?

People run the rat race 50 or so weeks a year. When they go on vacation, they want to relax and enjoy experiences that are very different from those in normal work and community environment. The last thing they want to do is pay good money to be in a socially threatening environment that puts them down rather than builds them up.

In primitive society, men were the hunters, bringing home the kill for the consideration and approval of wife and family. Their self-esteem depended in large part on their micro-societal acceptance. If the man was considered a good provider by his family, word would speed throughout his tribe or clan and his stature would be enhanced. Cultural anthropologists tell us that man today has these same, deep-rooted drives; consequently, he is loathe to present a vacation choice that won't meet with the acceptance of his wife and family and, of course, himself. A bad vacation selection today is akin to bringing home a tainted kill in ages past.

Consumer Psychology

Male vacation purchasers tend to move with extreme caution, making choices on the basis of previous enjoyable trips. Thus, of course, we're back to cruising's fundamental challenge: As most people have not cruised, the choice to forego a familiar land-based vacation and take a cruise is, for men, an intimidating unknown, perceived as a great departure from the normal vacation pattern, which requires a huge leap of faith. Curiously, most women have absolutely no problem taking the plunge, but then, they are descendants of gatherers, not hunters!

Women are far more intuitive than men. They can "see" the value of something they haven't experienced much more easily than men can. When a women enters a room full of people, she takes in the whole scene at once, seeming to grasp every detail in a flash. She'll notice immediately, for example, that a woman 25 feet away in a cluster of people, has a clashing orange-red purse with her blue-red knit suit or that the coffee table needs dusting. The man, on the other hand, is a linear thinker, absorbing details from point A to point B to point C. He enters the same room thinking: "I'm now looking at a (fuzzy) mass of people, I'm now discerning woman A . . ."

Most women "know" that they are going to enjoy cruising—it just feels right to them. That's why, in our experience, many women would kill or maim to be on a cruise. The problem is clearly with the males. Their linear thinking presents a huge obstacle to trial. Any additional obstacles, feeding negative perceptions, make the task of converting men to cruising even more daunting.

Against this background of consumer psychology, we have all the wrong images for today's cruising created by movies and television shows. One would think, then, that cruise advertising on television and in print would be carefully designed to break down the old stereotypes and present the cruise product as approachable, realistic, inviting, and unintimidating. However, the sharp decline in first-timers over the last ten years attests in part to the industry's collective failure to encourage trial. We argue that the cumulative effect of individual lines' advertising—sending confusing messages that not only do not overcome the obstacles to cruise marketing but reinforce negative perceptions—has brought this about.

Preaching to the Converted

That statement seems harsh. With so many factors at work, why does advertising take most of the blame? Because, as we saw above, it's the only thing the industry can truly control. It works two ways: when advertising is effective as a market expansion vehicle, it induces large numbers of first-timers to try this new, exciting vacation choice. These first-timers, in turn, sparked by their personal discovery, tell others about cruising with excitement and relish. Positive, word-of-mouth, third-party endorsement convinces noncruisers to try the product. (Remember, we know this is so because consumer research shows that cruising has both the highest customer satisfaction of *any* vacation and the cachet of a "new" experience—unlike "ordinary" land-based vacations.) When the advertising is *not* effective in bringing in a sizable number of first-timers, third-party endorsement is diminished.

The industry therefore loses twice: fewer immediate first-timers, and fewer "secondary," first-timers are induced to try the product because of the enthusiasm of the immediate first-timers they have encountered. It would be difficult to prove, but it's our view that the power of word-of-mouth endorsement diminishes disproportionately as these cruisers take more cruise vacations. The explanation for the phenomenon is as follows:

1. The more people cruise, the less excited they are about their discovery. It's old news after a while.
2. With subsequent cruises under their belt, people seem to acquire (and display) too much knowledge, which is offputting to prospective first-timers, who are overwhelmed by their

own lack of knowledge of the subject and frequently become intimidated and withdraw from the conversations of seasoned cruisers.

Savvy travel agents today recognize this situation and counteract it by promoting cruise nights exclusively for first-time cruisers, to which experienced cruisers are *not* invited. They learned this tactic by observing what happened when the crowd at a cruise show was mixed: the experienced cruisers told can-you-top-this stories and the first-timers stayed silent. It's intimidating to hear someone expound on the 64 ships he's been on, including, perhaps, the *Lusitania, Merrimac, Graf Spee,* and the *Bismarck.* Worse yet, a prospect may have asked a dumb question (perceived as "dumb" by experienced cruisers) and the cruisers in the audience roll their eyes in disgust at what they view as verbal flatulence. Trust us, this is immediately discerned by all the prospects in the audience who will experience subtle but very real discomfort. Is this a positive environment in which to sell cruises?

Perceived Obstacles to First-Time Cruising

Price
Cruising's "high falutin" image propelled by advertising strategies designed to increase a line's market share of existing cruisers not only runs counter to the successful, inviting appeal of most land-based vacation products, it also reinforces the noncruiser's concern about price. In 1994, Cruise Holidays, a franchise chain of independently owned cruise-only travel agencies, commissioned a nationally projectable consumer research study to determine why noncruisers weren't cruising.

As shown in Table 5.9, the perception that cruising is too expensive far and away explains most people's reluctance. About 51 percent of the respondents cited the high cost, an explanation offered more frequently than all other possibilities combined, and seven times more frequently than the second most cited reason—that they don't take vacations. (It's pretty hard for cruising to penetrate that subset!)

Table 5.10 shows that the picture is even more bleak. The perception of cruising as unaffordable persists across all household income groups. For example, 25 percent of households with

Table 5.9
Income

	Total	Under $20,000	$20,001–$40,000	$40,001–$60,000	$60,001–$75,000	Over $75,000
Think cruises are for people younger than you	14 1.8%	5 2.8%	5 1.7%	2 1.3%	1 2.6%	1 1.5%
Don't know enough about cruises	33 4.4%	2 1.1%	16 5.5%	10 6.3%	2 5.3%	1 1.5%
Are afraid you might get sea sick	49 6.3%	8 4.5%	17 5.9%	13 8.1%	2 5.3%	6 9.2%
Don't think you can afford it—too expensive	391 50.5%	119 67.6%	161 55.5%	67 41.9%	12 31.6%	16 24.6%
Think cruises are for people older than you	8 1.0%	0	1 .3%	2 1.3%	1 2.6%	4 6.2%
Don't think there's enough to do/cruise	43 5.5%	3 1.7%	15 5.2%	11 6.9%	6 15.8%	6 9.2%
Don't go on vacations at all	54 7.0%	13 7.4%	17 5.9%	14 8.8%	2 5.3%	5 7.7%
Other	148 19.1%	22 12.5%	48 16.6%	34 21.3%	7 18.4%	23 35.4%
Don't know/refused	35 4.5%	4 2.3%	10 3.4%	7 4.4%	5 13.2%	3 4.6%

Table 5.10
Cruise Objections by Category (Respondents Who Have Never Cruised

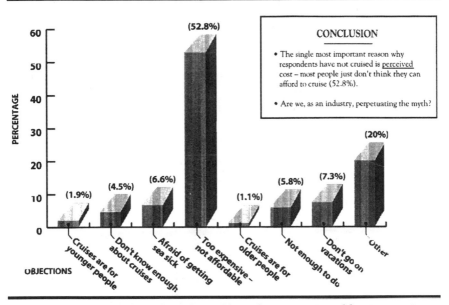

Source: Cruise Holidays poll conducted by Fabrizio, McLaughlin & Associates, Inc. (February, 1994)

a combined annual income of $75,000 and over—the top 12% of the households in the United States—cite the high cost of cruising as the biggest obstacle to purchase. Michael London, the wunderkind President of Cruise Holidays, commissioned the study because: "I wanted to confirm our beliefs relative to barriers to entry, which were based on our field knowledge gleaned from our Cruise Holiday offices." Curiously, London was able to detect the decline in consumer trial of cruising at the retail distribution level. Most cruise executives fail to acknowledge the problem, but London will admit what a shame the current state of affairs is: "Too many cruise line executives are obviously in denial—failing to grasp the importance of dealing with the affordability issue as well as other consumer perceptions of their products." CLIA, in 1994 commissioned a piece of consumer research, also nationally projectable, to determine obstacles to trial (adapted as Table 5.11):

Table 5.11
Most Important Reasons Never Cruised Before* (% Top 3 Box)**

	Noncruisers		
	Interested in Next 5 Years (%)	Not Interested (%)	Net Difference (+/-) (%)
It's too expensive	34	34	—
In this economy, it's not the right time to spend money on a cruise	32	31	+1
I go on vacation with my family and cruises aren't for kids	18	23	-5
I'm afraid of getting seasick	17	27	-10
I wouldn't be able to change plans once on ship	14	31	-17
If I become ill or injured, I might not get the best medical attention	14	13	+1
If I took my children, there'd be no chance to do anything on my own	14	11	+3
Little or no sightseeing on a cruise	12	21	-9
I couldn't be by myself because of too many people	11	22	-11
I'd be unable to choose where/when/and what to eat	9	11	-2
The food is not the best quality	9	8	+1
The ship might not be safe	8	15	-7

158

I wouldn't get to experience different people, places, or cultures	8	12	-4
I wouldn't be able to stay in touch with my family, friends, or job	8	10	-2
The nightlife very limited	8	8	—
I'd never meet anyone in my age group on a cruise	7	6	+1
There wouldn't be enough to do	6	16	-10
I wouldn't be able to participate in sports	6	12	-6
Accommodations are not as top notch as I'm accustomed to	5	9	-4

*Asked among total noncruisers who were given an expanded questionnaire.
**Top 3: Rating statement 10, 9 or 8 in terms of "critical decision to not take a cruise."

Note that the study looks at the most important reason on a cluster basis, ranked by how frequently a reason appeared in the top three choices given by a respondent. (In fact, a reply could theoretically include a large number of reasons, but the presumption is that the top three, irrespective of order, are the most important.)

Here, too, "It's too expensive" is the top-rated obstacle, mentioned 34 percent of the time, but the second reason "In this economy it's not the right time to spend money . . ." also suggests that a cruise is too expensive, especially when the consumers are opting for land vacations instead. If the top two answers are combined as "Too expensive," that response then dominates, at a frequency of 65–66 percent. It's also interesting that the perception of costliness, unlike most other obstacles, doesn't diminish among noncruisers who say they are interested in cruising in the next five years and those who say they are not. This certainly suggests the pervasiveness of the notion that cruise vacations are too expensive—with the clear implication that land-based vacations are cheaper and probably a better value.

Note that the fear of seasickness is the fourth obstacle for both groups of noncruisers, yet it is certainly not insurmountable. Noncruisers interested in taking a cruise within the next five years are considering cruising despite their concern, viewing seasickness either as a problem whose symptoms can be reduced with medication and/or Sea-Bands® or as a minor nuisance the risk of which is reasonable given all the good things that cruise vacations provide. Over the years, our anecdotal research among cruise executives and travel agents indicates that both groups believe that fear of seasickness is a sort of deal-breaker among consumers. However, the CLIA research suggests that this is not always the case.

But, you ask, if the industry is lowering rates, offering two-for-ones and other forms of discounting, and these prices are widely promoted via advertising and other promotional means, how can industry advertising be blamed for fueling the misconception that cruising is too expensive? Because the cruise industry has failed to generate a respectable percentage of first-time cruisers each year. Remember all that research that shows that for the majority of consumers the biggest obstacle to cruise trial is the view that it's too expensive. For any cruise line's advertising to produce results, it must effectively deal with and negate this misconception. Moreover, shrinking percentages of first-timers attest to the failure of the advertising; that the market-share strategies have failed is unarguable. The cause of the failure is straightforward. The beautiful people, with their fancy clothes and beautiful bodies, imply a degree of affluence—suggesting and reinforcing negative consumer perception. Just as important, the market-share advertising strategy, by definition, speaks to an audience of past cruisers. These ads have no need to proactively explain the experience of cruising. The noncruiser can neither understand nor interpret the value.

Larry Pimentel, President of Seabourn, is fond of saying that "consumers are used to unbundled, tip-of-the-iceberg pricing when encountering practically all land-based vacations." In other words, they know from experience that the advertised price of the resort is only a fraction of what they will end up paying, and they accept that situation. All-inclusive resort vacations, like Club Med, where the advertised price includes everything, garner less than 1 percent of the US and Canadian vacation market; people know even less about them than they do about taking a cruise and purchase them less frequently.

Consumers assume that the advertised price of a cruise is similar to that of a conventional resort. They don't realize the number of included features in a cruise price because market share advertising doesn't tell them. The plain fact is that new cruise shoppers compare the price of a cruise to what they are familiar with—resorts, and they don't know they are comparing apples to oranges. The lead cruise price, even after the "deal," seems, and is, much higher than the lead land price, which includes far less (as shown in Table 5.8).

Parenthetically, since 1984 Carnival has run seven different TV campaigns, averaging five or six 30-second spots per campaign, all of which featured at least two ads pointing out to noncruisers the items included in the cruise price. In one, spokesperson Kathie Lee Gifford, explains: "And just about everything's included in the price. All your meals are included, all your daytime activities, and your nighttime entertainment as well." This is logical and consistent with Carnival's market expansion strategy, in which the primary audience is the prospective first-time cruiser. With this focus, Carnival is dealing head-on with consumer ignorance and misperception of cruising obstacles to purchase (cost) and misconceptions (you need to be wealthy, gorgeous, urbane, and sophisticated to "fit in" and enjoy cruising).

The proof of Carnival's advertising effectiveness—against its target audience—is that it generates 60 percent first-timers, almost twice as many as the rest of the industry. As we mentioned earlier, the industry claimed that 40 percent of its passengers were first-timers in 1994. But take Carnival's 25-percent market share out of the calculation, and the rest of the industry's first-timers were only 33 percent!

Market Expansion—The Antidote to Overcapacity

We believe that a business strategy designed to capture a larger share of the existing cruise market is a poor one, not just for cruise lines but also for its primary distribution channel, travel agencies. Like many cruise lines, too many agencies ignore the larger vacation opportunity (the wider, lower-priced, land vacation level of the pyramid). Instead, they take the path of least resistance and sell most of their cruises to repeat customers, when the better approach would be one that focuses at least equally on promotion and sales to first-timers.

There is a widespread belief among marketing executives that is it easier to sell cruises (or anything else for that matter) to people who are already users than to go out and create new customers. That is true in most cases. The value of a loyal customer is much more than most people suspect—marketing experts often say it costs four times as much to win a new customer as it does to keep an old one.

This approach is especially appropriate with a product category in a mature market where the number of new customers is limited and therefore the probability of obtaining them is relatively low. Take laundry detergent. Marketing executives at Proctor & Gamble and Colgate-Palmolive know that some people seldom do their own laundry or don't mind wearing dirty clothes. And few of them, after being exposed to a powerful sales message on television, are suddenly going to start washing three loads a day instead of two a week. The name of the game is therefore to increase the company's share of the people who already do three loads of laundry a day, say mothers who are at home caring for young children.

The Myth of Market Share

The market share strategy is not the best one when there is a good chance of attracting many customers who have never used the product, as is most certainly the case in the cruise industry. What about Marketing 101 where you were taught that you can't create a new market but can only satisfy the needs of an existing one? Marketing gurus Kevin Clancy and Bob Shulman call this "Death Wish Marketing." They cite Professor Frederick E. Webster, Jr., a professor at Dartmouth's Amos Tuck School of Business. Webster says that people who believe this misread Professor Theodore Levitt of the Harvard Business School, whose classic article, *Marketing Myopia*, many feel started the marketing revolution. Levitt said that "Selling focuses on the needs of the seller; marketing on the needs of the buyer." According to Webster, executives who favor a market share strategy interpret Levitt to mean *existing* consumer needs and wants, and that's wrong. It's a myth, say Clancy and Shulman.

It's a myth "because it assumes that consumers (individual people, business executives, government officials—everybody who spends money for products or services) can always identify their needs and wants. What made Fred Smith (Federal Express), Ray Kroc (McDonald's), and Steve Jobs (Apple) so extraordinary is that they identified needs people did not know they had. They created whole new industries."

Creating a Desire

Remember what we said earlier about women's intuition? We were not being chauvinistic. Many scientists who have studied

[2]For a complete discussion of this and other marketing myths, we highly recommend *Marketing Myths That Are Killing Business: The Cure For Death Wish Marketing* by Kevin J. Clancy and Robert S. Shulman (New York: McGraw Hill, 1994). "A company cannot *create* markets" is Myth #50.

the brain know that right-brain thinking consists of hunches rather than logic, and women, who tend to think more with their right brain, are often more willing to take risks—to explore uncharted territory—just because it feels right. Men, for the most part, left-brain thinkers, need what they see as sound logical reasons to try anything new, but men can think intuitively given the right incentives. How many people wanted a personal computer twenty years ago? How many wanted to be connected to Internet two years ago? How many who had a computer and were connected to Internet felt a yearning to own Microsoft's Windows 95 before it was introduced in August of 1995? Not a lot, because these were new markets created by a simple understanding of the fact that people did want access to more information but didn't know how to get it or where.

It's not surprising that many travel agencies have been influenced by the cruise lines' marketing misdirection and attendant co-op money. ("Co-op money" refers to the widespread industry practice of giving travel agencies cooperative advertising and promotional funds to jointly promote the specific cruise line and the agency as the retail point of purchase for that line's products. More about this later.) Unfortunately, lucrative co-op money draws the retailer's attention toward the underlying strategy of the cruise line that supplies it—a market share strategy that will inevitably cause negative repercussions for the agency.

The Benefits of Market Expansion

To ignore the first-timers is an enormous missed opportunity for travel agencies for the following reasons.

Ease of Selling

First-timers are generally buying the broad concept of cruising and are not aware of the myriad available brands. They are less concerned about the subtle and frequently confusing market positioning of the various cruise lines. First-timers may have a strong brand preference (because of effective market expansion advertising and positioning and/or strong word-of-mouth endorsement), or they may have no brand preference at all, viewing a typical cruise in a more general way. Either way, the only sales effort required may be to match the desired itinerary, dates, or destination with available cruises. Repeat cruisers, on the other hand, can put travel agents through their paces for hours, querying them on nuances—and deals—of dozens of cruise lines!

Profit
The net profit of a cruise sale is 5 to 15 times higher than that of a land package. Yet the typical travel agency sells 10 land packages for every one cruise. A booking of two people on a cruise can equal the profit for a group of 30 people on a comparable land vacation.

Fewer Rebates
First-timers are largely unaware of the practice of rebating, where travel agents voluntarily give back a percentage of their commission to the customer as an inducement to make or keep the sale. However, many experienced cruisers seem to relish the challenge of securing the largest rebate. Perhaps it makes great table conversation on the cruise: bragging rights for the couple who negotiated the best deal. Could this be the adult version of king of the mountain? The "winners" are reinforced by their victories to try and "win" again with even greater rebates. The "losers," stung by their "defeat" are galvanized by their conviction never to be placed in that position again.

Agents have told us that some clients demand a rebate *after* the cruise as an inducement (bribe) to their continued patronage. In some communities, the practice of securing deep rebates is carried to ridiculous extremes. Prospective cruise purchasers will waste time and gas money to save an extra $10 or so on a $2,000 cruise!

Repeat Bookings
Cruising enjoys the highest customer satisfaction of any vacation, and satisfied customers are far more likely to return to the agency to book again. Roughly two-thirds of all agency business is repeat customers. It is the backbone of the business.

Ease of Booking
Cruise vacations are easier to book, since the cruise line handles many of the details of air scheduling, transfers, accommoda-

tions, meals, and so forth. Also, cruise and air/sea pricing is generally available one to two years in advance of the travel date, which is not so for most land vacations. Therefore, a travel agent can quote a price on an air/sea cruise when no comparable air/land price is available.

Overcapacity

Without sufficient first-timers, the industry will be plagued with overcapacity (because of under-demand). Cruise prices will fall, rebating will become rampant, and the profitability of selling cruises for the agency distribution system will be weakened.

The sobering fact is that unless this market share trend is reversed soon, the cruise industry will run the risk of becoming the same sort of boutique, out-of-the mainstream vacation it was thirty years ago. To prevent this, cruise lines must back up their image making with substance, and focus their marketing once again on the substantial group of potential cruisers who don't know what they've been missing!

6

Your Cruise Line GPS

Positioning and differentiation
of cruise lines

When Al Ries and Jack Trout wrote their classic treatise on positioning, the last thing they had in mind was the modern Global Positioning Satellite System, which establishes and tracks a ship's position by satellites placed in orbit by the government originally for defense purposes. Nevertheless, a parallel can be drawn. Ries and Trout were concerned with how consumers "position" products in their minds and use that information to make buying decisions.

GPS instruments assist sailors in viewing their position on the earth's surface and setting their course. Like sailors, consumers set a course as well—the routes they will follow to satisfy their needs and wants. They do this by assessing their environment and deciding what they need to do (or purchase) to improve it.

Positioning

There are, of course, several ways consumers make choices when they plan vacations. The principal ones (in order of importance) are recommendations of friends and neighbors, recommendations of a travel agent, travel brochures, travel advertising, and editorial material such as they are likely to find in the Sunday travel section of their local newspaper or *Condé Nast Traveler*.

Up to a few years ago, the cruise industry was relatively small. Thus, since the biggest source of new business for vacation products is the recommendations of friends and relatives, the general public knew very little about what it was like to take a cruise or the differences among the various lines because they were unlikely to know anyone who had ever been on one. At the same time, travel agents (another business that has grown very rapidly) were equally uninformed. Most of them hadn't ever sold a cruise, much less set foot on the deck of a cruise ship. Only agents who lived near cruise ports (principally Miami) had even seen a cruise ship from the outside, although most had an ample supply of colorful and often expensive brochures to distribute to customers who asked about them.

Few cruise lines advertised at all, and none on television. When Aaron Spelling Productions first introduced "The Love Boat," the "Princess" brand name was played down considerably because they wanted a generic cruise ship and Princess was not sponsoring the show—but simply providing the facilities. Indeed, one of the sponsors was Norwegian Caribbean Cruise Lines—the first and at that time the only line with a sufficient advertising budget to use commercials.

The program, moreover, did not project a realistic image of the cruise product. It appeared, for example, that the main duties of the principal characters (Captain, Purser, Ship's Doctor, and Bartender) consisted of mending broken hearts, matchmaking, and generally acting as social directors for the passengers. The staterooms, large by hotel standards, were outrageous by ship's standards!

Since it was a case of the blind leading the blind when it came to purchasing a cruise, agents typically handed a few brochures to the few customers bold enough to inquire and told them to call if they wanted to book passage. And very often agents didn't even do that. Many agencies had a wall full of brochures (they still do) and the cruise brochures were out there on display next to a Cosmos tour of Europe (11 countries in 10 days) or a week at the Hilton Hawaiian Village on the beach at Waikiki.

The image that people had of a cruise into the early eighties—
or, if you will, the position that the cruise vacation occupied in
the mind of the general public—was as a costly, stuffy (maybe
even pretentious) holiday best suited for affluent, sedentary,
middle-aged and senior citizens—in short, the country club set.
Those who did not fit that mold and took a cruise anyway did so
because they perceived it as a status symbol. But as Paul Fussell,
in his classic book *Class* observed, "The middle is the class that
makes cruise ships a profitable enterprise, for it fancies that the
upper-middle class is to be mixed with on them, without realizing
that class is either peering at the minarets in Istanbul, or hiding
out in a valley in Nepal, or staying home in Old Lyme, Connecti-
cut, playing backgammon and reading *Town and Country*."[1]
Cruise lines had little top-of-mind awareness as vacations since
they were not advertised visibly and were not sold often.

Ries and Trout point out that while positioning starts with a
product or a service, it has little to do with what you do with that
product. *Positioning is what you do in the mind of the prospect.*
Not that changes to the product or service aren't significant—
they can be, and cruise lines, like other hospitality products and
services, do change their physical appearance, food, features, and
price. But from a communications point of view, these changes
are made for the purpose of securing a higher degree of awareness, in other words, a stronger position in the prospect's mind.

Ries and Trout mention several ways to accomplish this. One
is by being first. Everyone knows that the first man to climb
Mount Everest was Sir Edmund Hillary. But who was the second? Who was the first person you ever fell in love with? The
second? It takes a little longer to answer those questions because, as Ries and Trout point out, the mind is like a ladder, and
for every product category there is one member that is at the top
of our minds, the one we think of first. Now, if you can't be first,
the idea is to find another way to establish a meaningful position
in your prospect's mind. Avis faced that problem years ago when
it grew large enough to compete on a national basis with Hertz,
the pioneer in the rental car industry. Hertz was number 1 and

---

[1]Paul Fussell, *Class* (New York: Ballentine Books, 1983).

[2]Al Ries and Jack Trout, *Positioning, The Battle For Your Mind* (New York: Mc-
Graw-Hill, 1981).

everyone knew it because it advertised the fact heavily. Avis couldn't say they were number 1, too because it simply wasn't true. Even if they had pursued a strategy of building more locations than Hertz, it wouldn't have mattered because Hertz had firmly established its number-1 position in people's minds.

What did Avis do? It positioned itself against the leader by saying "Avis is only number 2 in rent-a-car, so why go with us? *We try harder.*" The campaign turned Avis from a company that had lost money for 13 consecutive years to one that made a profit the very first year after they launched their campaign. Did Avis try harder? Sure. Their cars were very clean; their people were very nice. But the cars were, after all, the same ones that other companies rented. People who rented from Avis reported that they received good service, but there was nothing wrong with Hertz's service, either. The real difference had nothing to do with what Avis did to its cars or how accommodating its rental agents were; it had to do with how it was able to reposition itself in the minds of its prospects. If you got off a plane in Chicago and there was a long line in front of the Hertz counter, you went to the Avis counter. The same was true if Hertz only had small cars and you wanted a big one. You didn't go to the National counter or the Budget counter. Why? Because Avis was number 2. It successfully positioned itself as an alternative to Hertz—occupying the "heir apparent" or "crown prince" position.

Knowing Your Growth Potential

Cruise lines didn't have this problem at the beginning. In the early years no one company occupied the position at the top of the ladder of "cruises" in the consumer's mind, although NCL promoted itself as "America's favorite cruise line" for several years until mid-1984, when Carnival began billing itself as "The most popular cruise line in the world." There was plenty of business for everyone. Moreover, cruising was destination oriented, which meant that while there may have been more than one ladder in consumers' minds, they were for different destinations. People went on cruises then mainly as a way to visit and sample new destinations. Since different lines visited different ports, one easy way to pick a cruise was to decide where you wanted to go or what you wanted to see. Some lines promoted Bermuda, others the Bahamas, or different ports in the Caribbean, the Panama Canal, or Alaska. Carnival, Royal Caribbean, and Norwegian Caribbean cruised in the Caribbean. Holland America and Princess cruised to Alaska and Mexico. The preferred line—the one with the most awareness for each of these destinations—was different in many cases.

Positioning became an issue as soon as the industry grew to a size where many ships visited the same destination. And it became even more of an issue when the lines began to realize that they were selling vacation *experiences*. Surveys began to show that more and more passengers were looking at the ship itself, rather then the ports, as the primary destination.

One factor in determining your positioning is the kind of growth you can realistically expect to achieve. Say you are 99 percent confident that the number of new cruisers will increase at the same rate it has been increasing. If you are one of the leaders in market share, you can be reasonably certain that if the number of new cruisers overall grows by 10 percent, your new cruisers will grow by the same amount—providing you either have the capacity to absorb the growth or are new building ships to provide it. (Remember, in the eighties, when this evolution was occurring, the industry was operating at very high, 90 percent plus occupancies.) If you accept this assumption you see no need to position yourself as a better alternative to any competitor's line because there will be enough business for everyone (unless your capacity is going to grow by an increment larger than 10 percent in that same year). On the other hand, if you are not confident of growth, you need to take the view that "marketing is war" (a very common view among marketing executives in some industries) and that your growth is going to depend on increasing your market share by stealing customers from other cruise lines.

Positioning at Royal Caribbean

At Royal Caribbean, Executive Vice President Rod McLeod views the situation as a little of both sharing and war. To begin with, he is not entirely comfortable with the forecasts of passenger increases supplied by CLIA, although he has been its chairman on two occasions:

Rod McLeod:

CLIA is a promotional association, not a research institute, Jim Godsman's role (as CLIA's President) is to responsibly promote the growth of the cruise industry and to position it as a dynamic, growing, and profitable business. Even so, we don't pay a lot of attention to their figures—we have our own fleet model. I suspect CLIA's forecast in growth of passengers is "optimistic."

Remember, we're not selling open-heart surgery. The question we're asking is, Are you interested in cruising in the next five years? This is something a lot of people want to do, and 60 percent, or 71.2 million, say they will; 44 million definitely will. I don't think that number is overly optimistic. I do look at it as an enabling statistic, basically saying that people want to do this, there's a predisposition out there that cruising is something they would like to do.

That doesn't speak to the reasons they haven't, or may not, at this point. They may have barriers to entry and this is one of the problems. I'd like to have a Rolls Royce, but there's a barrier to entry. I think we have to understand that better and we have to shape and form our product to take advantage of that potential. There are a lot of people out there who are willing to work with us.

Some of that potential is people who say, "Yes I'd like to take a cruise—you know maybe for my twenty-fifth wedding anniversary." That's what old people do and we've got to overcome that. I agree with Bob Dickinson that we have a story to tell. The median age on the *Nordic Empress* in the summer is somewhere between 38 and 39 years of age. That shows that we are tapping into that younger market.

Now, as for growth in capacity, if you go back to September 1993, we forecasted the berth capacity growth for the cruise industry for 1995 to be 8.4 percent. Then in March of '94 we estimated that the capacity growth for the industry was going to be at 6.9 percent—lower then our original estimate. By June of 1995 we were projecting 1995 growth to be only 2.5 percent; in 1993 we were saying the 1996 growth would be 6.9 percent; and by March 1994 we thought it was going to be 10.9 percent—in

June 1995 we revised that to 9.4 percent. Ultimately, we believe it's going to be below that. Most likely the number of passengers and the number of berths will increase at the same rate between now and 1999 or 2000, but it may not be one to one. You have to understand the way we get capacity in the industry—one day you don't have it, the next day you do. It's not like package goods where you're dealing with percentage of factory utilization. But as an industry we're not concerned that capacity will increase more than the growth of passengers.

A lot of (future) growth depends on how smart we are and how we alter the product. The one marvelous opportunity we have—that marketers in this industry have—is the ability to shape and form the product like nobody else in the travel business can. You look at Bermuda or Hawaii or Miami Beach—they talk about average length of stay. We don't "talk" about it, we determine it!

Market Segmentation and Differentiation

Once the cruises lines had a fix on the growth of the market, whether it was their own or supplied by CLIA, they began to focus on issues of market segmentation and differentiation. Price is a major way to do that.

Security analysts, travel agents, and others talk about the luxury market, the premium market, the contemporary market, and the budget or economy market. Thus, Seabourn is luxury; Princess and Holland America are premium; Royal Caribbean, Norwegian Caribbean, and Carnival are contemporary; and Commodore and Dolphin are budget. Often these classifications are based primarily on price and amenities, but as Royal Caribbean's Rod McLeod points out, "There is a good deal of disagreement between the major lines as to how the market is segmented by product. We all have our own way of looking at it." RCCL does not subscribe to the standard classifications: "Unless your consumer and principal distribution system agrees with those particular labels I think they are irrelevant," McLeod says. "I don't think the world looks at us that way. Take the automobile industry. Look at the various players. If I say Mercedes to you and then I say Chevy, you now have certain specific attributes associated with those two names. These are related to price, style, and comfort. But people don't know enough about cruises to make the same kind of associations. For the most part, if you say Royal Caribbean, Celebrity, or Princess cruises to them, they can't make the same connections you just did with automobiles.

The Blurred Lines of Segmentation in the Cruise Industry

McLeod concedes that consumers do recognize luxury lines. But he believes cruise prospects are not able to draw a hard line of differentiation between premium and contemporary lines. McLeod has his own product segmentation system. He calls it the "Drinking Man's Guide to Cruising Segmentation":

> We have the champagne and caviar lines. These would include Seabourn and Sea Goddess. Then there are the Evian and granola lines, the specialty operators, where I would put Windstar. Next we have the wine and cheese lines, which I think we can further segment into imported and domestic. Crystal would contend that they belong in the champagne and caviar group, but I think they belong in the imported wine and cheese segment. Holland America and Princess are in the domestic wine and cheese category.
>
> Next lower on the scale after the wine and cheese lines there are the beer and pretzel lines. Finally at the bottom there are bread and water lines. We are in the domestic wine and cheese segment, but we're also in the imported beer and pretzel segment. Carnival falls into the domestic beer and pretzels category, and I would put Majesty in there, too, although they would like you to think they're domestic wine and cheese, but they don't conduct themselves that way. Bread and water lines are self-evident.

Although Carnival and Royal Caribbean are often considered similar, McLeod says, "Do I believe Royal Caribbean is better than Carnival. Sure I do. Why? Because we cost more. According to our best estimate right now [Summer 1995] we're about fourteen to fifteen percent higher than Carnival. You pay more and you get more."

Would that it were so simple. RCCL may cost more on some cruises some of the time, but with all of the discounting, rebates by travel agents, regional fares, and special promotions that are inherent in the cruise industry today (and probably always will be), it is difficult if not impossible, in our opinion, to make a generalized statement about which line is truly expensive. It depends where, when, and on what ship with what itinerary. In this respect it's like the airline and hotel businesses, which also deal with perishable commodities. Can you say that American costs more or less than Delta? Or that Hilton costs more than Marriott? Sometimes they do and some times they don't.

Even more to the point is the issue of cost. While there are surely instances when you pay more to get more, you don't always get more. You can't buy a new Mercedes for the same price as a new Oldsmobile yet, but Red Lobster restaurants sell fresh lobster for less than its competitors do. That's because they buy more lobsters and they serve them to a larger customer base. It's a simple matter of economy of scale.

Positioning and Segmenting the Cruise Lines

As you might imagine, several other cruise lines executives we talked with (as well as the authors) do not agree with McLeod's segments or, necessarily, in which segments they and some of their competitors reside. McLeod understands this and readily concedes that his is only one man's opinion of market segmentation. He does think it is a useful way of approaching the problem, however, noting that with the trend toward consolidation there will be fewer meaningful players, and this may result in some more niche marketers. As long as they have a valid niche that the consumer is looking for and recognizes, McLeod believes these lines may succeed, but to do this they must understand what a niche is, and he believes many operators don't.

Rod McLeod on Niches:

If you have an old small ship that is not competitive in the volume market, that in itself does not define you as a niche player. I mean that you can't say, "I have an old inefficient ship and therefore I am a niche player and I deserve to be here." From a consumer standpoint you're irrelevant. Consumers will say, "You have an old inefficient ship and we don't need you." If your prices are low you're a bread-and-water line, but you're certainly not a niche player. To me the niche players are up near the luxury segment, in Evian and granola. They are providing a unique service that the consumer is looking for and they do it very well. Those are the niche players I'm talking about. When we get into this rapidly consolidating industry, in terms of major marketing players, what we have to communicate to our prospects is our points of difference.

We have to understand that we're standing on the edge of what is in effect a new industry. We've come from an industry that we can look at 10 to 15 years ago as the early part of a race. There might have been 15 horses across the track—all of them running about evenly, maybe with some a little ahead or somewhat behind, but most clustered around each other. What has happened over those past ten years, particularly in the last five, is that a couple of the big horses with stamina—stamina being resources—have moved away from the pack. And in doing so they have gotten bigger. If you are a consumer in the grandstand you don't necessarily need a pair of binoculars to know who the players are—you're now seeing three or four and they're big ones. Their jockeys are wearing very distinctive colors, and they're coming around the track—you can't miss them.

Royal Caribbean

So, how does Royal Caribbean position itself? Who is its target market? "Let me to give you our demographic profile," McLeod says:

> I hate to typify where we are. We have flown in the face of marketing convention and our objective is to be all things to all people—within certain boundaries. Our average household income is $65,000 a year, and our median age is 44. The majority—67 percent—are married. Eighty-seven percent are from the United States and Canada. Thirteen percent are from every place else in the world. Fifty-three percent are first time cruisers, about twenty-four percent are Royal Caribbean repeaters, and the balance are brand switchers, starting out with someone else, and now with us.
>
> The income level somewhat suggests the education of people we have. They tend to have post–high school education—a

fair number are college graduates, certainly more than the norm. Their income level is greater than 50 percent above the median household income the United States. We are not walking down Park Avenue or Rodeo Drive looking for our customers, but on the other hand we're not browsing among the smokestacks, either. If you look at our positioning the way the analysts do, we bridge the lower end of premium and the upper end of contemporary market.

Princess

Rick James is Senior Vice President of Sales and Corporate Relations for Princess Cruises, the world's third largest line. Here is how he positions his line.

Well, of course, Rod has an interesting way of looking at things. I think it's a different way of slicing up the market and putting a different name to it, other then premium, deluxe, and so on. Everyone debates where they belong. Within the Princess fleet we have a mixture of ships with a mixture of destinations. I would suggest that we are in both the imported and domestic wine and cheese market, if you use Rod's scheme.

When you have the types of ships that we deploy, let's say in the European market, with some very complete itineraries, you provide a little different cruise experience then the seven-day Caribbean. We are somewhat different from our competitors in that we started out deploying on a worldwide basis and are now slowly creating in a bigger and bigger presence in the Caribbean. Our major competitors started from the opposite side of the fence—in the Caribbean and then slowly migrating to other destinations. That difference presents a unique set of opportunities and problems for us.

Part of the enigma is that we're not only for people who are 65 and older, nor are we only for families, nor are we only for any one segment. So, in fact, we have a great cross section of people, and that is why we ourselves have not spent a lot of time and effort trying to define who we are. Depending on the destination in the Caribbean, you'll see an average age on our ships in the area of 45 with an average income around $45,000. On a 12-day European cruise or a trans-canal cruise it obviously goes up. There guests are around 50 to 55 and their income is in the

$50,000 to $55,000 range. That happens because you're now into a two-week vacation.

When you talk about how we define ourselves, you have to remember that for all practical purposes we've already been defined by virtue of "The Love Boat" TV series. Right now, "The Love Boat" is in reruns in 93 countries around the world, so it is still very active. And one of the main things it has accomplished, from our point of view, is to humanize the cruise experience. It took away the mink stoles and steamer trunks, and while the program itself is a bit of a farce, it did bring a sense of "Gee maybe that's something I could do" because there are people on that ship like the viewer. So for us to have said, "No, our cruises are only for people fifty-five or sixty-five and older, or forty-five and older, would have diminished and restricted the market we're going after."

Effectively, by not defining ourselves, we get a huge cross section of customers. We say Princess is more than a cruise, it's the Love Boat, and by doing that we take our Love Boats and separate them from any other cruise that's out there. We expect the Love Boat to be whatever our passengers want it to be. Some will say its the hope of finding romance on board. Some will say that it's the romance of the sea. We want *them* to define it because by using their own definition they will always define it positively. The second we try to define what we believe a Princess cruise is, we're going to start excluding some of our potential market. We plan to continue our association with the Love Boat because of its strong awareness in the marketplace, but at the same time we are trying to better define what being on a Love Boat means. For example, our new ships built since the *Star Princess* all have an abundance of balcony cabins, and to many people that has become the signature of Love Boat ships.

Our positioning also involves spaciousness. Big ships do not necessarily mean that people are crammed in next to one another. Take a look at our new 100,000-ton ship, the *Grand Princess*. That ship will be carrying a similar number of passengers currently carried on 70,000-ton ships managed by some of our competitors. When we introduced the *Crown Princess* and *Regal Princess* everybody said, "How can you deliver a premium-class product on ships that large?" But we've done just that. It has nothing to do with size. It has everything to do with amenities. And the amenities that you build in break down the barriers to cruising—the things that stop people from taking their first cruise.

One reason we know that some people don't want to go on a cruise is their concern with regimentation. They know that they will have to eat at a specific time, the first sitting or the second sitting. So we're putting in a 24-hour Lido dining area, which allows our guests to eat at their convenience. Another concern is being too far away from family and friends and the office and not being able to contact them easily. We're putting business offices with sophisticated communications facilities on these ships—hoping that guests will enjoy their vacation but, again, taking away another reason for not trying a cruise.

That's why activities become important. We want to be able to conduct scuba classes on board and then take participants ashore in various ports so they can get their accreditation. For golf nuts we want to be able to build these automatic video golf courses where they can practice playing Mahogany Run on the ship and then, in port, go out and play the real thing. We want to be able to broaden our onboard activities so that there isn't a concern about regimentation and there is no worry about "What will I do all day" or the feeling that "Now it's bingo time and I have to go play."

I think taking a cruise is the greatest form of vacation and relaxation that anyone can have. I truly believe that, and I believe in trying to convince people to take that first step because I know that once they do they will come back over and over again. In the kind of stressful environment we work in today, taking a Princess cruise is something people should be doing for themselves.

Celebrity Cruise Lines

Although not one of the big three, Celebrity Cruise Lines, a relative newcomer, has enjoyed remarkable success according to many industry observers. The management are all veterans (the line is partly owned by the Greek Chandris family, who operated a budget line, Fantasy Cruises, for years. Their former Vice President of Sales and Marketing, Al Wallack, was the 1994–1995 Chairman of CLIA (Cruise Line Industry Association). Wallack, who came from an airline background, is one of the most thoughtful and knowledgeable people in the business. We asked him to tell us how Celebrity went about positioning its new line and its ships, the *Zenith* and the *Horizon*. Here's what he told us.

Al Wallack:

Everybody in this business establishes their style of service around a certain lifestyle. Ideally you want to create a lifestyle aboard your vessel that parallels the life style of your target consumer. But, let's take that just one step further, to the kind of lifestyle that people aspire to, because it's people's aspirations that we want to satisfy, not necessarily the mundane reality of their everyday life.

People in a leisure environment, in a cruise environment, have to feel it's something that they've always wanted to do—something that surpasses everyday life. From the very beginning we decided that our niche would be fairly broad. It would be that piece of the mass market that appreciates and understands quality service, a quality environment, and a very high level of cuisine.

We knew that we did not want to become a super-deluxe cruise line. From a practical standpoint we felt that the market at that end was too narrow and it was one that had some very serious players in it already, who appeared to be getting what there was to be had. We're talking about Seabourn, Sea Goddess, and that group. We also felt that with the demise of Sitmar and Home Lines [two premium brands that disappeared in the eighties] there was an opportunity to fill a void. Culturally we come from very similar roots, so we understood their product. These lines had occupied a wonderful position in the marketplace with great reputations, and they had a following.

We saw as our major competitors Princess and Holland America, and to some degree the upper end of Royal Caribbean. We included Royal Caribbean because before they became as large as they are now, they were considered a fairly upscale cruise line, at the top end of the mass market.

Understand, we absolutely recognize that the lines between the categories get blurred. They get blurred around ships and they get blurred around kinds of services you offer. Nevertheless, we felt we could distinguish ourselves and set ourselves apart by understanding the icons for quality and doing the kinds of things that support those icons.

Research told us, and we recognized immediately, that one of the most important icons for quality aboard a cruise was the dining experience. Most consumers, certainly in our target market, tend to define quality as place where one is served very good food in a pleasant and hospitable manner. We also believed that over the years, food on cruise ships has become like coffee mixed with chicory. In other words, over a period of time there has been some dilution of the quality of cuisine. I call this menu writing. The names of the dishes are written on the menu, but that's not what comes out of the kitchen and onto the plate. We decided that we would not just write the menus but deliver cuisine above and beyond what people expect to find in the cruise ship environment. In effect, we were going back to the classic period of ship travel, when some of the best restaurants in the world were on the great ocean liners. When you talk about the *Normandie* and the *Ile de France* and other great ships you tend to recall the ambiance of their dining rooms, their superior service, and the quality of their food. We felt that to some degree the industry had degenerated in that area and that we knew how to bring it back.

Then there were other icons for quality such as the European style of service and decor. From our point of view shipboard service had become very routine and had lost some of the personality that shipboard service used to be known for. When we analyzed the problem further, we recognized pretty clearly this was often caused by shortcomings in vessel design. When shipboard personnel have a difficult time working their way around the inadequacies of design, it takes away from the time they can spend developing relationships with passengers, understanding each other, and delivering personalized service. That meant that both in the cabin area and in the dining area—in fact, all over the ship—we had to create efficient and viable working conditions because the less time our crew spent overcoming hardware problems the more time they had to take care of our passengers.

Let me give you an example. If you design a galley where waiters have to make three stops before they can carry an entree from the hot table to tableside, you can almost guarantee that their delivery time will be slow and the quality of what they put on the table will be poor. If, on the other hand, you design a galley system that supports the efficient vectoring of the product, you'll get top-quality food in the dining room. If hot food is served cold, the waiter is blamed, but it may not be the waiter's fault. It may be because the soup tureen isn't in a place of the galley that allows the waiter to bring it out quickly. Moreover, if a waiter, from the furthest point in the dining room has to travel a significant distance through a circuitous route, you can guarantee not only that the food will arrive cold and late, but that, if the waiter has to go back into the galley for anything—a correction, a change of choice—it's going to take an inordinately long time, which will put the order of service completely off track and disappoint everyone sitting at that table. The implication of that kind of layout is that waiters will be reluctant to make changes and that's not what we wanted. A waiter who is reluctant to make changes is a waiter who is likely to disappoint the guest.

When we went about designing our ships, these kind of considerations became very important. An equally important element was our overall decor. We looked at a lot of different interior designs. Some we felt were very glittery; others we perceived as very austere and old-fashioned. Finally, we decided to turn to designers who had been designing in residential and commercial buildings. We wanted to achieve a look that you would be more likely to see in *Architectural Digest* than in a traditional resort environment, and to do that we had to rethink our notions about color schemes, trim, and furniture.

Of course, to succeed with this kind of strategy we realized that we would have to make a substantial investment up front. People who can afford it use the best possible materials, not because they like paying more but because they know that the best materials hold their color and their appearance much longer. Consequently, we bought the best possible rugs we could find, the best wall coverings, and the highest quality of fabrics because we knew that they would not only have an important initial impact but would wear better over time. We would have a superior product both short and long term.

You know, our kind of customer can tell when things are of high quality and costly. I think the environment you want to be in when you go on a vacation is one that surpasses your environment at home. You want to sit in a chair and say "Wow, would I love to have one of these in my living room." These seeming hardware issues are really life-style issues. Decor is a very important element of lifestyle, just as food is.

Norwegian Cruise Line

Kloster Cruise Ltd. has fallen on hard times in recent years. Recall that when the cruise industry started back in the mid-sixties, Knut Kloster was Ted Arison's partner. When they split, Arison, the poorer of the two, founded Carnival and pursued a business strategy of buying older ships, refurbishing them, and marketing them as fun ships. Kloster's Norwegian Caribbean Line (now Norwegian Cruise Line) comprised a fleet of brand-new ships that were the newest and nicest afloat. Since then the two lines' positions have been reversed. Carnival's fleet now consists of relatively new ships, and they have been adding more new tonnage than any other line. Kloster has been unable to finance this kind of expansion and has not put a new ship into service since 1993.

Thus, while Carnival, Royal Caribbean, and Princess, among others, have been able to capitalize on a number of new and quite beautiful vessels, NCL has had to find other ways to create marketing excitement. At one point they introduced a new concept in entertainment by producing an entire Broadway show once on every cruise, investing heavily in this tactic and positioning their line as offering the best entertainment afloat. Many travel writers and cruisers agree that they delivered on their promise. Unfortunately, that works only as long as your competitors allow it, and both Carnival and Royal Caribbean, whose newer ships had much more elaborate and expensive theaters, quickly and substantially upgraded their own entertainment.

Its perceived advantage negated, NCL decided to market a series of "theme cruises." Whether you were a country dancer or a football fan, there was a cruise for you. Many had celebrities and star entertainers connected to the themes on board to mingle with the passengers.

When Adam Aron became the President of Kloster Cruise Ltd., which at that time operated both the Norwegian and Royal Cruise Lines, he looked for a new approach. Already well-known as a marketing guru, he recognized that the product needed improvement (and he promptly brought in several experienced hoteliers to go to work on that), but they were still not in a position to order any new ships. So Aron began to look for the answer to their positioning not in the product but in the marketing.

Adam Aron:

In any industry it's vital that one differentiate one's products from one's competitors' products. When I went to business school, I was taught about product segmentation, product differentiation, and market segmentation. The model used was the detergent industry, in which what was inside the box was all the same, and yet some companies were going after fresher, brighter, or whiter clothes and others were saying that their product works in cold water or warm water. Still, inside the box the soaps were pretty similar. It's the same in the cosmetic business. With the sole exception of a particular scent, various perfumes are very similar. It reminds me of a wonderful Charles Revson quote: "In the factory we make lipstick, in the stores we sell hope." So it goes without saying that a smart competitor will differentiate himself as best he can from other competitors.

At Norwegian our slogan is "It's Different Out Here," which is a multiple play on a sea-based vacation as different from a land-based vacation. Our particular cruise line is different from other cruise lines. In our case, when that campaign was introduced the line itself was dramatically changing its quality levels of service so that there was an implication that we ourselves were different from the way we were before. Also, our very central, sexy advertising campaign, it's just as people thought the "it" in 'It's Better in the Bahamas,' referred to relationships between men and women. So another dimension to "It's Different Out Here" is that it inspires thoughts of what one might find in one's love life.

Having said that, I think Al Wallack is absolutely right when he points out that consumers don't have a clue what the differences are between lines, and that's because the industry is so small. There is, in fact, a lot of information available through consumer guide books and travel agents to help people distinguish between lines and ships. *Fielding, Berlitz,* and the *Total*

Traveler pull the lines apart by star ratings and numeric ratings, and there is no doubt that there are price differences between vessels, which indicate a relative level of quality.

Various ships gear their entertainment and activity to a specific age group. We own two lines, Royal* and Norwegian. Although on Norwegian our passengers range in age from 20 to 75, our ships are clearly programmed for a 43-year-old married couple with a very active life style. At Royal our average passenger is a 65-year-old couple. At Norwegian, life on board the ship is all about aerobics classes and "let's jog before breakfast." On Royal, jogging is prohibited on the deck because too many of our passengers commented that it was interfering with their enjoyment of the cruise.

Clearly there is a differentiation but also clearly consumers don't know about it unless they read about it in a guide book or ask. That's the role of the travel agent; who is knowledgeable about all of the factors I've been talking about and can answer questions about which lines are cheaper, which ones are geared for young people, middle-aged married couples, and senior citizens. They know who is classier, who is better, and whose entertainment is geared for each kind of customer. And they have a pretty good understanding and provide a very valuable service to consumers by steering them to ships they will like and away from ships they'll probably feel uncomfortable. on.

Holland America

For one more view on positioning, we spoke with Doug Falk, former senior vice president of marketing and sales at Holland America. Falk had come to Holland America from the position of President of Norwegian Cruise Lines; thus, we thought he might have a broader view about the positioning of the different lines, and he did. Falk told us that it is difficult to pigeon hole any cruise line in this or that category because it will typically span several categories, irrespective to labels. From his point of view, Norwegian Cruise Lines competes in the mass or contemporary market. He considers Carnival to be their biggest competitor, which suggests, of course, that NCL must position itself

---

*At the time of the quote, The Royal brand and was discontinued in early 1996.

to appeal to the same kind of people who would sail on a Carnival ship.

The problem is that Norwegian doesn't have any ships that look or act like Carnival's product. Whether that matters is another story, which we will discuss shortly. Falk does think however, that Norwegian is trying to achieve a more upscale position within the contemporary segment or mass market, but they don't want to be so upscale as to appeal to Holland America's traditional passengers. He rightly points out that whether a cruise line is considered upscale, and to what degree, depends not only on people's prior cruise experience but on their entire prior travel experience. This is an important point.

Doug Falk:

For some, a Norwegian cruise will fulfill their expectations of sex, sun, and gourmet food, and for others it won't. The expectations, developed by brand awareness, have a great deal to do with all of this. There's no doubt that Carnival's awareness as "Fun Ships" and Princess's association with "The Love Boat" give them some competitive advantage. Carnival has more of an advantage than Princess. It is important to own something, and if it's one word like "fun," that's the most powerful. The second most powerful is two words, and so forth. While Royal Caribbean's positioning may be working fine for them, in the final analysis I think it is much more difficult to remember that "You've got some Royal Caribbean coming" than it is to remember the "Fun Ship." Even if you do remember Royal Caribbean's promise. I'm not sure exactly what it means. I think the "Fun Ship" is the single best communication idea in our business, because it communicates what your experience is going to be. While "The Love Boat" is very memorable, it doesn't position Princess as clearly in terms of explaining what the Princess experience is going to consist of.

At Holland America our positioning started with a "Tradition of Excellence" that goes back more then a century. I think that says something about who we are and what kind of an experience we are trying to provide our guests. It doesn't have the memorability of the "Fun Ship" or "The Love Boat" for a number of reasons. To begin with, it hasn't been communicated nearly as strongly as the others by virtue of our smaller media budget. Our competitors outspend us—they run more television, for example. That's probably the paramount reason in my view. However, we are always and continually reviewing our strategic positioning.

In 1996 Holland America has made a significant change in its strategic positioning. They now believe that the 50+ age market represents their greatest opportunity in terms of growth rate and population increases. To capture this market effectively, the company unveiled a new multi-million dollar television advertising campaign focused on their exceptional service pampering and VIP treatment guests experience on board its ships. The theme of their new advertising campaign is "It's Time." In the commercials, viewers are asked to consider such questions as:

"When was the last time you were serenaded?"

"When was the last time someone remembered your name . . . your preference for wine . . . or that you liked your seabass blackened and your prime rib rare?"

"When was the last time you let your cares dissolve into the colors of the setting sun?"

The answers to all of these questions is that *it's time* to take a cruise vacation with Holland America. The commercials were shot using a revolutionary 85-foot Akela camera-crane which enabled the production company to produce exceptionally wide angles of the ship itself.

"This TV campaign is our largest ever," we were told by Jack Anderson, senior vice president, marketing and sales. "It is the lead component of an integrated communications program intended to claim a meaningful position: that Holland America equals Service, with a capital S. The ultimate objective is to fill ships and tours and build preference for our brand."

Carnival

Finally we come to Carnival; how does it position itself? The answer is, to compete in the broader vacation arena as a mass-market vacation product. Consumers make the Carnival purchase decision based on "value" (a lot of vacation at an affordable price), "choice" (a broad variety of amenities, activities, and popular ports of call), and "fun" (a pre-emptive claim that allows consumers to define their own vacation experience any way they choose). The acceptance of Carnival's product claims is validated not only by its own proprietary research (both qualitative and quantitative) but, more important, by the marketplace itself, whose enthusiastic response had Carnival sail more then 1,100,000 passengers in 1995, for a record 21st-year sailing in excess of 100-percent paying occupancy.

Carnival takes the view that it is competing in the *vacation market* and within that market the cruise segment competes with all alternatives that are positioned against the middle to upper end from a pricing standpoint. The company sees its broad contemporary appeal competing in the middle segments (versus a traditional "deluxe" product such as Holland America, a niche product offering such as Windstar, or a luxury or ultra-luxury entry such as Seabourn)—defined by price, product presentation, and itinerary options. It is able to keep that very sharp focus because its parent company, Carnival Corporation, owns these three cruise lines as well. Thus, Carnival Corporation provides a different product with a different market strategy and unique positioning for each of these distinct market segments.

Carnival's strategy is modeled after Proctor & Gamble. Carnival Cruise Lines sees as its "main competitors," primarily land-based resort and sightseeing destinations such as Orlando and Las Vegas. Secondary competitors include other cruise lines serving the contemporary market with similar itineraries and price points. Carnival does not believe that the market can be segmented the way Royal Caribbean does it in terms of wine and cheese and beer and pretzels. Its executives argue that champagne, wine, and beer are *all* contemporary products (they are certainly consumed in abundance on all cruise lines no matter what their cost or itinerary) and that Celebrity's approach of matching its product to the life-style of its prospects and guests is closer to the mark.

The Great Debate on Consumer Demand

Having looked at how some of the major players describe their positioning (and it is clear from the foregoing comments that some of them have not yet arrived at one), it is time to take a look at the major problem faced by all players in the arena: how to increase consumer demand. Despite disagreement on market segmentation and positioning, there is complete agreement that demand is a paramount concern—the question is what to do about it both strategically and tactically, and that is where we see a substantial difference of opinion.

With 25 new ships under construction or on order (each with building costs anywhere from $100 million to $400 million plus associated operating and marketing costs), the question on everyone's mind is how to fill them. Different lines have come up with different answers. Some feel that it is simply a question of awareness—if more people realize what a terrific value cruising offers and what a great vacation it is, then more folks will want to take one; all the industry has to do is go out and communicate that fact. Others feel that the real problem is not communicating with consumers but rather educating travel agents on the benefits that cruises offer their clients and motivating agents to do a better job of recommending and selling them. Still others argue that it is not an industry-wide problem at all and that each cruise line must choose the approach that works best for it. That may be to differentiate its products from its competitors and then, once the company has established these real differences, communicate them to consumers and travel agents. The proponents of this philosophy believe that if they build a better mousetrap the world will beat a path to their door. Others believe that all of these things need to be done. Finally, there is the school of thought that none of these expensive steps need to be taken. Everyone would like to take a cruise, any cruise, if they could afford it, and all that is needed is to make it cheap and accessible enough. We call this the "Field of Dreams—If we build it they will come" theory.

The 1995 Cruise-a-Thon

At the Omni Hotel in Miami, Florida, in July of 1995, 900 travel agents and 200 cruise industry executives and others associated with the business were gathered at a "Cruise-a-Thon" to discuss and learn how to sell more cruises and who to sell them to. The conference was co-sponsored by *Travel Trade* newspaper and the Cruise Line Industry Association (CLIA). The highlight of opening day was a panel discussion by leading executives in the business (including one of the authors) followed by a question-and-answer period.

There was an extraordinary interest this year within the travel agent community in selling cruises and there was a record crowd. The reason for the enthusiasm was an announcement earlier in the year by the major domestic airlines that they would no longer pay a blanket commission of 10 percent on the sale of domestic tickets. They would now impose a cap of $50 maximum commission, which in effect meant that an agency that used to receive a $70 commission on the sale of a $700 ticket would now only receive $50. As a result many agents were threatening to de-emphasize the sale of airline tickets and turn instead to selling more cruises and other vacation products where commissions run considerably higher.

Doug Falk of Holland America opened the panel with a few words urging agents to put together a marketing plan to secure more cruise business. What follows are the opening remarks of each of the participants in this discussion, most of whom the reader met earlier in this chapter. We have edited some of the remarks for clarity as in previous quotes, but otherwise what follows is exactly what was said after Falk's short opening remarks: Rod McLeod of Royal Caribbean opened the discussion by telling the agents that in fact there was no indication, as far as he could see, that they were selling fewer airline tickets and more cruises.

Rod McLeod, Royal Caribbean Cruises Ltd:

The distribution system itself has some problems. I would have expected that increased cruise sales would come from a distribution system that has in effect been disenfranchised by the airline industry, but we haven't seen that. We have not seen any significant change in the productivity of the agency distribution system, nor have we seen, when it comes to the airline industry, any reaction on the part of the distribution system to lessen their support of the airlines.

I think you have to not only attract more first time cruisers but attract more first-time customers. Less then 1 out of 5 leisure-travel dollars goes through travel agencies. Clearly this means that you have a problem in terms of credibility. As an industry, whether it be through an association or consortium or through your own individual efforts, you must begin to reach out and touch customers you haven't touched before.

Doug Falk of Holland America, in his opening address, referred to your sales and marketing plan. You need to have a sales and marketing plan of your own that targets new people in your area, the brand-new customers. We can't talk about holding cruise nights—and which are the best recipes to put on Ritz crackers on a cruise night—the problem goes far beyond that. Travel agencies are in danger as a distribution system. I want to see you improve your sales of first-time cruisers, your sales of repeat cruisers, and your sales of experienced cruisers. I want to see you sell more vacation travel.

Right now we're the fastest-growing segment of the travel industry, and that's over 20 years, and we offer the highest level of satisfaction. It is to be expected that as we build the cruiser pool there will be more business coming from experienced cruisers. As we expand our product and our product lines to new areas, we are bound to see people repeat more often. In our case it's 53 percent.

I grant you our industry has to adjust. But on the other side you can't ignore some of the issues in the distribution system. Among you there are people who have said there will be fewer travel agents three years from now then there are today—they're saying anywhere from 10 to 20 percent. It may even hit 50 percent according to some forecasts. Those figures are not coming from the supplier side; they are coming from your side. You've got the problem and you've got to address it. I compliment you for being here. I will compliment you even more when you take what you get from being here and put it into action when you get back home.

Bob Dickinson, Carnival Cruise Lines:

I think we're addressing the question to the wrong audience. The folks in this room include many who have been to conferences like this before, so we're preaching to the choir. All of you know that you need sales training, and you need it updated frequently. You know that 70 percent of discretionary purchases are made on evenings and weekends, and that means your offices have to open on evenings and weekends. You know, too, as Doug Falk said earlier, that psychologists say that you can't truly understand more then 10 or 12 products, so you really have to limit the number of products you sell.

I believe the agents in this audience clearly know that you don't lay brochures out in front of customers. You keep them in back where they have to ask to get them. You limit the amount of cruise lines to five or six that you hope to sell. And you have product seminars in your office—with your four, five, or six preferred suppliers. You don't try and sell everything to everybody; you specialize. A neurosurgeon makes an awful lot more money then a general practitioner. The people in this room realize that by not trying to succeed in making every sale, they will succeed in making most sales. They know that the average travel agent tries to be everything to everybody. They have every brochure, including the *Lusitania* and the *Bismarck*.

Successful travel agents, like you, know that they're not going to fulfill every request of every client. When prospects come in and ask about certain cruises, they're simply going to say, "I'm sorry—we don't handle that product." That is exactly what the Chevrolet salesperson says to someone who comes in inquiring about a Ford.

These agents also know that the way to develop productivity is to pay most of the compensation of your people not on a salary basis but on a commission or incentive basis. There are people in this room who have been in the real estate business and know that you don't stay in that business if you're not productive because you will starve to death. Their income is earned on the basis of commission. People in this room know that all their competition—other sellers of high-ticket discretionary items like real estate, automobiles, life insurance, and furniture—make their living on their commission.

Compensation is tied to productivity. So I think that rather than talk about that, I'll talk about us. I believe most of the problem really lies on the supplier side, not the distribution side. I am concerned that if the number of first-time cruisers went down to 40 percent last year, that's a failing grade for those of us in the cruise industry. It's not as much a fault of the distribution system as it is of our own industry advertising and marketing strategies.

Most cruise lines today are more interested in expanding their own market share rather than expanding the total cruise market.

The rest of the cruise industry—take Carnival out of it, carried roughly one third of their passengers last year as first timers. Carnival carried 60 percent first-timers. Most of the rest of the industry lost money, while Carnival had a record-breaking year.

Cruising enjoys the highest customer satisfaction of *any* vacation. It should be a vacation that everybody and his brother is selling and marketing successfully. When the industry is doing its job correctly, then all its ships sail full. Why? Is there a better vacation value today than cruises? I don't know of one. Is there a more satisfying vacation then cruising? All the polls say we've got the best product. So if we've got the best product, and we have the best values, and our ships aren't full, whose fault is it? How can we blame the distribution system when Carnival operates at 112 percent paying occupancy? The same distribution system that is selling our cruises is not selling the other guys. Therefore, I think we need to look at the problem from *our* side of the table.

Make no mistake about it—these are not trivial issues. Nine years ago, I remember one of us getting up at a meeting like this and saying "The distribution system doesn't sell. It doesn't know how to sell." Five, six, seven years later others started to say "You know, the distribution system doesn't sell." I got a lot of flack for saying that back then—I even found it necessary to have my secretary start my car! But the point now, today, is very simple from the distribution system's side. Enough of us in the cruise industry have finally gotten the sales message out. We knew there wasn't going to be a whole group of people running to sell cruises and vacations. Those people most affected by the commission cap were the corporate agencies that depend on business travel, and they aren't the people in this room by and large. If you repeat a message for nine years, folks are either going to get it or they're not going to get it. The ones that get it are here. They *know* what the issues are.

From the industry side of the problem, the situation has changed. There will be a 44 percent increase in passenger capacity from 1994 to the end of 1998. It's the biggest percentage growth in absolute capacity in the history of our industry. What nobody is telling you is that for the whole of last year, the cruise industry grew capacity but carried fewer passengers from North America than the year before. That's the first time in 20 or 25 years that's happened! It used to be that the whole industry rose on the tide. The biggest ships, the old ships, the new ships—all rose on the tide of balanced demand and supply. We can all remember days when the industry was operating at 90 to 95 percent of capacity. But the industry in the first quarter of this year [1995] didn't even operate at 80 percent.

To the people on this panel who say there are problems everywhere else, I say some of us should look right in the mirror and look at the messages *we're* sending out. What many of us are telling the vacation public at large is "My cruise line is better than other cruise lines." That makes no sense when most people don't understand what a cruise is all about because only 7 percent of Americans have even taken one. What good is it to tell prospects that my cruises are 50 percent off or 80 percent, or even 90 percent off when they don't understand what they're getting for their money? It seems to me that as an industry we are missing a real opportunity!

The fall of 1994 was a seminal event in our industry. Everybody misjudged the demand. If we send out messages in our ads and in our brochures that my cruise line is fancier then yours, and I need to have a $50,000 wardrobe and I need to have my breasts augmented and my teeth capped before I can step aboard, what are we talking about here? That's not what people want. We're scaring them away!

Al Wallack, Celebrity Cruises:

I think we need to focus on the fact that we're not moving forward at an evolutionary pace, we're moving forward at a *revolutionary* pace. Look at how this industry has grown. Look at what's going on in our business. We're growing from an almost infinitesimal industry to the pinnacle of the tourism business. And look at how we've grown in numbers almost geometrically over the years. There's a tremendous amount of interest out there in our ships. God knows, the media is interested.

I believe that both of us—cruise lines and travel agencies—have something to do. We have to raise the awareness of cruising, and we have to make sure that those people out there have a better understanding of what our business is all about—we're offering the most incredible vacation in sight!

We have to open the public's eyes and help them to understand contemporary cruising. We are not offering an old Fred Astaire and Ginger Rogers movie. When you do the research you find that the impediments to cruising have a lot more to do with the misconceptions about cruising than almost anything else. There are those who will argue it's price. I don't necessarily agree that that's the deepest and most important reason why people don't buy cruises because, God knows, what's advertised in the newspapers today are prices that no one ever thought of since the *Lusitania* sank! No, we have to ask ourselves how we present ourselves in the marketplace. Those of us getting new ships, of course, have to do more, and we're getting the fire power to do it.

There are several things travel agents can do. First of all, you should offer incentive programs for customers who have cruised with you before. It sounds simple, but it really works. Next, try to sell a cruise to everyone who comes into your agency—whether they ask for it or not. Just assume that when someone walks through your door they have C-R-U-I-S-E painted on their forehead. Believe me, you're going to earn a lot of money by doing that.

But that's not all. One of our problems is differentiation—if you don't know the difference between a Commodore cruise and a Royal Caribbean cruise, a Princess cruise and a Celebrity cruise, you had better learn. We are not offering a homogeneous, ubiquitous cruise product, though some agents talk about it that way. The bottom line is that we have to be more visible. We have a very competitive vacation product.

Finally, you need to understand that you are part of the world of retailing. Things are more exciting in the retail world than they are in travel stores in general. You sit behind your computers and seem very knowledgeable; retailers get out with the people. When people come in to see you, you call them shoppers; retailers call this phenomenon creating traffic. If you were selling handbags, if you were selling shoes, records, or books, you'd spend millions of dollars to create traffic. So if we all do our jobs, and goodness knows we could probably do them better, we will create this traffic. We want the browsers, but we want you to turn the browsers into grazers—get them to take a nibble. I don't think you should ever say, "They're only shoppers." If you can't shop, you can't buy.

Rick James, Princess Cruises:

I think one of the key issues we all have to deal with is the barriers to entry. That's one thing we don't talk about enough. We tend to focus on why we're not getting more cruisers from our own perspective, and in our advertising we can attempt to overcome those barriers. But quite frankly, if when you sit with those customers across the desk you can begin to get to those barriers, you can make a difference.

Now, what are some of the barriers? Price has been mentioned. That may be a factor in the 3- and 4-day market—the contemporary area. But when you talk to all the lines, it's clear that price doesn't apply equally to all of us. Be aware that there are a number of things out there like regimentation. There are still people who don't want to take a cruise because they think that they are going to be far too regimented. They also think about taking a cruise and say to themselves, "There's nothing to do. What am I going to do when I get on that ship?" or "I can't contact my friends and family when I'm gone." We—and I mean jointly—have not been doing a good job of communicating what our ships are about and what a cruise vacation is about. Another thing a lot of people believe is that cruises are not for families. I would suggest that there are products out there at all different price levels that are offering tremendous family programs.

When you go out and talk to people who say that they actually are interested in cruising but there are reasons they have not chosen to cruise, you tend to find these kinds of items. So whether it's through a CLIA-sponsored program or through the individual member lines—to the same degree that we send people into your offices, you need to understand those barriers to entry. You need to understand that we need to do a better job of training you in the kind of responses that will ensure that we take those barriers away.

Spenser Fraizer, Royal Cruise Line:

I think there's a lot of truth in what Bob Dickinson said. There's a necessity for us as an industry to question the messages we're sending into the marketplace and whether or not those messages entice consumers—baby boomers and others of all ages. I don't know that the cruise industry has really found the right message, but I do know there are actions to be taken on the distribution side as well. From where I sit there's too much focus on disasters rather than dreams. I think that while people are challenged by what's happening to Medicare, Social Security, and other bad news, it's our responsibility to make them remember what they've worked and saved for all of their lives. It's those rewards that these people have worked for. Part of their concern has got to be the quality of their life. There is something in the cruise experience that can help people find that magic they have been searching for—to find romance again. We have something that allows ordinary people to live their lives beyond the bleak prospects of what the years ahead may hold.

It's incumbent on all of us to once again become enthusiastic about selling cruises—to become focused not on computers but on our customers. We need to wake up and get excited about the great value of the cruise product today. I think it's also time for us to look at the most fundamental thing of all, and that is that there's nothing more important than getting out and working with you and your customers on a one-to-one basis. From your side the biggest single thing I can think of to suggest this morning is that you challenge your local cruise line sales representatives not to just come into your offices, drop off a brochure, and chat with you idly about what's happening in the industry today. Challenge them to work with you as full business partners. Sit down with the cruise lines you want to sell and create that sales and marketing plan with them, because until you have a marketing and sales plan you're not going to have anything to work with. Don't be satisfied when our representatives come into your office and simply deliver brochures—that doesn't reflect their best value for you, or for us. Just as television is going from broad band to narrowcast, it's time for us to get very focused on the value a cruise can deliver.

The Gospel Truth?

If the foregoing remarks sounds like an old-fashioned tent revival meeting, where the preachers urge the congregation to go out and get some of that old-time religion, it's not surprising. After all, these people on both sides of the podium were there to be saved. The agents wanted to sell cruises, and in fact there was a good deal of applause at many of the speakers' comments. And the speakers want them to sell cruises—their salaries and bonuses, to say nothing of the future of their companies, depend on it! What was said is what you might hear at any sales meeting whose purpose is to hype everyone up so they will go home and sell, sell, sell.

It's clear that with the travel agencies facing a loss of income as a result of the airline caps, and with the cruise lines facing a huge increase in capacity, everyone is virtually in the same boat. Or are they? In the next chapter we will try to sort through everything we have heard as objectively as we can, considering that one of us is looking from the inside out and the other from the outside in.

As we edit this manuscript in June 1996 a great deal has happened in terms of new initiatives to stimulate first-time cruise demand. Facing the onslaught of new capacity in the face of sluggish demand, Carnival has instituted the following programs in the first half of 1996:

Any vs. Your

Traditionally, all cruise line advertising has been tagged with the closing line "see your travel agent." Market research of non-cruise vacationers indicated that as many as 80 percent of these don't have a travel agent and are used to booking directly with the supplier. Focus groups indicated therefore, that cruise vacations were perceived as more difficult to book than their land-based competitors. As a consequence, Carnival changed its tag to "see any travel agent or call 1-800-CARNIVAL for information and a free brochure."

This created a minor flap in the trade press as some agents suggested that Carnival should at least say "see your professional travel agent." This was quickly sorted out when Carnival pointed out: (1) Why send a message to unwitting consumers that some agents are not professional? and (2) How could the consumer distinguish between the two? (We have yet to see an ad for Joe's Unprofessional Travel Agency!)

1-800-CARNIVAL

Using an 800 number in newspaper and magazine ads to accept direct business was a much thornier issue. Most cruise lines haven't been that brazen about going direct to the public. Never mind that most vacationers don't use travel agents.

- Almost every other vacation supplier except cruises widely disseminates its reservations number and encourages direct business
- Land resort and hotel vacations outsell cruising by 50 to 1
- Agents sell land vacations 10 to 1 over cruises. (The rest are booked direct.)

Carnival was facing a clear dilemma: It could no longer ignore that huge group of consumers who prefer to deal directly with suppliers yet it didn't want to, in any way, upset the travel agency distribution system that had made Carnival the "most popular cruise line in the world." "Bypass," the term agents use to describe a travel supplier's taking consumer bookings directly, is a four-letter word—as emotionally charged as the term "agent bashing." If Carnival, or any large cruise line, were seen as breaking ranks with travel agents the repercussions would be ominous. After all, travel agents selling away from a particular brand of cruise line could cause irreparable damage—a huge risk to take. Yet something had to be done if the industry was to communicate with the larger proportion of vacationers.

It should be noted, however, that virtually every cruise line does some direct business, usually under duress. The ATT 800 number information system allows anyone to access a cruise line's reservations department. In the case of Carnival, less than one half of one percent of its total business was direct.

Carnival devised a script for its reservations agents when dealing with a consumer who wanted to make a reservation. At the end of the booking, the Carnival agent would ask if they had a travel agent and if so they would automatically transfer the booking. If not, the Carnival agent would advise that should a travel agent be obtained prior to final payment, the consumer could notify us and we would happily transfer the booking. Carnival then announced this program to the industry through the trade press, while sharing the consumer research on the prevalence of vacationers' making their own plans. As one might expect, travel agents began calling the 800 number to test the program by pretending to be consumers. Once the fictitious booking was made, however, the travel agents would frequently hang up before the Carnival reservations agent went through the protocols described above. Carnival was thus accused of bypassing travel agents. The solution was simple: The order of the protocols was changed so that the reservations agent queried the consumer *before* the booking was made. Agents still test Carnival, but complaints are rare.

As of June 1996, we have about 6 weeks of data on this new program. The results are startling. For every consumer who had an agent at the time of booking, 18 consumers went out and found agents after the bookings were made. Hence, Carnival dubbed this program "thru-pass" (in stark contrast to *bypass*). Consumers were literally being passed through to travel agencies with pre-made cruise bookings. By annualizing these results, it's clear that thousands of travel agents will happily receive commissions from Carnival for pre-sold business. This is good karma!

The Carnival Challenge

Carnival has 41,566 agency locations in its data base for the United States and Canada. In 1995, 29 percent gave them *no* business at all! At the other end of the spectrum, 7.5 percent are what we call vacation retailers who sell, on average, two Carnival bookings (2.2 guests each) per week. The remainder, 63.5 percent are what we describe as random agent vacation bookers who give Carnival, on average, only 8 bookings a year (certainly a random occurrence)! Half of this group gives Carnival just one to four bookings a year while the top 15 percent of this group gives them two bookings a month . . . a sign of hope! But 60 percent of their sales come from only 7.5 percent of the agencies.

As Carnival represented 25 percent of the industry's cruise passengers last year, we believe these data realistically describe the dramatically varying cruise and overall vacation sales pattern within the travel agency distribution system. Discussions with other vacation suppliers (tour operators, hoteliers, and cruise lines) confirm this analysis and show similarly and frequently even more, skewed results.

It's not surprising then that virtually every vacation supplier—but Carnival—has for many years not even attempted to call on most or all of the random agent bookers or zero producers, focusing their field sales efforts instead on those agencies that are, or are trying diligently to become, vacation retailers. In their words, these suppliers are "fishing where the fish are."

Carnival, on the other hand, has always directed its sales force to call on all agencies to generate cruise sales—especially by training and motivating agents to become vacation retailers or sellers, not just order-takers. However, because Carnival's strategy is unique, even though they have the largest vacation sales force in the travel industry, their competitors' (land and sea) concentration on the top agency accounts occasionally causes Carnival to lose market share in a high producing agency, as Carnival's sales resources are spread more broadly throughout the agency community.

Bob Dickinson notes: "How long can we afford to call on everyone? It's challenging to be the Lone Ranger! We'd like to continue indefinitely. After all, this strategy has made us the most popular (and profitable) cruise line in the world! We won't *ever* change the strategy *if* we can find a sufficient number of agencies (out of over 34,000) who are willing to change and become vacation retailers."

Hence, the Carnival Challenge. This program is designed to identify random bookers and zero producers who are willing to change, adopt proven sales concepts, and meaningfully grow their Carnival business. As a result, they will earn an extra $15,000 a year or more in commission income—far more than the average agency lost as a result of the airline commission caps. Carnival's commitment, in return, is to pledge to work closely with these agencies, not just at the field sales level but at the highest levels of their management to ensure these agencies achieve their goals. Producing 100 seven-day equivalent guests (a three- or four-day guest counts as half) will place the agency's production well within the ranks of Carnival's successful vacation retailers. Moreover, adoption of their proven sales techniques will invariably result in more overall vacation sales with greater earned commissions from tour operator, hotel, and other cruise line sales as well. The whole vacation industry will be the beneficiary of these efforts!

Predictably, many agencies won't respond to the challenge. That's their choice . . . they don't have to sell vacations. Ironically, however, it's a few of those very agents who tend to be the most upset when its pointed out that most agents don't know how to sell and as a result are, at best, haphazard order takers of vacation travel. Carnival forecasted that 500 agencies would take up the challenge. In the first month, over 1,000 agencies responded! The response, as well as the early results of building and executing individual agency business plans, is very encouraging.

The Carnival Vacation Guarantee

In May 1996 Carnival introduced another cruise industry first—a vacation guarantee. Its purpose is to encourage a portion of the huge group of potential cruisers who are sitting on the fence by providing an option to leave if they don't like the experience, just as they usually have with a land vacation. The perception that they can bail out is important, but the reality is that Carnival expects the vast majority will enjoy their vacations. Carnival made the guarantee valid for a limited time period (August 8–November 22, 1996) so that there would be an opportunity to measure the rise in demand brought about by the guarantee. Guests must notify the reception desk on board prior to the first port of call if they are dissatisfied and desire a refund. Carnival will reimburse the cost of coach air transportation from the first non-U.S. port of call back to the port of embarkation. The refund would be pro-rated according to how many days of the voyage were left at the point the guest disembarked and would be mailed within 30 days of completion of the cruise. "The financial risk to Carnival in offering such a guarantee is minimal given the extremely high satisfaction rate among our guests," said Dickinson.

7

Now Hear This

*Marketing communications—
a view from the bridge*

Imagine that we have just started a new cruise line, which we'll call Hospitality Cruises. It will have a fleet of five large ships in the 70,000-ton class and thus compete for passengers with the major cruise lines for business. As Vice President of Sales and Marketing for Hospitality Cruises our job is to formulate a marketing communications strategy . In this chapter we will take a closer look at some of the elements that go into such a plan—the situation we are facing as we enter this new business, our communications channels, our target market, our positioning, and our competition and their creative strategy and advertising messages. With this exercise we can focus on what the major players are (or should be) doing now and why they are doing it, and assessing as best we can their effectiveness. In this way we will gain an understanding of promotional strategy in the cruise-line industry.

The Present Situation

The place to begin, as with many such plans, is the situation as it exists in the marketplace today. Even though we have not yet designed our own product we do know quite a bit about the cruise market from data obtained from the Cruise Line Industry Association (CLIA) and other sources. We also have published speeches as well as off-the-record comments made by the CEOs and marketing and sales officials of the major lines and their advertising agencies, in which they assess the situation they face in their positioning, if they have one, and in their advertising strategy.

Market Size/Potential

Since 1970, the industry has had a compound annual growth rate of 10 percent per annum. The prospect for continued market expansion is favorable, although, as we learned earlier, the forecasts provided by CLIA may be overly optimistic within any given time frame.

In the past 20 years an estimated 40 million passengers took a deep-water cruise (two days plus), and nearly 40 percent of total passengers were generated in the last five years alone. Of those who cruised in the past five years, the average number of cruises per person was 2.4 in the same time frame—or one every two years.

Over 71 million Americans have an interest in taking a cruise, and 44 million say they'll take one in the next five years. We believe that the year 2000, as many as 8 million passengers per year will cruise.

Primary growth opportunity at the moment is among younger prospects 25 to 39 years old, families with children, and singles. However with the "graying of America," the size of the market for older cruises should increase rapidly. In 1990, only 17 percent of Americans were over 60 years of age. By 2025, that figure will stand at 27 percent. Older individuals typically have more disposable income and those who are retired have more time for travel. In short, cruise appeal versus that of other vacation categories will continue to be broad-based.

The Target Market

The demographics of the cruise passenger are fairly broad, with potential cruisers coming from all ages and walks of life, with the economic wherewithal and inclination to spend at least $100 per day per person. The longer and more expensive the cruise, the older and wealthier the passenger.

On the whole, however, there is not as great a difference in age, sex, or income as one might suspect among those who have an expressed an interest in cruising. For example, 57 percent of men are interested in cruising, while the figure for women is 63 percent. When viewed by household income, cruise prospects comprise 56 percent of households which earn between $20,000 and $39,000 and 62 percent of those between $40,000 and $59,000 and 66 percent of those who earn more than $60,000. Sixty percent are singles and 59 percent are married folks.

First-Time Cruisers

Various sources indicate that at most only 7 percent of the population has taken a cruise. Therefore, most of the growth in passengers will have to come from first-time cruisers. According to a 1994 CLIA study, 40 percent of cruisers are first-timers and 60 percent are repeaters. As a new entrant into the market place we will have decide whether to depend heavily on first-time cruisers or, if we do a good job of positioning ourselves, go after repeat cruisers from other lines.

Competing with Land-Based Vacations

Given the rapidly expanding capacity in the business (32.3 percent more berths between 1995 and 1999), all of our competitors must also attract a significant number of first-timers to their brand to survive. However, we can expect them to continue to try to hold on to their current customer base through relationship marketing efforts. It should be noted that these hot prospects are regular vacationers—that is, they are not stay-at-homes but like to travel and have taken trips by airline. They are for the most part adventurous people who like to see new sights, have new experiences, and meet new people. Travel researchers characterize them as more willing to take risks than those who prefer to stay home.

We know that among those who have expressed an interest in cruising, significant numbers take at least one vacation per year, travel internationally periodically, prefer to travel with friends, and have typically stayed at resorts. Bill McFarland, President of HMS McFarland & Drier in Miami (Carnival's advertising agency) believes that ultimately "the land-based resorts are the enemy." That is to say, he believes that's where we need to look for our customer base, not among existing cruise lines. Apparently the resort business sees it the same way. In a story in the *Miami Herald* about a $12-million renovation of the pool area at the Bal Harbor Sheraton on Miami Beach, David Fine, Director of Sales and Marketing is quoted as saying, "The Sheraton improvements are aimed at pulling leisure travelers away from cruise lines and other major resorts." The story goes on to say that the hotel plans to hire a cruise director "to orchestrate outdoor entertainment, including games, jugglers, food, and music."

Now there's a new concept for you. A hotel with a cruise director! But then why not? They tried to turn the great *Queen Mary* into a land-based resort, but unfortunately, even Disney couldn't pull that one off!

Gilbert Trigano, who founded Club Med, told us that his original concept was based on the idea of providing guests with "a land-based cruise." The Club's GOs (*Gentil Organisateur* in French or "congenial hosts" in English) handle all of the tasks at a typical Club Med except housekeeping and maintenance, mingle freely with the guests (GMs or *Gentil Membres*), and in fact perform many of the same duties that the cruise staff on a modern ship handles.

All Noncruisers Are Not Alike
We note that not all noncruisers represent an equal potential given the economic and leisure time requirements. Even within the appropriate profile, noncruisers represent a spectrum of the likelihood of taking a cruise. At one end is the noncruiser who will never cruise. That they say they would like to take a cruise doesn't mean they ever will. (Both of us would like to climb Mount Everest. We'd also like to own a vineyard in France and a chateau to go with it, but we probably won't.) At the other end of the spectrum

is the noncruiser poring over brochures and deciding which cruise to take next month. That's the one you can count on to be a "float" on someone's line somewhere in the very near future.

Barriers to Entry

In between is that large group who would enjoy a cruise and can afford one but who have one or more of those "barriers to entry" discussed by industry executives. The four barriers most often cited are price, boredom, confinement, and seasickness, and there is some degree of all of these among our best prospects.

Price? Maybe they can afford a cruise now, but if their employer is in the midst of downsizing or re-engineering, their vacation dollars might be better off in the bank until the storm blows over—if it does!

Confinement? We don't feel confined in a ship that's 12 stories high and the length of 3 football fields, but some people might.

Boredom? If you're a couch potato and your idea of fun is watching every live football, baseball, and basketball broadcast, you're going to be bored on just about any cruise ship sailing the seas right now. The beer and pretzels you can get, but many of the games you can't.

Finally there are a few who really do get seasick even when the ship is docked at the pier, and we won't be able to change their minds no matter what we tell them!

So, as we contemplate a marketing and communications program for our new cruise line in the current increasingly competitive environment, we see it is toward the latter end of the spectrum that the near-term battle must be waged—for the potential passenger who already has a high propensity to cruise, not for the one who needs to be convinced on the merits of a cruise vacation. The others will come along in the future as their friends come back and tell them what a great vacation they had.

The Appeal of Cruising to First-Timers and Experienced Cruisers

Studies have consistently shown that a cruise is very appealing to most people. Indeed, among those who have taken both, a cruise is considered superior to a land-based resort. In a CLIA study among persons who had taken both a cruise and a resort vacation in the last five years, for example, 32 percent reported that they were more pampered by the staff and the same number said that their cruise vacation was better organized. Twenty-nine percent said that they were more satisfied with the dining experience on the cruise; 13 percent found their cruise vacation more hassle-free, and 11 percent reported that it was more relaxing. Fifteen percent said it was a better value for the money. About the only negative was accommodations. A cruise cabin is by necessity and design smaller than an average resort room, and 15 percent of those who had taken both found the resort accommodations superior. However, it is not really fair to compare a ship at sea with a building on land and if customers understand that their cabin will not look like the ones on television and movie sets, which are in fact Hollywood sound stages, there is ample evidence that they will not be disappointed.

Aside from studies by CLIA, we'd be leaving out a good story if we didn't report on a 1996 survey conducted by *Cosmopolitan* Magazine and Royal Caribbean Cruise Line on "Sex At Sea." Ninety-five percent of vacationers polled rated cruises as "extremely or very romantic" compared to land-based vacations. Among the top 10 romantic activities of passengers, having sex on board topped the list with almost half the cruisers—48 percent—saying they had sex up to six times on vacation as compared to their usual once or twice a week at home. According to the *Cosmopolitan* press release "a full 80 percent said they felt more amorous at sea, with most passengers—58 percent—unable to wait more than 10 hours after embarkation before dropping anchor in the sea of love."

After vacationers take their first cruise, there is a very high level of satisfaction. As we pointed out the figure industry-wide is 80 percent. In truth, virtually all vacation types create a high level of satisfaction. In other words, most people report being satisfied with their vacation whether they take a cruise, stay in a resort, rent a condo for skiing or a cottage by the sea, take a package tour, or simply visit friends and relatives. That's one reason why vacations are so appealing. However, when CLIA asked these same vacationers to state which kind of vacation they were "extremely satisfied" with, 41 percent said a cruise, which was the highest score received by any of the vacations mentioned. Package tours and visiting friends and relatives both received 29 percent "extremely satisfied" ratings, while resorts received 24 percent. Eighty-five percent of those who had taken a cruise in the last three years expressed an interest in taking another one, and the mean time-frame was within one to three years! Note that since first-time cruisers have only been on one ship, they define the experience as highly satisfactory irrespective of whether they are sailing on the *Fascination* or the *Crystal Harmony*. Price, amenities, and even ports have little to do with satisfaction levels—an important point to consider when we think about positioning our new company.

Among those who have never taken a cruise but would like to, expectations are high, often because of what prospects have heard from experienced cruisers and travel agents and what they have seen and read in editorial material and advertising messages. Focus groups of prospective cruise passengers indicate that people who are interested in a cruise like the idea of abundant food, visiting exotic locations, nightly entertainment, getting closer to nature while at sea, and having the time and space to enjoy themselves.

Why People Don't Cruise

Now, when we look at people who have never taken a cruise and ask their reasons for not cruising we see an entirely different picture.

A study by CLIA in 1994 showed that price and a concern about the economy are major barriers to trial. Among those with some interest, the disinclination to mix cruises, children, and seasickness were secondary reasons. Other concerns were "I won't be able to change plans once on ship." "If I'm ill or injured I might not get the best medical attention," "If I took my children, there would be no chance to do anything on my own" "There's little or no sightseeing on a cruise," and "I couldn't be by myself because there are too many people."

In fact, we have seen that many of these are pure misconceptions, and we debunk them one by one.

Seasickness. Passengers seldom get seasick on cruises—not only do modern ships have elaborate stabilizing systems, but they tend to cruise in protected waters. Moreover, cruise ships have access to elaborate satellite weather forecasting systems and can easily outrun any storm system. Even in the hurricane season, cruise ships continue to sail on schedule for the most part, simply diverting to other ports when necessary and thus avoiding most if not all of the bad weather.

Change of Plans. When you board a plane going from New York to Los Angeles, or the Orient Express from London to Venice, or a Cosmos Grand Tour of Europe you can't change your destination plans, either.

Illness and Injury. Good medical attention is available *within minutes* on a cruise ship 24 hours a day—try that in hotels, resorts, or any other form of vacation we know of. A few years ago, on a PBS documentary on a round-the-world trip aboard the *QE2*, the ship's doctor said that many of the people aboard were either in very fragile health or sick and were on the ship to recover. They knew that if they needed help the vessel had, among other things, a completely equipped operating room.

Things to Do. Take a look at the daily calendar of any cruise ship on a day at sea. On one from a Holland America Caribbean cruise aboard the *Westerdam* there were 49 different activities. In addition, there were two religious services on board that day, a meeting of Alcoholics Anonymous, shopping in the ships' boutiques, eight movies shown on closed-circuit TV in the cabins, and two movies shown in the ship's movie theater.

Value

Nevertheless, we have to recognize that not everyone sees things the way we do. Take economy and price. If people are nervous about keeping their jobs or having enough to pay the rent, they postpone vacations and delay big-ticket items. That's the way it is and that's the way it has always been during times of economic uncertainty. Moreover, a cruise is paid for up front, typically 60 days up front. People are not used to writing several-thousand-dollar checks for their vacation in advance—even when it's a terrific value. Besides, the concept of value is subjective, there is no universal standard as to what constitutes it. Harold Kassarkian and Thomas Robertson, in their book on consumer behavior, point to one study in which consumers defined value in one of four ways:

1. Low price
2. Whatever I want in a product

3. The quality I get for the price I pay
4. What I get for what I give

They conclude:

> These four consumer expressions of value can be captured in one overall definition: perceived value is the consumers' overall assessment of the utility of a product based on perceptions of what is received and what is given. Though what is received varies across consumers (i.e., some may want quantity, others high quality, still others convenience) and what is given varies (some are concerned only with money expended, others with time and effort), value represents a tradeoff of the salient give and get components.

Whether a cruise is a "good value" depends not on what *we* believe that is but on what *customers* believe that is (always keep your eyes focused on the customer), and that depends on what their idea of value is. So we need to make certain that we explain why a cruise is a good value using the customers' frame of reference. We think, and we believe that people who have taken cruises also think, that you get a lot of high-quality service for a low price, compared with what you would pay if you bought those same services (transportation, lodging, dining, sightseeing, and entertainment) á la carte instead of packaged on a cruise vacation. That's what makes it a good value.

Segmenting the Market

In 1995, CLIA released the results of its Cruiser Segmentation Study, the purpose of which was to identify and profile distinct consumer segments within the cruise market. Segmentation studies are very useful because if you can get a better fix on the kind of people who already enjoy any product or service and what percent of the market they represent, it becomes easier to decide which segments you should target for future marketing efforts. You can also create different marketing messages for each segment, stressing the appeals and benefits that are most important to them. If, as this study did, you also learn something about customers' media habits, you know not only what to say but where to place your message so that they are most likely to see it. The

16-page study, which was mailed to 2,800 recent cruisers and returned by 86 percent, sought to answer these questions:

- What are these segments like in terms of demography, lifestyle, and general attitudes?
- What is their cruise behavior?
- What are their perceptions and needs with respect to cruising?

Cruising's Segments

The study identified six distinct segments of past cruisers. Members of each resemble each other (and are different from members of other segments) in many respects that have to do with how they approach cruising.

The two largest segments comprised Restless Boomers (33%) and Enthusiastic Baby Boomers (20%). Both include those roughly between the ages of 30 and 55, a group of forty million households that by the year 2000 will make up 30 percent of the population. Other segments are Consummate Shoppers (16%), Luxury Seekers (14%), Explorers (11%) , and Ship Buffs (6%). Let's take a close look at each of these segments and see what we know about them.

Restless Baby Boomers

These are the newest to cruising. They enjoyed their cruise experience and would like to do it again, but cost may be an impediment because they are price conscious, at least for now. The average age of this group is 44, more than half are college graduates, three-quarters are married, and their median household income is $58,000. They are also at this point still inexperienced as travelers and are trying different vacation experiences. They vacation as a family and see themselves as average Americans: thrifty, family-oriented, and not particularly fashionable or cultured in their own opinion. They also like outdoor camping and attend pop/rock concerts. They do not read newspapers or magazines as much as other groups do.

Enthusiastic Baby Boomers

These are somewhat older than their cousins (the average age is 49), not as well educated (only 38 percent are college graduates), and not quite as affluent (median household income is $55,000). They live intense, stressful lives and generally look to vacations for the escape and relaxation they offer. While folks in this group shop for value, they are willing to spend what they have to get what they want. They see themselves as fun-loving, willing to try new things, physically active, and fashionable. Other leisure activities they enjoy are sporting events, video games, and clubs and discos. Like the restless segment, they read newspapers and magazines less than other groups do.

Consummate Shoppers
This group is constantly looking for the best value (not necessarily the cheapest) in a vacation and in a cruise. They definitely enjoy cruising as long as they can get a good deal. As you might expect, they are somewhat older (55 on average). Almost half are college graduates, 71 percent are married, and their average household income is $60,000. They see themselves as well traveled, average on most characteristics, and, of course, thrifty. They spend their leisure time reading for pleasure and attending the theater. They are heavy television viewers as well.

Luxury Seekers
These cruisers can afford, and are willing to spend money for, deluxe accommodations and pampering. They are somewhat younger than consummate shoppers (averaging 52 years old), 61 percent are college graduates, 73 percent are married, and their average household income of $95,000 reflects their ability to pay for what they want. They are often last-minute planners, extravagant, and willing to pay for quality. They view themselves as very well traveled, ready to try new things, successful, physically active, and cultured. Their leisure-time activities include concerts, boating, sailing, skiing, and golf, as well as museums, classical concerts, and sporting events. They watch television and listen to the radio less than other groups do.

Explorers
These are well-educated, well-traveled individuals with an intellectual interest and curiosity about different destinations. They are an older group (average age 64), educated (69 percent graduated from college), and fairly well off, with an average household

income of $81,000. They like to visit different vacation places, they are not looking for a rest, nor do they want pampering. Their leisure hours are spent somewhat in the same manner as the Luxury Seekers, except that they are not into physical activities to the same extent. They watch TV and read books and newspapers.

Ship Buffs

This last group are the most senior segment (68 on average). They are educated (60 percent college graduates) and able to afford to travel ($78,000 household income), and 67 percent are married. They have cruised extensively, like it, and intend to continue. They are not particularly physically active, family oriented, or fun loving, and they are reluctant to try new things. They spend their leisure time reading and attending the theater, watching TV, and reading both magazines and newspapers.

With this information we can formulate some reasonable ideas about the marketing messages that would appeal to the various segments. For example, we would want our message to Ship Buffs to remind them of the on-board experiences they enjoyed in the past, and reinforce them, and we would be wise to tell Explorers about new destinations. Consummate Shoppers will pay attention to special rates and promotions, whereas luxury seekers need to be reassured that their expectations of a "pampered " experience will be met. Baby Boomers need to be told about the fun and excitement of cruising, as well as its affordability.

The Competition

When planning a marketing communications program, it is fatal to assume that you are advertising in a vacuum. Others are out there as well, and whether or not their messages are in the best interests of the cruise industry, they do appear in newspapers, in magazines and Sunday supplements, on television, and in other media. Consumers may see those messages and form judgments from them about a cruise versus a land vacation or which cruise they prefer.

Note that we used the word *may*: If the advertising is not effective there is ample evidence that no one will see it and no one will be influenced by it. According to published figures, five cruise lines spend in excess of $10 million annually on measured advertising media. Given that kind of money, it is a safe bet that to a varying degree those campaigns have been noticed. The five big spenders are Carnival, Celebrity, Norwegian, Princess, and Royal Caribbean. Since we know roughly what these companies spend and something about where they spend it, we can compare their communication strategies.

Their Positioning

The logical place to start is with the comments we heard in Chapter 6 on how these marketing officials positioned their companies. In any communications program the messages flow from the positioning. In other words, the advertiser should be communicating his positioning: This is who we are, this is what we are, this is how we are positioned in the spectrum of products out there.

Remember, real positioning focuses on customers' needs and wants, not on the product. It has nothing to do with the product itself but everything to do with what people think of it. As Adam Aron suggested in Chapter 6, look at package goods like laundry detergents, which spend many more millions of dollars than any cruise line jockeying for position. As many as 40 different detergents are on supermarket shelves today. Some are positioned to get rid of grease; others kill germs; some work better in cold water; and others make your clothes come out whiter than white or smelling fresh. Are these detergents really that different? Do consumers really care? The answers are no on both counts. Most shoppers recognize that soap is soap. They also know that just about all of the detergents make their clothes smell fresh, get rid of grease, and work in cold water, but it doesn't matter.

The positions and brand names are useful tools of marketing and advertising, but the differences are seldom crucial to making the sale *except when everything else is equal*, and *everything else is seldom equal.*

Some brands have superior advertising. In the history of laundry detergent marketing campaigns like "Stronger than dirt" and "Ring around the collar" catapulted their brands into first place overnight. Whether or not you're a smoker, consider the Marlboro Man, who positioned Marlboros as a brand for real

men. Was this achieved by injecting male hormones in the to-
bacco or shaping the cigarettes to look like cowboy boots? Don't
kid yourself, Marlboro cigarettes are just like everyone else's.
The positioning is something that happens in people's minds,
not in the product.

Going Straight to the Source

When you get right down to it, a ship is a ship. You can have a
different menu, and a different decor, but that isn't enough for
people to choose one cruise over another. How do we know this?
By taking a ride on the Information Superhighway!

Several million Americans belong to an online service connected to their personal computer. America Online, Compuserve,
and Prodigy are the largest and all of them have travel bulletin
boards on which members exchange opinions and give advice.

We monitored the cruise bulletin board on both Compuserve
and America Online as we wrote this book, and it became clear
to us that while most past cruisers do have a favorite ship or
even a favorite line, their choices have nothing to do with the
product attributes the lines themselves say are their differentiating features. People who like Carnival may say they enjoyed the
food or the ports or the shows, or some combination of the
three. Those who like Royal Caribbean say the same, as do the
ones who prefer Princess or Celebrity. Take a look at the following representative messages from America Online's cruise bulletin board. What is important is not whose cruise they liked but
the *reasons* for enjoying the cruise:

> My husband and I have taken both a Carnival Cruise and a Big
> Red Boat cruise to the Bahamas, and by far the better cruise is
> Carnival. We took our three children with us and they had the
> time of their lives!
>
> We booked a New Year's cruise on the *Sun Princess*. The
> price is good. We've been on several Princess cruises and have
> had excellent service, entertainment, ports of call, and of course
> food.
>
> I sailed the *Horizon* to Bermuda and loved it. My parents
> cruised RCCL and Celebrity and found them comparable.
> Celebrity had bigger cabins and RCCL, better service.

My wife and I just returned from our first cruise ever. This was aboard the *Fascination* and we just loved it. All of our needs were well cared for and there was nonstop entertainment. Dinner each night was a different theme. Our waiter and busboy were the best.

We sailed on the *Meridian* last fall and just returned from a 3-day RCCL cruise on the *Nordic Empress*. We much prefer RCCL. Ship maintenance was much better, and there were better activities much better done (the snorkeling program was excellent). The ship was extremely stable (no seasick problems). The *Meridian* was a confusing, gerrymandered ship that we never really got oriented to. Of course, our favorite line is Holland America, but RCCL runs a close second.

We got even better insight when we asked experienced cruisers whom we anonymously interviewed on cruises they took during the past year to give us their opinions:

We went on Norwegian Cruise Lines *Dreamward*. It was very nice, but we didn't like the Western Caribbean. There was nothing there to buy. This time we decided to go through a travel agent. We wanted to try the Eastern Caribbean, and she had heard good reports about Holland America. She got us a better deal too—last time I bought from the cruise line directly. We're going on Celebrity's *Zenith* in a couple of months. We used to go to Las Vegas three times a year, but now we like to cruise.

We were on the *Princess* last month. It's the same as Holland America. We've taken our kids on Royal Caribbean and Carnival. The cabins are too small on RCCL, and the service was friendlier on Carnival. We decided to take this cruise because of the price. It's cheaper then Royal Caribbean.

We've been on forty cruises, one every two months. We're addicted. We have 40,000 miles on Holland America—they gave us a special emblem. We like other ships, too. The *Costa Riviera* was fun. They had a man with a monkey going around the ship and served pizza all day long. We also love Carnival's *Jubilee*. It's a beautiful ship.

You can see that while people noticed the hardware, the activities and service were equally or more important in the few opinions we quote here. For the most part, none of these comments played back the executive positioning lines we heard earlier. True, one couple who sailed Carnival said they had the time of their lives, which is very close to Carnival's "fun" positioning. But the people who liked Princess didn't say it was a "Love Boat", and one couple who cruised Celebrity and Royal Caribbean found them comparable. Another enjoyed Holland America, Costa, and Carnival—three very different products with very different positioning.

What happened to the "icons of quality" that Celebrity has tried to incorporate in its positioning? The fans of RCCL did not talk about receiving what they felt they were entitled to, although RCCL has spent bundles promising it to them. Holland America has positioned itself as the only line with an Indonesian and Philippine crew and no tipping, and while one respondent said it was her all-time favorite line, she didn't mention specific reasons. Some mentioned Holland America's service, but just about everyone was equally captivated by the service aboard their favorite cruise.

True, we have only noted a few comments here, but during research for the book we interviewed 150 passengers at random aboard five cruise ships, asking why they had picked that specific cruise. Almost never did people play back the positioning that had been described to us. On Holland America, for instance, many commented about the fine food and entertainment, but so did the guests on Royal Caribbean, Carnival, and Norwegian.

The implications of this are quite clear and support our hypothesis that the differences among the major lines lie not in the way they build their ships or in the food they serve: They exist in the hearts and minds of their guests. They are to a large extent shaped not only by the guests' cruise experience but by the advertising and other marketing communications, that have created a personality for the brand.

Advertising Messages—a Reality Check

Carnival

Carnival's positioning and advertising message has been consistent for the past 22 years. For all of that time their ships have been the fun ships. In a typical Carnival TV commercial, spokesperson

Kathie Lee Gifford gives us a tour showing us the disco, the dining room, other public rooms, and the featured show, stopping to say hello to other celebrities on board such as George Foreman, Richard Simmons, and Robert Wagner. All this time she may be singing a Carnival jingle.

> "In the morning, in the evening
> Carnival's got the fun
> Sunny weather, all together
> Carnival's got the fun"

or

> "If they could see you now
> Out on a fun ship cruise
> They'd never believe it
> If your friends could see you now"

The commercial ends by asking for the order: "Take a three, four-, or seven-day vacation on Carnival—the most popular cruise line in the world."

Kathie Lee Goes Down to the Sea in Ships

In terms of recall and recognition, Carnival's television ads, created by HMS McFarland and Drier Advertising, dominate all others. Research shows that Carnival is clearly perceived as fun-filled with lots of things to do day and night, high energy, moderately priced, and for young and old everyday people. An important part of this, of course, is Kathie Lee Gifford. A spokesperson in advertising whom people trust, admire, and can identify with works, and, like Carnival's advertising message, Kathie Lee has been around a long time. Her role has evolved from simply showcasing the product to acting as an endorser and a solicitor of testimonials from other celebrities, but she always remains the official spokesperson. Certainly not everyone likes her, but regardless of what consumers may think of her personally they believe what she tells them, and what she tells them is that no matter who they are, they'll have fun on a Carnival cruise. Carnival's commercials also make the product itself the star of the commercial. Because of the distinctive and innovative decor of their ships, all of which have been designed from top to bottom by Miami architect Joe Farcus, there is a real advantage to showing as much of them as possible, and the company does. As well as interiors, Carnival commercials show scenes from their shows, close-ups of dinner menu items, and exotic drinks.

These two classic advertising formats, spokesperson-testimonial and product demonstration and presentation, combined and used consistently over a long period, have produced the most memorable brand image of any cruise line on television today.

Carnival's print advertising is consistent with its television sports. One magazine ad depicts dining, disco, the casino, a show, Camp Carnival, the Nautica spa, shopping, a couple strolling on the beach, the ever-present Kathie Lee Gifford, and a romantic interlude on deck. The headline reads, "If You've Never Taken A 'Fun Ship' Cruise . . . It's Time To Test The Waters." The copy is unpretentious and explains how what Carnival offers is different from other resorts' offerings (both on land and at sea). It is a classic example of persuasive advertising designed to do exactly what the television ads do—explain the product:

> For the ultimate vacation, sail aboard one of Carnival's magnificent floating resorts. No other resort vacation can compare, because a 'Fun Ship' cruise is the vacation of your life at an affordable price. You'll find playful days on deck and sparkling nights filled with lavish entertainment. The 'Fun Ships' offer you spacious staterooms, outstanding service, Las Vegas style revues, dazzling lounges, the largest casinos afloat, exquisite food, and our extensive Nautica Spa fitness program . . . plus many more Fun choices. Best of all, you get your air fare, accommodations, meals and entertainment all for one low price. It's your best vacation value . . . "

Clearly the ad stresses price and value, which ample evidence from advertising research shows is one of the most effective appeals you can use, particularly in terms of audience recall.

The Strategy
Carnival's former Vice President of Marketing, Karine Armstrong, who subsequently served in the same position at Royal

Caribbean and is now Vice President of Advertising at Princess, is in a unique position to comment on all of the campaigns used by the major lines, since she has played a role in all three. She says, "What Carnival has done, and it's been such a boon to the industry, is taken a lot of the mystery out of who should go on a cruise. That was the objective. People want to have fun, but everyone has their own interpretation of what fun is. To some people that means from the minute they get on till the minute they get off, they do everything. They eat everything, they participate in everything, and they just have the time of their lives. They have to be taken off on a stretcher! To others, fun means going on board and dropping out. Their idea of fun is lying on the deck, reading a book, not participating in anything, and having a very leisurely vacation experience. To them, this is fun. Carnival demonstrates in its advertising that people have many options. They let them know that all of that stuff is there, but they can do it all or nothing at all, as we used to say when I was there."

Armstrong's evaluation of Carnival's advertising and Kathie Lee is this: "they make the point brilliantly, quite frankly. Television viewers recognize their advertising. They may love Kathie or hate her, but she shows them beautifully what there is to do, as well as the relaxing side."

Princess

One of the most recognized advertising and public relations campaigns for a cruise line (according to some research we have seen) also uses a spokesperson whom people trust and like. Princess's campaign built around Gavin MacLeod, Captain Stubing of "The Love Boat". Curiously though, while MacLeod is a logical spokesperson for Princess, in the series he was surrounded with movie stars and older couples in tuxedos, in a somewhat heavy-handed presentation of Hollywood-style romance.

MacLeod told us that many people believed he was the real captain of the ship. His dry cleaner in New York one day asked quite seriously "Hey Captain, who's driving the boat?" and he heard the same question hundreds of times while the show was in production. One lady who presented herself at the Purser's office shortly after a Princess cruise left port and asked to see "Captain Stubing." When the Purser explained that there was no real Captain Stubing, he was a fictional character created for the TV series, the lady was incensed. "I bought a ticket on this boat just because I wanted to meet Captain Stubing." She was not interested in meeting the real captain and demanded that she be let off at the next port and her money refunded!

"The Love Boat"—the Boat You'll Love

One of Karine Armstrong's jobs at Princess is "to turn that perception around from being a boat where you'll find love to a boat that you'll love being on. We want people to perceive our Love Boats as ships where they'll love the food, the entertainment, and their cabin, as well as their cabin stewards and waiters. We want them to say 'I love the whole experience.' " Armstrong admits she has a way to go to accomplish this, but expects Princess' new advertising campaign, developed by J. Walter Thompson, to produce results. "We want to tell people that you will love the experiences that the boat will bring you," she says. "I firmly believe that this is an esoteric product. We're appealing to people's emotions. People put a lot of effort into planning their vacations, and so they want them to be as rewarding as they dreamed they would be. We want them to love the boat. We want them to know that we will love them. That is reality, and that's what we're doing."

In fact, the first-time Princess passengers whom we talked with, who are of all ages and from all income groups, didn't pick their cruise because it was a "Love Boat" but because it went to the right place for the right price, and their travel agent or friends told them they would enjoy it. Even so, there is no doubt that it helps to have a name and a face that people remember, and Princess achieved that objective years ago. In the past, Princess's advertising was destination oriented. In a typical spot Gavin MacLeod might be standing on a Princess ship as she sets sail. He says, "In Alaska no one else can quite do what Princess can. You see, no one else has more ways to Alaska by land and sea than Princess. You'll see it in a way you never thought possible. Princess, it's more than a cruise, it's the Love Boat."

While he talks we see scenes of Alaska. The visuals are a combination of photography and art that gives the whole place an appearance of a storybook land.

Print ads similarly showed a Princess ship passing glaciers and mountains, with a headline that read, "Let Us Make The Journey Worthy of the Destination," and destination-focused copy: "Alaska. Mt. McKinley against a cobalt sky. A towering wall of ice crashing into the sea. An eagle soaring overhead. Let Princess take you on a journey that no one else can. On the Love Boat . . . "

Unfortunately, several other lines, including Holland America, feature the same destination in its ads and offer similar benefits. Thus, Princess's advertising is not preemptive and must concentrate on better ways of defining what the Love Boat experience is and why no one else can duplicate it. Karine Armstrong recognizes that challenge.

Royal Caribbean

Of the major cruise lines, the one that spends the most on network television advertising—more than 50 percent of their total media budget—is Royal Caribbean. This is consistent with the lines belief, expressed by Rod McLeod, "driving not only brand awareness but brand differentiation. The best way to affect people's attitude toward a product is television. It tends to be far more strategic than newspaper—it's not a retail medium."

You've Got Some Royal Caribbean Coming

Royal Caribbean's advertising is beautifully produced and elegantly executed by McKinney & Silver Advertising. In one typical spot, we first see a flag fluttering off the stern of a ship while a male voice says, "A sparking ship on crystal waters is coming." A smiling woman adds, "They would do anything for us there." The male voice continues, "The perfect lobster is coming. Memories are coming. Seven days in Royal Caribbean's Caribbean are coming. You've got some Royal Caribbean coming." Scenes include islands, beaches, and palm trees. RCCL's print ads use the same theme. One double-paged spread is headlined "Everyone Has Some Royal Caribbean Coming," and the body copy is short and direct:

> A group of high school teachers from Atlanta. A recently retired couple from Los Angeles. The girl next door—her mom, dad, and younger brother. All sorts of people from all over have

cruised on Royal Caribbean's sparkling ships. All over the Caribbean—all over this whole, wide, wonderful world for that matter. They come to rejuvenate. To have the vacation of a lifetime, the vacation they deserve. An experience they'll always remember. All of which is to say, you can trust us with your hard-earned vacation. We're cabin stewards who remember your name and wine stewards who remember your wine. Plus all the things other cruise lines offer . . .

We asked Rod McLeod to explain the rationale behind RCCL's slogan, "You've Got Some Royal Caribbean Coming." Here's what he told us:

First of all we think people view vacations as an entitlement, and that entitlement is defined differently by different people. I deserve a good vacation because I've just gotten a divorce and I need to get away; I've been working very hard and I need to get away; I haven't taken a vacation in ten years; my wife just died; I just put my kids through college; my family is entitled to a vacation. These are all reasons for getting away. They define to a certain degree what we mean when we say "You've got some Royal Caribbean coming." What we're seeking to do is differentiate by defining what we call our brand personality; what I mean by brand personality is this: Next year we have to attract 5 billion people to "sleep with us," so we should at least be charming. We are the nice people down the street that you'd like to get to know; we are the nice guy in the car pool that you'd like to get your family to know—good company to be with. One of the ways we do this is by telling true stories, which appear in our advertising and our brochures.

McLeod pulled out an ad showing a cake decorated with roses and the words "Happy Divorce." The headline is "Our Chefs Prepare Each and Every Creation With Love: and the copy reads:

Needless to say, Divorce Cake isn't on the menu. But when a passenger jokingly requested the iced and layered confection, our Executive Chef Peter Kofler eagerly obliged. He baked and decorated a cake honoring, well, the less celebrated side of matrimony. The maitre d' presented it to the table. And with great flourish (along with a few cheers) chopped it in half.

While we fully sanction the institution of marriage, the moral of our story is this: stop at nothing to love, honor, and obey the whims of our guests . . . You've got some Royal Caribbean coming.

Birth of a Slogan

Karine Armstrong remembers quite well from her days with RCCL how that campaign was born. McKinney & Silver, the advertising agency, believed that Royal Caribbean was not doing enough of its own chest pounding; they were not telling consumers and travel agents how good they really were, and they needed to put that stake in the ground. The agency's intent was to replace the word "vacation" with the words "Royal Caribbean" in consumers' minds. "Vacation, leisure, good times, great benefits— Royal Caribbean wanted to take the place of those words and feelings. Instead of saying, 'I've got to go on a vacation,' customers would say, 'I've got to go on Royal Caribbean . . .' It would become part of the language of cruising, like the 'Love Boat' already has."

Armstrong doesn't think that the campaign achieved its objective. "Looking at the tracking research, I don't think it's set. It's not there in people's minds, and I don't think a lot of them get it. I do agree that a lot of people aren't taking vacations the way they used to, and that it's important to remind them that they deserve to get away and be pampered and taken care of. But I recall our Chairman Richard Fain saying he wanted every ad to pay off on that promise, and that part of it doesn't seem to be coming through. When travel agents are tracked Royal Caribbean comes out very high. But from the consumer side they're still light years behind the awareness factor of Love Boats and Fun Ships. Carnival and Princess are the only two cruise lines that have successfully identified themselves in consumers' mind in the industry."

RCCL and Carnival—All the Same Boat

Ironically, Armstrong adds, "Royal Caribbean ships are decorated in a manner that some people consider more tasteful than Carnival's decor; however, when it comes to onboard service, quality, and presentation of food, I think Royal Caribbean and Carnival are equal. Royal Caribbean's cabins are not as good as Carnival's with respect to size, but there are some things that Royal Caribbean does better than a lot of the rest of us, like trying to get you to the ship without multiple air connections. Most lines will get you to the ship, but they don't care if it takes several connections because they're trying to get the lowest possible cost. I have nothing but the highest respect for RCCL, but in their own minds they're positioning the line as delivering a higher product then it actually does."

Armstrong adds that by spending more money on television than anyone else they have achieved some degree of success in the same way that Chinese water torture is successful—drip by drip. "If they tell you enough times, "we're upscale," eventually you come to believe it. But she adds, "if you take out the European and other exotic cruises [which are very different packages] and look only at the Caribbean, they're after the same person."

We might add that Carnival and Royal Caribbean *get* the same person. The demographics of both lines' passengers, in terms of income, age, education, and occupation, are very similar. The differences are the same kind you might expect between the people who read *People* and those who read *Time* or those who drive a Ford and those who drive a Chevrolet. These differences have to do with price, styling, or availability, or what their best friends have told them.

While we have the utmost respect for Armstrong (and she's was very generous in providing material for this chapter), we might comment that decor is a matter of taste. Armstrong misses the point when she says that Royal Caribbean's ships are designed more tastefully. Carnival's interiors are not designed to look like an elegant resort or a private yacht, nor do they necessarily reflect the personal taste of designer Joe Farcus, whose own living room is not filled with neon lights and kinetic sculptures. They are carefully designed to make Carnival cruisers feel like they have left the real world and been transported to a land of *Sensation, Fascination, Imagination, Ecstasy, and Fantasy.* It is what Carnival calls Entertainment Architecture. Its land-based equivalents are found in Disney World and Las Vegas. It's fun and exciting. This look doesn't appeal to everyone any more than the *Wizard of Oz* or *Snow White* is everyone's favorite movie. It's this consistency of product and promise that makes Carnival's formula successful. Delivering on the promise is a major issue in cruise line advertising, as we will demonstrate shortly.

Celebrity

Celebrity Cruises, a premium line, up until recently put all of its efforts in print (although as Al Wallack told us earlier they intended to go on television and began running their campaign in 1996). Their ads are clever and pretty, and they are good because they do what advertising should do—promise a meaningful benefit in their headline and pay it off in the copy. One ad shows a Celebrity ship sailing in a luxurious sunset. The headline reads: "An experience like this usually begins with the words 'Once Upon A Time.'" Another, also showing a ship at sail, reads, "Is the closest you've gotten to calming blue water lately the office water cooler?" A third, showing a beautifully presented dinner entrée, reads, "Exotic ports, whirlpools, a casino, a rather nice health club. And oh, an occasional snack." The copy in this ad pays off the promise in the headline and the photo:

> We know no one goes on a cruise just to eat. But don't be surprised if in between our endless array of other pleasures, some of the finest cuisine you've ever sampled crosses your palate. After all, we have placed internationally acclaimed chef Michel Roux in charge of menus for our entire fleet . . .

This is good, solid advertising that makes a serious attempt to differentiate Celebrity's product from others'. Even so, there are two problems with it that are not unique to this line. First, Celebrity hasn't spent enough money to begin to achieve the degree of awareness necessary to make an impression in this business. Second, while Michel Roux is a unique chef and his recipes are first class, many other lines serve superb food as well. It takes a very discriminating palate and a chance to sample the food on every line in a short time to detect the nuances of one line's cuisine compared to other's. In other words, it's not a promise that only Celebrity can or does make.

The Ad Campaign—NCL and "The New Constitution"

While Carnival, Royal Caribbean, and Princess have garnered the most awareness among consumers with their advertising, by far the campaign that stands out is the one launched in 1994 by Norwegian Cruise Lines. Created by the San Francisco agency Goodby Silverstein & Partners (although it clearly shows the hand of Norwegian's President and marketing guru Adam Aron), the campaign was simple and logical—take the focus off the ship and put it on the benefits of taking a cruise. This was good strategy because NCL, unlike its competitors, had no new ships to focus on, so it made sense to change the rules of the game.

The television spots were extraordinary. *Advertising Age* picked them as the best in the travel category *and* in the cinematography category, calling them "smoldering passion in black and white." The magazine described the spot it particularly liked this way: A "silky-voiced, shapely young woman recites various elements of a 'new constitution for the world (among them 'Article 1, Section 3, we shall form a more perfect union' and 'Article 4, Section 7, work shall be abolished') while she and a male companion frolic, embrace underwater, and go boating in tropical settings." The spot closes with a shot of one of NCL's ships.

NCL's magazine ads were equally innovative. One showed the head and shoulders silhouette of a sultry woman, her hair wet. There was no headline, and the copy, using a variety of type sizes with no punctuation, read:

There is no law that says that you can't make love at 4 in the afternoon on a Tuesday

shall not study a sunset or train butterflies

must pay tax on itemized moments of pleasure

may not have extra mushrooms with your steak

can't disembark in Tortola and stay there

must pack worry along with your luggage

can't learn about love from a turtle

must contribute to the GNP every single solitary day of your life

absolutely must act your chronological age not your shoe size shall maintain strict economies of emotion

can't make love again at 5 in the afternoon on the Tuesday
we spoke of earlier

because the laws of the land do not apply

the laws are different out here

These ads stood out in another way as well. Conventional
wisdom (based on some solid readership research done by ad
agency Ogilvy and Mather) says that ads with black backgrounds
and white type are not read as much as ads with white backgrounds and black type. But these ads were according to Roper
Starch Worldwide—the research firm. The NCL magazine ads
scored higher than average on the basis of readers who remember having seen an ad in a particular issue of a publication, who
noted who the advertiser was, and who read more than 50 percent of the copy.

The Magazine Publishers Association awarded its prestigious
Kelly Award, including $100,000 in cash, to the agency for NCL's
campaign, which in addition garnered a prize from the One Club
of New York and a CLIO.

Adam Aron points out with justifiable pride that no other
campaign in the travel industry has ever won so many awards.
Even so, he has had to defend the campaign with virtually every
one of his competitors, who for the most part have violent reactions against it.

The Critics

Rod McLeod, who before rejoining Royal Caribbean, was President of Norwegian Cruise Lines, has this to say:

> I think it's finely crafted advertising. I think they've done a
> beautiful job with production values—very well done. My only
> concern, and it's really Adam Aron's concern since I'm looking
> at this as an outside observer, is whether or not the advertising
> is consistent with the product. Is what the advertising says
> about NCL what the NCL product is? I look at that advertising
> and I say to myself, that's not what any of us do. It's from the
> high-fashion genre of advertising, like Calvin Klein's Obsession
> commercials. It's a very high-fashion, trendy, new-age type of

communication. If I were to impute an objective to that, I'd say it was to talk to affluent first-time cruisers.

I think you could find this kind of experience on Seabourn or Sea Goddess. But there's a level of pampering, of peace and tranquillity, that comes through in this campaign that you're not going to find on a 1,500- or 2,000-passenger ship, so it's out of sync with the product. But to be fair, if you asked me about Carnival's advertising or asked Bob Dickinson about my advertising—well, its like taking Rembrandt to see a Michelangelo and asking if he would do it the same way. I think we would all do each other's advertising differently.

We agree with McLeod. Advertising is an art as well as a science, and every artist sees his subject differently. What is interesting in this case is that while everyone in advertising applauds the campaign and many creative directors from other agencies would give their eye teeth to have done it, we could find no one in the cruise industry (who doesn't work for NCL) who likes it. And the primary reason has a lot to do with Rod McLeod's comment, "That's not what any of us do."

We also asked Karine Armstrong for her evaluation of this campaign, and she pulled no punches.

It's different out here. How nice for them, how wonderful. But is it selling any cruises for them? I don't think so. I think this campaign scares people. Granted, passengers don't want to see people in polyester suits as their cruise mates, but they don't want to be surrounded by the most beautiful people on the planet, either. It's intimidating to both men and women. Men look at that and say, "Ye God, these are the women who are going to be on there with me? That's kind of cool." How do you think wives feel about that?

And think of a woman at home, watching this with her husband, who is sitting there in his shorts with his pot belly hanging out. She's in her housecoat or robe and looking at him thinking, "Yeah right . . . he's going to get me under a shower or behind a rock and kiss me on the neck. You might as well believe in the tooth fairy. Harry and Edith aren't going to do that on a cruise. Sure, everyone would like to have a vacation like that, but it ain't gonna happen. Maybe [NCL's] just going after the people who go to La Costa Spa. If so, that's great. But the travel agents know that they don't deliver a product like that.

Armstrong mentioned her brief time working with Aron at Hyatt after she left Carnival, admitting, "He knows how to sell stuff." But she feels that his campaign ignores the fact that most consumers haven't been on a cruise, don't know what one is like, and need to be realistically enlightened. The NCL campaign does not do that.

Doug Falk, formerly at Holland America, and before that President of NCL (they've had a lot of them) also has serious doubts about the campaign:

> I think the campaign is partially right but also partially narrow. Right in that it is arresting, it's intriguing, and it's unique, those are all important elements of a good advertising campaign. Narrow in that it misses the mark by appealing to a small slice of Americans. I'm not sure that in the long run [NCL is] giving themselves the best opportunity to build a broadly based franchise. Many potential cruisers will not find that sex-oriented advertising appealing. You know, most of us in this business have spent our career on either the East Coast or the West Coast, where our ships are. But many of our passengers come from the Midwest, and they see the world differently.

Carnival's Bob Dickinson, too, is critical of the NCL campaign for basically the same reasons. "It's fanciful," he says. "Instead of helping the industry attract new first-time cruisers it is harming all of us by projecting an image that turns off a huge segment of our potential market. Moreover, NCL's continuing poor operating results suggest that the marketplace has simply not embraced it."

The Response
Adam Aron:

"All of this criticism is coming from the chief marketing officers of other companies, whose advertising has not been similarly praised. There is no doubt that it is revolutionary. It took a certain amount of courage to run it because it is different from what most airlines and hotel companies have run before. And it's hardly surprising that when you take a significant risk to break category, the more conventional thinkers in the category are going to be bothered by it.

It's also true that you measure advertising by its results, not by whether your competitors snipe at it, and in our case there are two very interesting statistics. Our occupancy has risen faster than any other cruise line in the industry this year, and our customer satisfaction rates are higher than before the campaign broke.

The campaign has been highly noticed and talked about. Jay Leno did a monologue about it, and an entire Phil Donahue Show, on which I was a guest, was devoted to it.

Let's look at what you want an advertising campaign to do. You want your advertising to be noticed. Clearly ours has been. For an advertiser with a $20 million budget, it has received attention far beyond what that sum would ordinarily justify. You want an ad to sell your product, and the fact that our occupancy has grown faster than any of our competitors' suggests that we are doing that.

If our advertising was raising expectations that we couldn't deliver on, you would expect that when people go on one of our cruises they would come back disappointed. Our satisfaction ratings are higher than they've ever been in 20 years: Ninety-six percent of our passengers say we're meeting their expectations onboard. The industry average is 90 percent. Actually, as many as 65 percent say we're exceeding their expectations. So its important that in the last two years our competitors have seen our advertising but they haven't sailed on our ships.

Then there's the question of being too upscale. Calvin Klein and Guess Jeans do not sell their products to millionaires. Those products are sold to everyday Americans. When I was on the Donahue show the women in the audience were hooting and hollering at the scene where the couple embraces in the outdoor coral rock shower and the woman strokes the man's chest. And Donahue's audience are not elitist Brahmin aristocrats.

Our advertising is very sophisticated and very sultry, but that doesn't mean it intimidates average consumers. My basic view of selling is that most consumers are aspirational, and if you talk down to them they think your advertising is pedestrian."

Aron also addressed what he calls the three-percent body fat issue. This is the complaint the people in his ads are too perfect, that they don't look like the people who sail on Norwegian Cruise Line ships.

My simple retort is that in their own mirrors that's precisely what the people on our ships look like, which goes back to the whole notion of aspirations. The cosmetic industry is not a quadrillion-dollar business because people think they look bad. It's such a big industry because people want to make themselves look as good as they can. When a woman walks out of a beauty parlor, she thinks she's pretty even if she's not.

Our advertising doesn't intimidate prospects because they can't identify with the models. The people in our advertising represent the fantasy of who our passengers want to be.

I don't agree that we're scaring people away, I think we're doing a nice job of expanding the market for everyone. For 20 years this industry has been marketing in the same ways to the same constituency, and that's middle-class clientele. They have been using sensory overload as the driving motivation to take a cruise—so many islands, so much food, so much sun—and we continue to think people find that appealing. We're showing a different side of what cruising can be. It's escapist, it's unusual, it provides them with experiences they've never had before. Beyond that, I venture to say that with all the pressures they have in this day and age, two-income couples find that their love life in the eighteenth year of marriage is not what it was in the honeymoon year. And there's something very appealing about putting those pressures aside for a week and falling in love with your wife or husband again.

Seeing the Trees for the Forest

Is there an easy resolution to this debate? Probably not. One reason is that all of the lines try for as broad an appeal as possible, but end up attracting different segments of the market because their different products appeal to different people—with different incomes, of different ages, and with different life styles. They all need to attract new cruisers, but these new cruisers need to be those who will like what the lines have to offer. Since most consumers haven't been on a cruise and can't tell one ship from another, any advertising campaign that depicts cruising as an off-putting experience will threaten the portrait that other lines are trying to paint of what cruising is all about.

The issue is whether folks are intimidated by the ads or drawn to them. Remember, the name of the game is differentiating yourself from your competition in a way that will attract the most customers to you. The Cruise Line Industry Association tries to promote cruising generically, but that can be a real challenge, somewhat akin to the National Restaurant Association launching a campaign promising that we will enjoy eating out at any restaurant no matter what it looks like and what it serves. Obviously, it won't work because we've all been in a variety of restaurants and we know how to make an informed decision. But we haven't all been on a cruise, and therein lies the heart of the dilemma. All we know is what we are told.

If the industry really wants to grow it, needs a unified approach. But what's good for the forest in this case may not be good for all of the trees. The bigger trees, which constitute the bulk of the forest, operate under the laws of nature and create an environment that is most comfortable for them. Within the same forest there can be several different environments—thickets full of vines and undergrowth, hummocks, and glens. Smaller species may not be able to thrive in any of these and fight fiercely for their existence. To some extent that is what is going on in the cruise industry today—survival of the fittest.

At the beginning of this chapter we tried to imagine what we would do if we were to start a new cruise line, specifically how we would position and market it. As you can see, it would be difficult because the current players seem to have covered the waterfront. However, that doesn't mean it can't be done, as Adam Aron explains: "I haven't given much thought to what the next hole waiting for someone to drive a truck through it will be. You have to assume, though, that there is always such a hole if you have a talented client and a talented advertising agency working together with the clear intent of finding it."

We agree with him. Everyone in the industry is waiting to see where Disney Cruises, due to debut in 1998 with two ships, will find the hole. They've got the talent and the money to drive a very large truck!

8

Pieces of Eight
Making money on the high seas

You and your spouse have decided to spend a week in a resort destination . . . say Honolulu. You go to your travel agent or call your favorite hotel's toll-free reservation number, and get a rate on a per room/night basis. Room choices may be ocean front, ocean view, junior suite, etc.—maybe five or six in all. The rate of the room type you choose times the number of nights is the price you will pay. Life is simple, yes? No, of course not. It just appears that way, which gives most land-based vacations a huge advantage over cruising.

First, the room rate is expressed on a per-night basis, creating the lowest possible price (unless it's called the "Love Nest Motel" and rents by the hour). Second, purchasers know (or they think they know) exactly what they are receiving for their money: a room, maid service, and the no-cost amenities of the hotel such as the lobby, beach area, and pool. If the hotel has a gym or spa, more often than not, they will pay a per-diem fee for usage.

The purchase decision appears to be small and totally manageable. The hidden costs or costs that don't seem to count in the price include breakfast, lunch, dinner, snacks, daytime activities, drinks, tipping, cover charges, taxes, cabs, and so forth. Why these items don't seem to enter into the perceived cost of a land vacation is curious. Perhaps people feel they will incur many of these costs anyway—after all, they do have to eat—and even staying home, they are likely to spend money on drinks and entertainment. Perhaps some vacationers overlook these costs because they might persuade them not to make the vacation purchase. Remember, many Americans approach high-ticket, discretionary purchases like vacations with a certain Puritan-ethic ambivalence. They are sinners who don't necessarily deserve to indulge themselves, especially when people are starving in India or Rwanda; what's more, they have to save for the proverbial rainy day.

The self-delusion of regarding only the cost of certain items as part of the vacation creates a low, more justifiable, purchase price. In reality, the cost for food and drink is significantly higher in a resort than at home—where few people eat out for breakfast, lunch, and dinner, let alone late-night snacks. In the captive environment of a resort hotel, food prices for one breakfast could feed a family of four for a day's meals, and a six-pack of beer bought at home is a fraction of the price of the same beer ordered at a resort. Most video rentals are under $3.00, where an in-room rental may bring $7.95 plus tax. In short, while consumers can omit these costs when they figure the cost of a vacation, there is a definite premium on these items at a resort. The premium is even higher when the resort is seasonal and/or removed from mainstream commerce, as any tropical island is.

Take Bermuda. Everything there is imported, so you can count on paying 25 percent more than in the States. The shipping costs alone, which are calculated on bulk not weight, send the price of something as small as potato chips through the ceiling! Also, Bermuda has no income tax. The government's revenues come primarily from duties collected on all imported goods, which add considerably to the purchase price of the items for the hotel—everything from soap to napkins, from soup to nuts. Finally, the markup on the already inflated costs is higher than in the States because Bermuda, like all of the islands in the Caribbean, is very small and there is limited competition. You can't get it cheaper at Walmart because there is no Walmart, and if there were it would probably have to charge the same as everyone else because there are only 61,000 local residents. That merely compounds the problem, resulting in high prices to the consumer.

Land-Based versus Cruise-Based

The paradox, then is that the typical, unbundled land vacation sports a low initial purchase price on the room but high subsequent costs. Cruising, on the other hand, has an unavoidably high initial price because of its all-inclusive nature, but fewer subsequent costs, like drinks, and shore tours, which are generally lower than those for land vacations. For this reason, cruise pricing generates a high incidence of sticker shock. Given cruising's roots as an expensive, elitist vacation, high brochure prices seem to confirm a noncruiser's suspicion that a cruise is simply out of reach.

The cruise industry, through its marketing organization, the Cruise Line International Association (CLIA), attacks the apples-and-oranges comparison of land and cruise vacation prices by giving seminars to travel agents on comparably equipping and pricing the two vacations. Between 1980 and 1995 CLIA estimates it trained 86,323 agents. Unfortunately, there are roughly 250,000 travel agents in the United States and Canada and 10 percent or so enter or leave the industry each year. Moreover, in the greater scheme of things, cruising represents about 7 percent of travel agency revenue, and only about 1 percent of its transactions. The infrequency of agency sales and the relative lack of importance of cruising in the full-service agency's "big picture" probably means that agents forgot what CLIA taught them about cruise versus land-based vacation costs.

Another factor that influences the way vacations are sold is that, in our experience, a good many, if not the majority, of travel agents have a very foggy understanding of clients' vacation-purchasing rationales. The reason is simple: They don't buy vacations the way everyone else does. When agents take cruises or stay at resorts, they travel free or at significantly reduced rates, and they expect and receive upgraded airline seats and accommodations when available. Indeed, most agents' knowledge of vacation products come from familiarization trips on which they are wined and dined at little or no cost to themselves. In many cases their employer picks up the tab so that others in the office can get a firsthand briefing and the agency can say, "Our people have been there." The result of these freebies and VIP treatment is that when they sit behind a desk and quote a room rate of $150 a night for a hotel in St. Thomas at a resort they just visited and for which they paid the agent rate of $25 a night, they sometimes question in their own minds whether the room is really worth that much or even feel guilty about selling it at that rate. Agents don't think the same as their customers, or pay the same prices when they travel, so many of them are not as sensitive as they should be to consumers' notions of pricing in general. They are often at a complete loss when comparing cruises and land vacations because their own experience is so at odds with the real world.

All-Inclusive Vacations—Competitors or Not?

A small but not insignificant number of land vacations are all-inclusive resorts such as Club Med or Sandals. It is estimated that some 1 million North Americans purchase such all-inclusive vacations each year—only about one-fifth the number who took a cruise last year. Nevertheless, comparing such vacations with a cruise presents a problem from the opposite extreme. All-inclusive land packages include tipping, virtually all daytime activities, and even in some instances alcoholic beverages and wine—items not included with most cruises.

Aficionados of the all-inclusive vacation, and some travel agents, are urging cruise lines to emulate this approach. They believe that unless cruises become more inclusive, the Club Meds and Sandals may erode cruising's popularity. This is an issue worth pondering.

Shore Excursions

Offering everything at one all-inclusive price would be difficult, if not impossible, for any moderately priced cruise line, for the following reasons: (1) It would highten the perception that cruising is too expensive by increasing the initial purchase price; instead of growing the business, it would shrink it. (2) It wouldn't be possible to include all shore excursions (not even the luxury lines do that). These adventures, whether landing on a glacier in a helicopter or snorkeling among tropical reefs, are an important and memorable aspect of any cruise. Every port-of-call has a varied menu of places to go and things to see, and their costs and availability vary. Some tours are sold out almost as soon as the ship sails because space and time are limited. Imagine a shipload of unhappy people who couldn't see what they wanted to either because it wasn't offered or not everyone could get on it. This is not a problem for all-inclusive resorts (which don't offer excursions off the premises for free either). Only on very small, exploration-type cruises, such as those to Antarctica where everyone goes ashore in Zodiac boats, is pricing to include shore excursions feasible.

Tipping

Tipping is another perceived all-inclusive advantage. Usually the only cruises lines that include it in the price are the expensive, luxury ones like Cunard's *Sea Goddess, Silversea,* and *Seabourn.* Holland America, which is positioned as a premium line, and at a much lower price level than the one we've just mentioned, tells its passengers that tipping "is not required." But, our research suggests that most passengers are so captivated by the level of service they receive that they end up tipping their waiters and cabin stewards, anyway. Indeed, many of us are so conditioned to tipping that we consider it almost un-American not to.

The danger with a no-tipping policy, especially in the hospitality industry where there are large numbers of low-paid employees, is the inherent risk of poor service when the staff isn't motivated to perform at their best to earn tips and thus increase their income. The small luxury cruise lines manage to avoid this problem because, through higher ticket pricing, they can afford to pay their crews more than they could earn virtually anywhere in the world on land or sea for doing the same job. If passengers complain about their hospitality and service levels, crew members can be easily replaced.

Certainly, the cruise industry cannot and should not ignore all-inclusive resorts as competitors (remember the founder of Club Mcd in Chapter 7 who said he was inspired by cruises when he formulated his concept).

All-inclusive vacations have achieved a relatively small penetration of the overall vacation market among North Americans, and we suspect that they tend to appeal to a lifestyle somewhat different from that of the average cruiser and cruise prospect. Nevertheless, even though Club Med isn't and never will be a meaningful substitute for, say a Carnival Fun Ship cruise, travel agents and their clients are still often tempted to compare prices of the two.

Issues in Selling Cruises

Commendably, the all-inclusives have done a superior job of price stabilization. There is little discounting of the product as operators are content to run their facilities at 50 or 60 percent occupancy if necessary to maintain their price integrity. It's much easier for them to do this because their operations have substantially lower fixed costs than cruise lines. Moreover, because there are so few brands—Club Med and Sandals dominate the Caribbean for instance—companies can diligently enforce nonrebating policies at the agent level. Remember, a *discount* is a price reduction offered by the supplier, while a *rebate* is a price reduction offered by the travel agent that represents a portion of his or her commission.

Rebates

Butch Stewart, the successful owner of Sandals Properties, says he simply refuses to accept bookings from agents who rebate any of their commission. The agent community knows this and respects his power to enforce the policy. Because rebating is not illegal (in fact, it is encouraged by the federal government as a pro-consumer policy to effect lower purchase prices), cruise suppliers can only control it by exercising their individual rights to deal with any travel agent they choose, which means not dealing with agents who operate counter to the cruise line policies.

However, because there are so many cruise lines and no line has captured the lion's share of the market, and because of the unhealthy imbalance between cruise capacity and consumer demand, any unilateral enforcement of an antirebating policy risks losing a share of the rebating agent's business. A cruise line can put an individual agency on a "no-sell" status (meaning either not taking the bookings at all or taking them but not paying commissions) when, for example, the agency's sales tactics are judged to be anti-consumer and thus harmful to the line's reputation. However, no cruise line, in today's market, can afford to put hundreds if not thousands of agents on a "no-sell" status to stop rebating. Doing so would stop rebating of the company's product, but it would also cause irreparable harm to its business.

An Example

If agency X has been threatened with a no-sell status by cruise line Y because of rebating, and actively sells ten cruise lines, it simply moves line Y's business to one of the other nine cruise products. Line Y's product is thus out-priced in agency X because of its rebating policy. Whatever price cruise line Y set for its products is in line with the market; that is, the other lines' pricing. But by not accepting rebating, it now must face a 5- to 10-percent price disadvantage (the extent of the rebates its competitors enjoy). In a price-sensitive environment, this doesn't cost line Y only 5 percent of its business but much, much more. The line's competitive share of the rebating agency's business might drop from 10 percent to 2 percent—a decline of 80 percent in the best case. If agency X refuses to stop rebating, line Y has no choice but a no-sell, reducing its share of the agency's business to zero!

Now, factor in the cumulative effect of a widespread antirebating policy unilaterally enforced by cruise line Y: Perhaps a thousand agencies, which account for 20 percent or more of the line's business, would shift away 80 percent of their business on that line, costing the line at least 16 percent of its total business! No cruise line can afford to embark on an antirebating program that would put it a such a risk.

For these reasons, most lines look the other way and ignore the rebating issue altogether. Carnival, for example, has a policy of prohibiting rebated rates from being advertised in public media. If the Carnival name, which is trademarked, is used in an ad, the company can control its use. Offenders are sent cease-and-desist letters and almost always quickly comply with the policy. As a matter of interest, Carnival's policy also applies to advertising group rates in public media. The theory is that such restrictions gives all agencies in the market a level playing field when it comes to promoting the Carnival product in newspapers, radio, television, and billboards.

This may be as good a time as any to look at why some travel agents rebate. This is a very low-margin business, so shaving your commission to give a client a few extra dollars off doesn't seem to make sense from an economic point of view. However, agents view rebating as a tool to help them increase their market share. If one travel agency decides to rebate, say, 5 percent of its commission on a travel product such as a cruise, and other agencies in the area fail to match that, the price advantage the agency can offer consumers should result in increased cruise sales. This presumption is based on the perception (and frequently the reality) that most cruise purchasers, 60 percent of whom are experienced cruisers, will shop around to find the best deal. Consequently, an agency rebate can make the difference between a cruise sale and "I'll check with my husband."

Once one agency starts rebating in a market, even if infrequently, many other agencies will begin to rebate for fear of losing business. The risk here is not simply a lost commission on the cruise sale but the even more serious threat of a lost client. This might be a long-term client, who presumably (remember, no one knows for sure) has given an agency all of her travel and vacation business, not to mention referrals to associates, friends, and relatives, which means that all the future business, as well as those valuable past and future referrals, will be lost. By not offering a rebate, the agency never even gets a chance to match, let alone better, the rebate deal offered by a competitive agency. Even worse, many agents are concerned that this lost client may somehow feel cheated by the agency she has been loyal to all of these years, or systematically taken advantage of. Because the client receives a lower price from a competitor that uses rebates to make a sale on a cruise it follows that maybe, just maybe, her former agency was overcharging on *all* past business!

Commissions and Rebating

Cruising has a high initial purchase price because of its bundled nature. The actual dollar amount received by agents in commission when they sell a cruise is higher than when they sell a land vacation. Moreover, the rate of cruise commission, for most agencies, averages about 14 percent versus 11 percent for the land-based combined commission rates. Fourteen percent commission on a $2,000 one-week cruise for two people yields $280 in commission for about an hour's effort, and rebating by as much as $100 still yields a net commission of $180 on the sale. By contrast, a $1,200 one week land package at 11 percent commission yields $132—less than half the cruise commission. There's less commission to work with so there's a much lower tendency to rebate. In addition, as we mentioned earlier, the few high-priced all-inclusive land package operators have been able to effectively discourage rebating of their products.

Telemarketers

Cruise rebating is further encouraged by the nationwide marketing of so-called 800-number cruise specialists, many of which use rebating as a standard marketing tool. This can range from rebating "only when we have to" to a standardized rebate of a predetermined percent on all business. To listen to some retail agents, however, you'd think, it was 50 percent or more!

This is a case of perception versus reality. Because of their visibility, a result of aggressive cruise marketing, these national telemarketing operations appear to local travel agencies as a huge threat to their mom and pop operations. Agents frequently offer a rebate in anticipation of their prospects' succumbing to a national operator. Yet, the truth is that their actual volume simply doesn't warrant this concern. These national operators account for less than 5 percent of Carnival's business. It could be much less if agents truly closed the sale. An analysis of Carnival's individual booking statistics reveals that, on average, 65 percent of all cruise bookings fail to materialize, but 95 percent of all deposited bookings stick. These data probably are representative of the entire industry. Given this, our rule of thumb is simple: *The key to stopping the shopping is GTM* (getting the money).

Options

The 75 percent failure rate of nondeposited business is the fault of travel agents who have not mastered the art of properly closing a sale, but instead offer their prospects an option. An option on a particular cabin at a particular price was designed originally to facilitate arrangements between the cruise lines and their travel agents, but it was never meant to be discussed with prospective customers. Why? An option means that the agency has the specific reservation for a given period of time, and check or credit card number must reach the cruise line before that specified time expires. If it doesn't, the option is automatically canceled. Customarily, unless space is extremely tight or the booking is very close to the sailing date, options are generally given only for seven days. After that, the cabin goes back on the market. It is not unusual for a cabin to have as many as six or seven options on it before it is finally sold.

When an agent gives a prospective client an option, he or she is saying, in effect, "You have seven days to change your mind. You can shop for a better price here in town or by calling one of those national 800-number agencies." Is it any wonder why the cancellation rate of optioned bookings is so high? Getting a deposit, on the other hand, is a commitment on the part of the prospect. Once folks make a deposit, by check or credit card, the likelihood of their changing their mind is sharply reduced, 15-fold based on our data.

Deposit Psychology
Real estate brokers have understood this principle for years. They will willingly take a $250,000 house off the market, even during a busy selling weekend, for as little as $500 earnest money. It is called "earnest" money because writing such a small check—less than one-half of 1 percent of the purchase price—says the buyer is in earnest—he or she really wants the house and fully intends to buy it. Obviously, if this wasn't so in practice the vast majority of the time, brokers would demand and get a more substantial deposit, but they don't have to do this because when a buyer makes even a small deposit on a home, their purchase decision is made and they stop looking.

Another reason for booking failure is that travel agents are often reluctant to recommend just one product to prospects, preferring to provide them a whole range of vacation options to consider. This is silly. Shoppers confronted with a whole host of purchase options are likely to discuss them with friends and relatives, who either add their own options, further confusing the issue, or send them to another agency to clear up the confusion!

Research of over 5,000 travel agents indicates that agents' primary fear in a selling situation is rejection. They feel that if a client doesn't buy one of their recommendations, they are somehow diminished, and that makes them feel uncomfortable. This is hardly earthshaking news—just about everyone who doesn't like selling lists fear of rejection as a major obstacle to be overcome. Asking for the order and getting the deposit is, of course, the moment of truth in any sale. At this point you find out whether your efforts have paid off—whether your suggestions have been accepted or rejected. When they're rejected, it is a terrible moment! That's when your fear of failure become a reality.

Fighting the Fear

In our seminars around the country, we consistently point out that these fears are without foundation. No travel agent we know of has ever been killed, maimed, assaulted, or battered for requesting a deposit. If the client says, "I'll think about it," the proper response is "I can understand that, but it would be a good idea if you get back to me quickly, because that way we will improve our chances of obtaining the same or comparable space and we have a really roomy cabin now." The implication is scarcity—rooms like this are not easy to come by, and there is nothing deceiving in saying this because it is the truth. Every day closer to sailing rooms are sold and so there really are fewer choices remaining.

Trust us, scarcity sells. It is a proven technique that helps people make up their minds to buy because they do not want to delay their decision only to find that the exact cabin they wanted or, even worse, the sailing date they planned on is no longer available. The drawing power of scarcity is especially strong with high-ticket, discretionary items such as vacations because of the ambivalence we discussed in Chapter 4. If a prospective purchaser decides to take the plunge and make the purchase, the purchase better be available or he or she will be terribly frustrated!

Cruise Commission Caps?

The domestic airline commission cap on tickets over $500 has lead many agents and travel writers to suggest that the cruise lines follow suit on their products. The reasoning is that the majority of cruise lines are losing money and may view this as a significant cost-cutting measure. For most cruise lines, as for airlines, commissions are the largest or second largest expense. (Depending on the line's percentage of air/sea business, air fares could be the largest.) But perhaps just as important, lower commissions would stop rebating altogether or at least reduce the amount of the rebate to some insignificant level.

Whether any of the cruise lines will take this tack remains to be seen, but the risk of unilaterally lowering commissions is great, paralleling that of curbing rebates. The agency distribution system in the United States, remember, it is still largely shaped by the airlines, with a few notable exceptions such as cruise-only and some full-service agencies that are vacation oriented. Given the threat of a widening imbalance between cruise berth capacity and consumer demand, most lines have been paying higher commission percentages, not lower ones. There are no definitive data on the subject, but our best guess is that average cruise line commissions climbed from about 12.5 percent in 1985 to 14.5 percent in 1995. That represents an increase of 16 percent overall but of 80 percent over the base 10-percent commission. Override commissions (those paid beyond the base 10-percent commission) have nearly doubled as cruise lines ferret out and reward cruise-producing agencies. Most cruise lines have a sliding scale of commission payment percentages based on sales productivity (either measured in dollar volume or head count). The concentration of cruise sales in a relatively small number of agencies—relative to the 41,000-plus total agency count in the United States and Canada—suggests that not only are these agencies benefiting from higher commission percentages, but their higher mix of cruise business is heavily influencing the individual cruise line's average commission payout.

Carnival's Experience

Carnival is an example of the industry pattern. Roughly 28,000 agencies did business with Carnival in 1995, representing nearly 70 percent of all U.S. and Canadian agencies. In other words, almost one agency in three produced no business at all! If nothing else, this is a clear indication of the strong agency orientation toward booking airline tickets.

On the day the airline commission caps were announced in February 1995, Carnival announced it would increase its commission to the 12,000 plus agencies who had not sold a Carnival cruise at that time, from 10 percent to 12 percent for a six-month trial period. The idea was to jump-start agencies that were financially affected by the cap situation to sell cruises. Carnival even offered a sales call by one of its representatives within seven days of a request by one of these agencies. The sales rep would provide product information and sales material as well as sales training to help the agency change its thinking from the order-taking mentality of an airline ticket agency. Remarkably, fewer than 400 agencies took advantage of this offer and developed *any* business during the six month trial. Considering that Carnival is the largest and most popular of all lines, and thus theoretically the easiest to sell, that's a fair indication of what's going on industry wide.

The Moral
The conclusion, then, is that while increased commission structures can and do motivate agencies to grow their cruise volume—if they are already cruise producers—they do little or nothing to motivate agencies who are neither oriented nor inclined to sell cruises or for that matter, to sell any other form of vacation other than visiting friends and relatives (VFR).

Our Carnival story is not the only one of agency inertia. When the airline commission caps were imposed, Royal Caribbean's Rod McLeod expressed his opinion (shared by many leading travel agency business strategists) in the trade press that the caps would finally force thousands of agencies to turn to the profitability of selling cruises to offset the caps' financial effects. However, at the 1995 CLIA/Travel Trade Cruise-A-Thon held in July in Miami, McLeod told the audience of agents, with disappointment, that the anticipated surge of cruise bookings simply had not materialized.

The End of an Era—the Florida Commission Base
In 1994, three lines, Royal Caribbean, Princess and Celebrity, acting independently of one another, announced that they would abolish the Florida commission base, wherein Florida agents received a base commission of 15 percent compared to the indus-

try standard of 10 percent. This anomaly had its roots in the $19.95 and $29.95 1-night and 2-night cruises offered from Miami in the fifties and sixties, before the modern cruise business became established. Back then, a 10 percent cruise commission was simply too low to attract agents' attention and motivate them to sell these new products, so a 15-percent inducement—the Florida commission—was created. It did the job and became institutionalized as the industry standard.

Whether the three lines initiative to create a level playing field among all (Florida and non-Florida) agencies made any material change in the commissions paid in Florida is a matter of conjecture. After all, what difference does it make if a Florida agency had a base commission of 15 percent and an override of 2 percent or a base of 10 percent and an override of 7 percent? In both cases the agency gets 17 percent for its efforts. Bear in mind the hotly competitive Florida cruise market—Florida was the leading cruise producing state in 1995, accounting for 18.3 percent of overall North American sales.[1]

Florida will at least maintain and probably enhance its market share in future years, so it's highly unlikely the initiative will hurt any of the three lines as they vie for their share of this important market. In all probability, the net effect will be a change in the base for *non-producing* agencies from 15 to 10 percent. In view of Carnival's experience after raising commissions because of the airline cap, this will turn out to be a nonevent, akin to speculating whether a fallen tree makes a noise in a forest if no one is there to hear it.

A Myriad of Tariffs

Put aside rebating and commissions, and we still have the prospect considering the seemingly high initial cost of a cruise versus an unbundled land vacation. And there's a further complication: There's not just one brochure price for this cruise, or three or four as with a typical resort hotel, but eight or twelve or twenty depending on the complexity of the cruise ship's state-

---

[1] *1994 CLIA Passenger Industry Carryings Report*

room breakdown. With most cruise lines, the prospect is confronted with a grid of prices that reflect not just stateroom size (like a hotel room) but location, with higher decks commanding a premium over lower decks. Then consider the choice of inside and outside staterooms, this is further complicated when some lines and travel agents refer to staterooms as cabins. What images must pass through a prospective first-time cruiser's mind when he hears an agent ask "Would you like an outside cabin?" He is probably picturing a gleaming white ship steaming out of port with large ropes trailing behind—each attached securely to rustic cabins bobbing up and down on the briny deep. The "cabin cruisers" are sitting in rocking chairs on the front porch, enjoying their voyage. Outside cabins, indeed! Old habits die hard, even though the trend in the industry is to emulate our land-based resort competition and refer to these accommodations as "ocean view." What other kind of view would you expect to find on a ship ? Naturally, they sell at a premium over inside staterooms, which have no view.

Pricing Combination

If you factor in seasonality, in which the price fluctuates with the time of year to adjust for the ebb and flow of consumer demand, the complexity of prices is further compounded. A hotel with 4 room categories and 3 seasonal prices generates 12 possible price combinations. A cruise ship with 12 room categories and 3 seasonal prices results in 36. It definitely seems that the cruise industry goes out of its way to make a purchase as daunting as possible. But why? The answer is that, with the exception of some small luxury and specialty lines like Sea Goddess, Windstar, and Seabourn, most lines want a large variety of stateroom prices to allow a blend of revenue possibilities. By having a few "loss-leader" type cabins, they can advertise a cheap lead price without committing too much inventory to it. In theory, based on sufficient demand, the line can then sell out all its staterooms at full tariff. If the demand isn't strong enough, the company simply keeps offering to resell the lower-priced categories that are selling and upgrading the passengers in those accommodations into the higher-priced accommodations that are not selling. More about this in yield management.

Discounting

Although this philosophy sounds simple enough, the real situation is dauntingly complicated. That is because brochure tariffs for most mainstream cruise lines have little or no bearing on the real prices that cruise products fetch in the market place. That cruise brochure tariffs are inflated is an understatement! In fact, unduly high brochure tariffs are worsening a bad situation in an industry that is already a victim of sticker shock because of the bundling of its product and carrying the burden of price complexity because of a dizzying array of accommodations choices. How did they get in such a mess? In the late seventies, when berth supply was tight and demand vigorous (remember the Sitmar ads we mentioned earlier?), cruises generally sold at or near brochure tariff. Yes, there was some upgrading going on. This was the case when someone paid for a category 4 inside twin/king stateroom on the lowest deck of the *Jubilee*, for example, and ended up in a category 7 inside twin/king without paying the $150 per-person difference, or when someone paid for a specific category with the guarantee the he would be in that category at a minimum but probably end up doing better (for which the passenger was willing to forgo receiving a cabin number at the time of booking). Most of the time, however, the brochure tariff price of the stateroom was the one that was paid for the cruise; in any event, on just about every cruise some passengers paid the price published in the brochure, although not necessarily the price for the specific accommodation received.

Then came the huge capacity increases of the eighties and nineties, and brochure tariffs simply weren't getting the job done. Ships weren't filling and the industry embarked on a long and irreversible path of discounting. Now, we may ask, "Aren't upgrades and guarantees a form of discounting?" Not to split hairs, but no, they aren't. Both pricing schemes are in fact sold at tariff, as we have said. Discounting, on the other hand, is a supplier-based pricing scheme that departs from tariff, creating a whole new lower pricing structure for the product.

It All Started with Sea-Savers

The first wide-spread discounting scheme was NCL's Sea-Saver fares. These were capacity-controlled, cruise-only, run-of-ship (no stateroom numbers) rates that applied for bookings within 30 days of the departure date. Sea-Savers were introduced in July 1980 to deal with huge increments of unsold inventory resulting from the recent introduction of the *Norway*. They were soon followed by Carnival in January 1981.

Holland America introduced "free air" in the fall of 1980. In effect they discounted their air/sea cruises by eliminating the air add-on charges, which had compensated them, partially at least, for the round-trip air fare between the passenger's home city and the ship's departure port. Free air lasted only for the slow fall season of 1980 to stimulate demand depressed by national recession. In 1982, Carnival, too, eliminated their air/sea add-on á la Holland America, but then increased their base tariffs in 1983 and after to include the effect of the air-add-on in the base. In other words, a winter 1983 1-week cruise was priced from $950 including free air, versus $810 and an average air add-on of $150 for a total of $960 for a comparable cruise in the winter of the previous year. As the company was able to recoup the entire air add-on (by 1984), the discount disappeared and a new tariff scheme was born. At the same time that free air was priced into the base tariff, Carnival also provided a cruise-only travel allowance for cruise only passengers, who, we assure you, had no interest in subsidizing the air cost of fellow passengers!

Free-air pricing was quickly matched by the other year-round Caribbean operators, but they, too, quickly abandoned it for a new tariff scheme. The reason was simple: Agent feedback to Carnival in the fall of 1982 was overwhelmingly in favor of free air. At the time, about 75 percent of the Caribbean-based cruise business was sold on an air/sea basis. (This was before the airline frequent-flyer programs were established. Now, less than half of the business is sold this way as more folks take advantage of amassed frequent-flyer miles to obtain "free" air.) Before, agents had to sell the cruise in two pieces: the cruise itself and then the air add-on; now free air eliminated the second step, and ironically, agents preferred the more bundled, higher priced air/sea product.

Market-Specific Promotions

The mid-eighties saw a plethora of discount programs offered by various cruise lines, probably the most common of which was the market-specific promotion. If a cruise line needed a "push" for a few months to either top off a series of sailings or to prevent the total disaster of half-empty ships, it would select one or more cities for a city-specific air/sea deal. The cities were chosen not only on the basis of their ability to produce sales with a "deal" but also because there was a minimum amount of business already on the books from those cities for the sailings in question. The latter consideration ensured a minimum level of dilution—with hardly any business already booked, the market was virtually undisturbed. Little or no refunding or upgrading of existing business, group or individual, was needed. Nor were agents upset that their group promotions were undermined, because any group activity had already proved to be fruitless. If there was a large piece of group business on a specific, isolated date or two in the series, the cruise line would simply "black out" the dates from the promotional offer. This was a dangerous game, but if the line was careful it could be successful with a minimum of disruption. Occasionally, the group would want to move to one of the non-blacked out dates, and the cruise line took the dilution hit.

Because this promotion (a euphemism for discount scheme) was capacity-controlled, the offer could be withdrawn at any time. This is an important feature of any discount program, as it protects the line from "giving away the farm" if the price set for the deal proves to be too low, resulting in more demand at that price than the line is willing to provide in terms of berths. Also, because the program is limited to specific markets, there is simply no disruption in the unaffected markets. If the program got underway in, say, eight cities and that proved insufficient to fill the needed capacity, one or more additional cities could be added to secure the needed demand.

The scheme was not without a cost however: City-specific promotions required city-specific advertising messages, generally involving the Sunday travel sections of the local papers as well as occasional local spot television. Table 8.1 shows two newspaper ads whose sole purpose is to promote city-special discount programs. And don't forget that additional cities mean additional acquisition costs in incremental advertising. Timing, too, is always a consideration in such programs because they are typically developed four months out or six months at the latest

Table 8.1
Examples of Market-Specific Newspaper Ads

from the time of the sailings. Timing is crucial, as the early results of the promotion must be analyzed to determine what additional actions are necessary. Are more ads needed in the same cities? Are more cities needed? If so, which cities and how soon can the ads be placed and run? (For a national advertiser, it usually takes at least ten days between the time an ad is ordered and when the ad appears. When a vessel is 60 days away from being partially empty, 10 days seems like an eternity to a marketing executive!) Because of these factors, prudent planning suggests that a line have a contingency plan for their deals that is on the shelf and ready to be rolled out quickly if necessary.

Market-specific programs allow the line to test different levels of discounts and advertising messages for relative effectiveness. Because the program is market-specific, whatever is done in a given city is limited to it. It doesn't affect any other city-specific or national program that the line is offering. However, a disadvantage of the program is the possibility that it will disrupt the national advertising message of the line and undermine the prevailing national price structure. When a cruise line bombards Chicago, for example, with a great deal for certain sailings of certain ships in the fall, what message is it sending about:

1. Its other ships?
2. Its sailings during the rest of the year?
3. The validity of its normal (nondeal) price structure?

What is the long-term effect of ads in the *Chicago Tribune* for a $799 one week air/sea program—ads which may run for three months to the exclusion of any other advertising by the line—on the long-term pricing structure, which may call for a $1,099 lead price in the winter? Will consumers react and buy the $799 deal but will there be a backlash, when it comes time to promote the winter higher-priced product? We know intuitively that there will be. There is always a price to pay, in the long-term, for "quick-fix" discounting, and that's true in most marketing cases. Consumers get conditioned to buy at a "sale" price and reason that there will always be another sale—all they have to do is be patient until it comes along. In the group cruise business, as in the group hotel business, it's an issue of expediency: the soft-sailings of today versus the unknown demand of tomorrow.

One thing is certain: If the soft sailings of today aren't dealt with effectively, there may not be a tomorrow for the cruise-line marketing executive to worry about. In the cruise industry particularly, which is intolerant of the occupancy levels hotels accept, the needs of today, the next few weeks, or the next couple of months, always seem to take precedence over the unknown supply–demand equation of tomorrow, and at least up to now the industry has been consistently optimistic about its future. Like Scarlett O'Hara, they believe that tomorrow is another (and better) day!

Itinerary

Another important consideration in pricing is the itinerary and/or destination. Alaska marketing, for instance, had its own peculiar pricing history, very different from that of the Caribbean. Here the practice has been to present an early booking discount that expires on, say December 31. The intention is to create an up-front demand for this very limited (by both capacity and season) Alaskan product, which does about 18 1-week sailings a year. If the line is successful with its up-front pricing, it reverts to tariff. However, if the anticipated number of bookings needed to fill the ship by sailing time is inadequate, the early-booking deadline will be extended, usually with the cruise line's spokesperson citing "popular demand" and the line's "inability to handle the onslaught of bookings." Later, if the pace of bookings fall short of topping off the summer sailings, say in April-June, the lines would be extremely creative with all manner of last-minute discount programs—as they are highly motivated to fill this high-yield capacity.

One of the favorites of Alaskan cruise marketers is the special agency deal, special prices that only a limited number of high-producing agencies can obtain. Known for being aggressive promoters and marketers, these agencies are given these "last-minute" preferential deals in the hope that they will motivate the agencies to provide extra business by either generating new customers or luring some away from another cruise line. (The line offering the deal isn't too choosy as to where the business comes from, as long as it materializes.) The smart operators keep track of the incremental business that individual agencies develop to determine whether it makes sense to continue to extend them the preferential deal in subsequent years. As lines know from sad experience, there's no necessary correlation between the promises of smooth-talking, charismatic travel agents and sales results. By their very nature, preferential pricing deals work most effectively when they are kept quiet in the marketplace, not unlike private sales by a clothing retailer. Some agents seem to get more enjoyment out of telling the other agencies about their special deal than expending the effort necessary to produce the business.

Juggling Fares

Most of these discounting schemes essentially reward prospective cruisers who want to make their cruise purchases close in to the time of sailing. As cruise lines judge what market stimulation (discounting) is needed by the pace of bookings (how a particular ship and sailing date is filling in comparison with how it has booked in the past for that particular time of year), any delay in booking patterns makes this decision process problematic. (When you see enough of them you notice that most cruise marketing and sales executives have gray or white hair.) First of all, the shift in bookings throws off the validity of the previous history—in effect, a new pace has developed with no comparable data to triangulate it with. Secondly, the new close-in booking pattern gives the line far less time to take corrective action to stimulate demand. When in doubt, the lines stimulate demand on a close-in basis thus perpetuating the problem by rewarding purchasers who delayed their purchase decisions with lower-priced cruises. At the same time, group business suffers because these last-minute discount deals tend to undermine the once-favorable group rates that the agent may have obtained perhaps a year prior to the sailing. If they were promotional in nature, groups tend to fall apart, costing the agent time and money. Frustrated, the agent is leery of booking future group business.

This system was not working and something had to be done. In 1992, it was. That year Royal Caribbean successfully introduced a fleet-wide, year-round advance-purchase program called, aptly, Breakthrough Rates, which was quickly matched in one form or another by the other large cruise lines. Only Celebrity held out, publicly opposing these programs for two years. Al Wallach, Senior Vice President of Marketing, claimed in the trade press that it was presumptuous of cruise lines "to dictate to consumers when they had to purchase." Finally, with little fanfare, Celebrity succumbed to the industry trend and trotted out an advance-purchase program of its own, rewarding those who purchased well in advance of the sailings with the best rates.

Breakthrough pricing and its imitators start out with their lowest rates and then, based on how the sailing is filling, the rates are raised in discrete intervals. The discount is thus lowered until on occasion, tariff is reached! In a sort of reverse strip-tease, the dancer starts off scantily clad and, as the performance goes on dresses until she is, hopefully, fully clothed.

This kind of pricing makes eminent sense. It rewards those who have tied up their money the longest. It lengthens the booking pattern because it places the biggest discount in the hands of those who book earliest. And, in general, it restores a measure of much-needed price stability into the market, which is critically important for market growth.

Pricing a discount is certainly an art. The cruise line has to anticipate the response from the marketplace—a function of a varying price elasticity of demand. Some lower price point will produce the required increase in consumer demand necessary to fill that portion of the unsold capacity the line is willing to give away at that price. Too small a discount (too high a price) and there will be insufficient demand. Too deep a discount (too low a price) and the unsold capacity quickly sells although it could have been sold at a higher price, and revenue is permanently lost to the line.

Is It Time to Reposition Tariffs?

In the past few years, when demand did not react as anticipated, a number of cruise lines advertised two-for-one rates (see Table 8.2), which meant that one person could cruise for free if the second person in the stateroom paid the tariff price. Airlines do the same thing (they did it first). While these promotions are effective—they catch the eye and make the phone ring—they also suggest to consumers that brochure tariffs are probably too high. Undoubtedly, the lines maneuvered themselves into this position through a combination of optimism, survival, and ego: optimism, that the next year will always be better and therefore the brochure tariff will (finally) become realistic; survival, in which executives justify their existence (and next year's expense budget) on the revenue budget propped up an increase in tariff and net yields; ego, the most subtle yet most powerful influence of the three. What cruise line wants to reduce its brochure tariff and thus send a signal to the marketplace that the line is somehow "less" in quality or stature than before, or, perhaps more important, that by re-pricing downward it has reduced its ranking and positioning when compared to its competitors? (Never mind that the product was egregiously overpriced on its face and only sold because of an arsenal of discounting weapons.)

Proponents of the status quo argue that the consuming public truly loves a great deal—no one wants to pay "sticker price"

Table 8.2
Examples of Two-for-One Newspaper Ads

for anything. People want to save money, and the more they can save, the more willing they are to buy. High brochure pricing provides the platform or base from which to deeply discount the product. If you move to lower, more reasonable pricing, discount levels are reduced and the deal won't seem as attractive. Without an attractive deal, demand will lessen and lines will be forced to lower prices—that is, deepen the discounts. Deeper discounts from lower brochure pricing, they argue, means lower yields for the line, so let's maintain and even increase brochure pricing!

Yes

The other side of the coin says that high brochure prices will frighten would-be cruise purchasers when there is no reference to real prices. Remember, a cruise vacation's all-inclusiveness already "forces" even realistic pricing to appear too high when compared with unbundled land vacations. We think the issue is not how much a person saves, but how much she pays for the product she ultimately buys. If a prospective vacationer takes three brochures, a cruise with ridiculously high pricing and two realistically priced resort or sightseeing vacations, which will appear to provide the best value? Which will seem unreasonable in comparison?

At least two cruise lines, Royal Cruise Lines and Holland America, had addressed the problem in a somewhat Solomon-like approach. Their brochures feature discounted rates in a column right next to the brochure tariff. Prospects can understand what they are paying (the discounted rate) without the products appearing too cheap relative to competing lines (as their high tariffs are consistent with those of direct competitors).

The downside to this strategy is that it carves the deepest discounting stone. What if a line overestimates future demand and prices the discounted rate too high? Trapped with the published discount, it has no choice but to obviate the brochure deal and peg a lower price, and this is easier said then done. What do they do with those expensive brochures? Scrap them? If the line has a second, lower tier of discounts, it won't achieve its goal of realistic published rates but only its published discounted rate. But, if it underestimates demand with this device, at least it has an escape through capacity control of the discount. This indicates the perishability of this discount in the brochure and suggests that the cruise price will move by discrete but unspecified iterations all the way to tariff if demand warrants.

It will be interesting to watch the evolution of published discount pricing: Our guess is that it's offering a bandaid to a cancer patient. One thing is clear: the industry desperately needs to portray its value advantage over land vacations more effectively than it has done before now.

Groups

Groups are an important component of cruise sales, probably accounting for about a quarter or more of the total sales. Group business can be affinity groups like Kiwanis organizations, garden clubs, family reunions, or alumni groups, or it can be open promotions wherein agents block group space with a cruise line to secure a favorable rate and concessions, and then promote the group to their client base and/or the general public through advertising and public relations. Either way, the agency books the space to ensure, as much as is practical, that the inventory will be available to sell when it promotes the group.

Concessions

Availability is the most important aspect of group development, but group pricing and concessions are also important. Agents need an attractive "deal" to provide prospects with an incentive to get on a specific ship on a certain date. Locking in the lowest rates gives the agency confidence and enthusiasm in its group promotion. The concessions are equally important because they can help lower the price of the group cruise and thus make it a more attractive package.

The Pied Piper
The biggest concession, typically, is a complimentary berth for a tour conductor, or "Pied Piper" as he or she is known in the trade, who is often the person organizing the tour. (Your priest is organizing a trip to the Holy Land and you decide to go along with him—he's the Pied Piper.)

For years the industry standard was one free berth for every 15 bases paying passengers. In other words, the 16th person was free, equivalent to a reduction of 6.25 percent of the overall price of the group if the tour conductor was prorated against the basis two guests. Instead of giving it away, some agents split the revenue from the earned tour conductors' space—giving some away to true group leaders and prorating the rest to further reduce everyone's cost. Today, though, some cruise lines are *very* creative, offering tour conductors (or TCs as they are called) for as low as one free for six!

Other Concessions

Other concessions may include free or reduced-rate cocktail parties on board ship for the group to socialize privately, shore excursions, on-board credits, donations to charity, and advertising dollars to promote the sailing—just about anything you can imagine. Group travel is an important segment of the overall vacation travel industry, so it's vital that the cruise industry be fully competitive with its land-based vacation competitors.

While we believe that group cruising is a superior value, it does suffer from the same pricing handicaps that individual cruise products do: the perception of a high price because of cruising's all-inclusive nature; and inflated brochure pricing—a practice not generally found in the pricing of land-based vacation products which are realistically priced with rare discounting; and price instability—resulting from cruising's unique determination to fill every berth. In the fall of 1994, for example, the cruise industry generally overestimated demand and inadvertently, but frequently, undercut the group rates that had been promoted for the period. Our guess is it will take some time—two to three years—for many of those group promoting agencies to rebuild their confidence in group-cruise pricing. The smart lines realize this and have developed pricing policies that should ensure that the situation won't recur.

In any event, tour operators and resorts offer their products with virtually no price instability. So it behooves cruise companies to stabilize group pricing quickly. Imagine what would happen if consumers truly understood the inherent value of cruising as we have explained it in this book? Demand would exceed capacity, not the reverse, and price stability wouldn't be an issue!

Charters

A special form of group pricing is a charter hire, in which the group or organization has exclusive use of the vessel for a contracted period of time. This exclusivity can provide a huge range of features unique to the chartered cruise experience. A charter could take a ship out of normal sequence or pattern and create one or more unique itineraries, provided that at the termination of the charter the ship is in the right place on the right day to return to its normal, advertised schedule. Occasionally, the charter may take the ship and reposition it in another trading area, moving a Miami-based ship to New York for three weeks, for example. The charterer is expected to pay for the unsold positioning days when the ship deadheads (sails without passengers) between Miami and New York at either end of the charter. If the ship is returned a day before its normal cruising recommences, the charterer is expected to pay for the unused day.

That "Charter" Feeling

Having a ship exclusively for the use of one organization creates a special feeling of camaraderie on board. It's the ultimate private party. All passengers have something in common, there are no strangers, and everyone feel very special, and "on the inside." As with any large group event, its common to celebrate such a happening with T-shirts or other items. Back home, these commemorative articles seem to have a special cachet: This was a one-of-a-kind experience!

Religious groups and fraternal organizations are obvious choices for charters. Not so obvious are collectors, Super Bowl attendees, Trekkies, and cruise 2000 participants—all drawn by a strong common interest or hobby. In these cases, the charterer promotes the cruise in the special-interest magazines and newsletters of the group, trusting that the appeal of being with like-minded folks, interacting, and celebrating their hobby or special interest will be a powerful enough draw to be successful. And many charters are—hugely so! We predict that people's growing thirst for affinity (which is less often quenched these days through the nuclear family and the community) will make special-interest groups and charter cruising a larger component of cruise's business mix in the years to come.

Sometimes charters don't hire the whole ship, merely half of it. For example, Budweiser took over the entire second seating of a ship, which allowed them to have speeches and themed parties in the dining room as well as a special second-seating show with their own entertainment. To compensate the other passengers, who were all assigned to the first seating and the early show, Budweiser offered free beer to everyone on the ship for the entire cruise!

Charter Pricing

As a point of consumer protection, all charters must be legally contracted and then filed with the Federal Maritime Commission (FMC). Some unscrupulous promoters advertise and sell charters that they booked on a speculative basis, hoping to fill a ship. Of course, if they fail to hit the numbers, no one goes and the deposits of everyone are at risk. Sometimes all of it is lost—the promoter claims that the money was used up in administrative and promotional costs. While it's a federal offense to promote charters that haven't been contracted, occasionally an agent or travel broker has a large group that could perhaps be sufficient to fill a ship if the response to the offer is strong. Some cruise lines will provide a partial charter for the initial size the agent is able to financially secure, with an option to secure the balance of the space within a stipulated time. Even here, though, the promoter can't advertise or imply exclusivity on the ship until the full charter agreement is signed and secured.

From the cruise line's prospective, the charter hire (price) should reflect, at a minimum, the net yield of what the vessel would realize for that sailing date, under its normal operation, plus pricing to recover any incremental cost of lost on-board revenue for the period. Chartering to a group of 2,000 teetotaling, nongambling, Polynesian frog worshipers can truly put a cramp in on-board revenue, so this needs to be anticipated and offset by a higher charter price. Some lines go after charters aggressively— with a very sharp pencil—because they like the compression a charter creates. They reason that the charter business is virtually incremental, forcing their normal demand for the sailing to compress, in other words, shift, into other dates or other ships of the line's fleet. This fill-up of demand will result in higher rates for those sailings. As a result, those higher rates can theoretically justify a lower price for the charter hire itself.

Normally, there is no incremental acquisition cost (advertising and sales efforts) for charters—a fact also used by some lines to justify lower prices. Frequently, two or more cruise lines with competitive ships on competitive routes will compete for the same charter. It's not uncommon for a smart charterer to play one against the other.

Seller's Remorse
In the quest to be successful, lines can bid too low and end up with a case of seller's remorse. What's fascinating about this is that the demand compression caused by the charter also affects the direct competitors. If three lines, for example, offer 1-week cruises out of San Juan on virtually identical itineraries, and they are competing on a charter bid, sometimes the two lines that don't win will make more money than the "lucky winner." Because of their greater availability of space in that same time period, they can capture more of the compression of normal individual and group demand, at higher yields, than the winning line—a result of the fact that some travel agents as well as some of their clients view these lines, rightly or wrongly, as interchangeable. Sadly, some travel agents feel it's more appropriate to first offer their clients another line's product on the same date, rather than the product of the one they originally selected on a different date on the same weekend but on a different ship. This is obviously a result of the commoditization of the travel industry we spoke of in Chapter 4, as well as the agent's unfounded unwillingness to suggest an alternative date to the client.

Yield Management

Yield management, a business tool that emerged in the late 1980s in the airline industry, has appropriate applications in the cruise industry. The focus is on yield rather than revenue because it gives management a much clearer picture of the profit impact of pricing decisions. For example, the revenue of an air/sea booking, for comparable accommodations, will always be greater than a cruise-only booking. Yet, if the related cost of the airfare, transfers, and hotel (if occasioned by the flight connections) is greater than the revenue increment, less the commission paid on the additional revenue, the yield on the cruise-only booking is higher than the air/sea booking. Table 8.3 gives an example.

Clearly, if we want to maximize revenue, we will encourage sales from Seattle. If we want to maximize yield, we will discourage sales from Seattle—either by increasing the air add-on or, if free-air, raising the category available for sales to Seattle-area residents. By raising the minimum category available from category 4 to category 7, the price increases by $120. After a 10-percent commission, the yield improves to $908—comparable to the other product prices in the table.

Note that we have used a 10-percent commission structure for ease of example. The proper way to calculate the yield is to use the weighted average air/sea and cruise only commission costs that the line is experiencing. While individual lines differ, on average, the industry-wide commission is estimated at 14.5 percent in 1995.

The Goal
The goal of yield management is to maximize the obtainable yield on a given sailing, recognizing that the sailing is on the market for perhaps a year and that demand for that particular

Table 8.3
7-day New York Cruise Booking
(Inside Accommodations)

| | Air/Sea | | |
Gateway	*Chicago*	*Seattle*	*Cruise Only*
Revenue	$1295	$1395	$995
Less commission	130	140	100
	$1165	$1255	$895
Less airfare/transfers	260	455	0
Net yields	$905	$800	$895

date and vessel will ebb and flow over this purchase period. At time of sailing, the objective is to carry the most passengers at the highest *average* yield. "Average" is the key term here, because just one price for the product will not accomplish the goal under most circumstances; a mix of prices, and resultant yields, will result in an average yield. Every sailing has a booking pattern or pace that can be accelerated or slowed by price manipulation. The current booking pattern for, say, a New York–Bermuda 7-day cruise for the last Saturday in August is compared with the booking pattern for the same ship in previous years as well as for sailings of that ship around the sailing date. If the present pace is behind prior years, prices can be reduced to stimulate demand; if the pace is brisker, prices can be raised to maximize yield. Over a one-year period, pricing may be manipulated daily, hourly, or weekly as needed. Sophisticated automation quickly compares booking patterns and recent trends and responses so that management can decide if further action is needed.

In Table 8.4 notice the shaded area. It represents an expected range of weekly booking activity that either historically filled the ship (if the ship operated previously on that itinerary and season) or is expected to fill the ship based on extrapolation of reasonably analogous data. The arrows point to cumulative booking patterns outside the desired range. When the arrows point up it indicates that demand is insufficient to fill the ship in the remaining selling time. Consequently, pricing mechanisms need to be eased (lowered) to stimulate demand. If pricing is lowered too much, demand exceeds the pace range (the downward arrow), suggesting that the line is selling at too quick a pace, leaving money on the table that it hopes to recoup by tightening the pricing mechanisms, selling the remaining inventory at a slower pace but with higher yields.

Adjusting Pricing Mechanisms Can Take Several Forms:

Mild

Taking guarantees allows the line to ease pricing by selling unspecified higher-cost inventory if available at lower prices.

Giving upgrades specifies a level of higher-priced inventory that will be sold at a lower price. For example, selling a category 6 stateroom at a category 4 rate (a two-category upgrade).

Table 8.4
Yield Management Demand Range

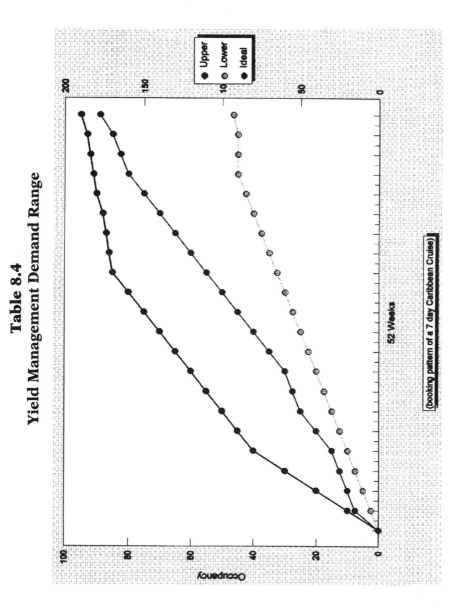

(booking pattern of a 7 day Caribbean Cruise)

Adjusting the minimum rate applies to air/sea bookings where the minimum stateroom rate available is a function of the cost of the round-trip's air component. The "normal" minimum category might be category 6 for the Seattle market traveling to San Juan. If required, the category can be lowered to 5 or 4 to stimulate demand from that market (with many lines offering 100 air/sea cities or more, obviously a varying number of cities can be adjusted.)

Moderate

Adjusting the level of the advance purchase discount rate. All advance purchase programs have "stair-step" price increments built in, which allow the line to reduce the discount (raise the rate—improve the yield) as demand warrants. In theory, once a new discount level is established, the line is not supposed to lower it again. Under most circumstances, this is the case, but occasionally, as in the fall of 1994, lines misguessed demand and the rates were adjusted down again (this is considered severe)—causing a certain amount of disruption among agents and clients who booked earlier at a now higher rate. These passengers need to be protected at the new, lower rate or be upgraded to better accommodations. In any event, once the new discount level is established, changing the pricing structure, all the "mild" price manipulations can be applied to the new base.

Market-specific deals. Discussed earlier, these programs, while severely discounting price in specific, local markets, don't have much effect on the overall market.

Severe

Best available stateroom. This is a first-come, first-serve program based on one flat attractive price. The problem is that the best staterooms sell first, giving the biggest savings to those who act quickly. However, the line has to set the price low enough that the lesser accommodations also appear attractively priced or the ship won't fill. This type of program is usually a desperation, close-in move as it tends to reduce yield (on the better inventory) too drastically. A variation, without this difficulty, is a two-rate (inside, ocean-view) best available program. On the other hand, the two-rate version has significantly less "sex appeal" in the newspaper!

Two-for-one. This is a sure way to stimulate demand but the line has to content itself with no more than 50 percent of brochure tariff. It can be even worse, as all mild manipulations can be applied with this program if the sailing is a dog!

Lowering or eliminating air add-ons. Some advance purchase programs, like RCCL's Breakthrough rates and NCL's Leadership fares, separately price the air component based on specific markets or regular zones. Reducing or eliminating the air add-ons, which are a significant component of the initial (and, in theory, the lowest) price is a pretty severe action when done nationally, but moderate when done in local markets, regionally, or for specific groups, such as senior citizens.

Stand-by fares. These are deeply discounted cruise-only rates that are typically available within thirty days of departure. They tend to be promoted in the local drive market, perhaps within 300 miles from the port of embarkation.

As you can see, the industry has numerous pricing mechanisms to stimulate or retard demand as necessary to fill its ships. To maximize yields, some lines like Royal Caribbean and Carnival approach yield management with highly sophisticated computer programs that monitor booking activity similar to those used by airlines; other lines manually gather relevant data. Either way, the success of yield management is in the decision process—how to interpret the data in today's market conditions and how much of which price mechanisms to manipulate. High-volume cruise lines may need to review data hourly; low-volume lines, with lower booking activities, are significantly less volatile.

Whether demand is strong or weak, each decision to change a price, and the amplitude of the change, is critical to maximizing yield. As an extreme example, a few years ago one line faced a critical lack of demand in the spring for its upcoming fall season. The line selected a rate scale it thought would fill its ship and offered it to travel agents for both groups and individuals. The ship was sold out by early summer; however the groups materialized faster and in far higher numbers than anticipated (because of the low rate) and by early fall the ship was actually well oversold. Obviously yield was not maximized, costing the line many hundreds of thousands of dollars in profit. A few senior managers left that company that fall to pursue other interests!

On-Board Revenue

On-board revenue is a key to profitable operation of a ship and is thus a key to the jobs of the hotel manager, the food and beverage director, the casino manager, and the cruise director. Look at it this way. If the marketing people have done their job, the ship is going to sail full. Everyone has already prepaid for their ticket, and the only variable left that will determine the overall revenue (and ultimately the overall profitability) of a voyage is how much is spent on board. A number of factors determine how much money people will spend on board a ship, and successful operators understand that these are all critical if they are to succeed in maximizing on board profit. Believe it or not, one of the most important of these is the design of the ship. The single largest source of revenue on board most ships (especially in the Caribbean) is the sale of beverages. For some reason, drinking and vacationing go together in the minds of many people, or at least those who enjoy cruising! Whether it's a Piña Colada by the pool, a Rum Punch in the disco, cokes in the teen club, brandy in the show lounge, champagne at the caviar bar, or wine at dinner, money is spent on beverages every day by virtually every passenger. And because beverages are purchased duty free by the lines (and often in the country of origin, thus saving transportation charges as well), the sale of beverages can be much more profitable than it is for hotels or restaurants ashore. Therefore, one key to making money and satisfying guest needs on a cruise is simply to have a lot of beverages available in a lot of places and at all times. A second key is to make certain that those places are not simply accessible but very attractive and highly visible.

This is where ship design enters the picture. Good ship designs incorporate a lot of bars and serving stations. The idea is that you should be able to get a drink wherever and whenever you want it. Equally important, designers recognize that since the sale of drinks is as often an impulse buy as it is a planned purchase, bars need to be situated in high-traffic areas. In a well-executed ship design, the most convenient way to go from your cabin to the dining room should take you past a lounge of some sort, where you can stop for a cocktail before dinner or a drink afterwards. And because most ships sail in warm waters, you also need a highly visible bar by the pool—or even in it! In fact, one can argue that there should be a bar everywhere! Some lines even station waiters near the library in case people want a drink while browsing.

The key, of course, is to not make people feel that they are expected to buy a drink. We have heard passengers complain that on some ships you can't sit down anywhere "without someone trying to sell you a drink." We've also heard complaints that "there's no place around to get a drink." Remember, one of the main attractions of a cruise is that it is supposed to be inclusive (and it is, when you consider the main components of transportation, lodging, and food), and some passengers can get turned off very quickly if they feel that an effort is being made to pry open their wallets or purses while on board. But the truth is that selling goes on all of the time all over the ship, as we will see, and it makes all the difference in the world when it comes to the bottom line.

In addition to beverages being readily available, it is equally important that there be an opportunity to consume them. It seems obvious enough, but in fact providing this on a cruise, where every hour is chock-full of opportunities to do things is somewhat of an art. The artist in this case is the hotel manager, who, as we said, "orchestrates the vacation experience."

Take a Royal Caribbean 3-day cruise on the *Nordic Empress* from Miami to Nassau. Passengers for this cruise board the ship between 1 P.M. and 3:30, and sailing is at 4. They have arrived from all over the country. Some have traveled less than an hour from their Florida homes, while others have been traveling all day from California or even Europe and South America. As soon as they have unpacked, they begin exploring this magnificent ship. Some are hungry and want to have lunch, others immediately change into their swim suits and start on their long-awaited tan. It doesn't matter. The Pool Bar opens at noon and shuts at 7 P.M. The High Society Lounge opens at 2:30 P.M. (an hour and a half before sailing) and remains open until 1:30 A.M.—a full hour after the last show presented that evening. The Strike Up The Band Lounge is open from 3 to 4:30 and has a "Welcome Aboard" presentation by the Cruise Director, and again from 5:30 to midnight for casual drinks before and after dinner and shows. Then there's the Carousel Pub which opens at 11:30 A.M. when the first passengers are allowed on board on the day of departure and stays open until 2 A.M., which is late enough for most passengers but not everyone. The Casino is open from 6 p.m. to 3 A.M., and although drinks are available at the Casino Royale Bar during gaming hours, the place for winners to celebrate and losers to commiserate is Royal Caribbean's trademark Viking Crown Lounge, which opens for the first time at 5:15 P.M. and stays open until 7 P.M. (for a before-dinner rendezvous) and re-opens from 10 P.M. to 11 P.M. for a Teen Club gathering and then stays open for adults until 3 A.M. The only time there are no bars open that first day is between 4:30 and 5:15, when everyone is required to attend a lifeboat drill. As you might expect, there is a daily drink special—on this opening day it's a "Paradise Cocktail"—a mixture of gin and apricot liqueur with orange and lime juice. In a souvenir glass one of these concoctions can cost $5 or more.

Look Ma—That's Us!

The bars are the biggest source of on-board revenue in many cases but they are hardly the only one. When you board just about any cruise, the ship's photographer is at the gangplank to photograph the start of your vacation. He or she will take a picture of you at least two or three more times before you leave the ship. Everyone gets their picture taken shaking hands with the Captain at his reception, when they're dressed to the hilt and thus look their best (often in a rented tuxedo, which is another source of on-board revenue). Then there's the picture of all the passengers at every table. Coming down the gangplank is another photo opportunity—next to a prop such as a sign saying where you are ("Look, mom. This is us getting off the ship at Cozumel!"). When you buy the pictures in a gallery, which is usually posted in another high-traffic area (outside the dining room where people line up before dinner is one popular venue), you'll pay somewhere between $6 and $12 depending on the size and the number of photos you purchase. Assume a ship carrying 2,000 passengers sells only 2,000 photos—one per person per trip. Using the $6 minimum figure, you can see that the revenue from those photos will be $12,000. If the ship is in service 50 weeks of the year doing two cruises a week (a 3- and a 4-day,) that's $1,200,000 in photos alone. On 7-day cruises of course it's likely passengers will buy more than one photo. And these photos cost only a few cents to take and develop using the automatic film-processing equipment on board. Many ships now also sell a video of your cruise vacation. If you sign up for one, they're able to ensure that you will be a featured player. Videos are a popular item, priced around $30 on most ships.

The Casino

It's a myth that the casino is the biggest money maker on the ship. As we pointed out, on most ships the beverages do better. Typically only about 30 percent of the passengers gamble while the rest watch. In truth most people do not take a cruise to gamble. The casino is not open 24 hours a day or at all when the ship is in port, so gambling opportunities are limited. Rather, gambling is regarded as yet another diversion the ship offers along with shopping, partying, eating, sightseeing, and a host of other activities. For the most part, those who do gamble spend around $10 a day, though a few cruise lines are now developing "high roller" programs to attract some of the big spenders (more about that later). From an operator's point of view, running a casino aboard a cruise line presents some different problems from those on land. For instance, on land if someone is suspected of cheating they are simply asked to leave. But on a cruise ship the suspect is a paying guest and needs to be handled differently. Because gaming is a first-time experience for many cruisers and some genuinely don't understand the rules, cruise ships tend to be more flexible than land-based operations, where everything is black or white. If a passenger loses $5 because they didn't understand how to bet, some cruise dealers are more apt to return it to them than they would be on land. Shipboard dealers, incidentally, usually gain their experience on shore and are rarely trained on board. The pay is in the neighborhood of $1800 monthly plus room and board, and they receive around six weeks off every year.

For those who are put off by slot machines and blackjack, there are other gaming opportunities if they just want the thrill of betting. Carnival runs bingo games with minimum jackpots of $600 and $700 on its 3-day cruises to Nassau, horse racing, a daily lottery where participants can win as much as $50,000, and a Scratch-and-Match game where winning tickets are worth up to $1,000.

Shopping

Shopping is another important source of on-board revenue. Studies show that many people rank the quality of their vacation experience by the number and variety of shopping opportunities. The cruise lines have responded accordingly. Shops are not open in port because local governments insist visitors patronize local shops. It's not difficult to understand why. One study of cruise passengers made by Bermuda showed that the average cruise passenger spent $90 while on shore. At sea, shops are big business and their prices on items like liquor and perfume are competitive to those of the merchants of the ports that they visit. They even have special sales on the last day of the cruise. The cruise lines have learned, incidentally, how not to give up all of the revenue their passengers spend in port. Most lines allow merchants to promote their shops on board the ship, usually in the cruise director's "port orientation" talk, which describes the various tours that are available, where to eat and shop, and suggested good buys. Some lines show samples of participating shops' merchandise or stage a fashion show. Others include advertisers in a "shopping video tour" shown before the ship reaches port.

Where shops are promoted by the ships, a customer satisfaction guarantee by the line usually accompanies the merchandise. In any case, the cruise line charges a fee to the shops who choose to participate in these promotions. A note of caution to cruisers: In many ports, stores not part of the ship's official program promote themselves by handing out flyers on the pier, often featuring "lucky cabin number" gifts. Supposedly, passengers who occupy certain cabins and show up at these shops receive special prizes. Unfortunately, these schemes are not always legitimate— unscrupulous merchants in some ports post numbers of cabins that don't exist or that they know to be unoccupied.

Mud Baths, Anyone?

Another popular source of revenue is the beauty salon and spa, where passengers can get massages, mud baths, facials, hair styling, and more. A vacation is a renewal experience, and what better way to renew yourself than to change your hair style, have a facial and perhaps a massage or herbal wrap? As with land-based spas and resorts, you can easily spend $125 in a half a day at sea in a modern spa, and the available time and convenience makes it an almost irresistible buy for many. Often the massage appointments for a 7-day cruise are fully subscribed by the second day out!

Shore excursions are one of the most popular parts of any cruise and can be extremely profitable to the line. Why? Because the revenue produced by the shore excursions on some lines frequently exceeds the bar revenue, and the profits on these items are enhanced because in Alaska both Holland America and Princess own some of the tour infrastructure (such as buses, rail cars, and day boats).

Places to Go, People to See

Not unreasonably, people are often fearful of exploring a new place on their own—especially if they do not speak the language. The success of shore excursions, however, has everything to do with the ports of call and the tours that local operators have been able to develop. In some ports, like St. Thomas, sightseeing is not very popular. The preferred thing is to take a taxi into town and shop. Nevertheless, there are dozens of boats that can take you to a private beach for the day, snorkel trips, and even a submarine ride.

Other small island destinations might not appear to have a lot to see or do, but have been able to develop a number of shore excursions that sell very well. Nassau, for instance, has at least 14 that we know of, including a 2-hour bus sightseeing trip ($17), a glass-bottom boat ($16), Coral World Underwater Observatory ($20), Paradise Island and Crystal Palace Casino Shows ($34), and a scuba trip for certified divers ($60).

Alaska is primarily a sightseeing destination for observing wildlife and nature's last frontier. These sights cannot be easily sampled simply by strolling around Skagway or Juneau. In Juneau, Princess, which calls its shore excursions "Adventures Ashore" offers a 3-hour raft trip down the Mendenhall River (including some mild rapids and a stop for a salmon snack) for $94 ($62 for children 6 to 12), a 3-hour tour including a 50-minute floatplane ride to Taku Glacier Lodge, where passengers are offered a traditional alderwood-fire salmon bake including all the wine and beer you can drink for $185, a 2-hour helicopter glacier tour for $151, and a 5-hour sport fishing expedition for king salmon for $150. There are also nature walks ($54), a Yukon dance hall revue ($17), and a chance to pan for gold ($33). In Ketchikan, you can go mountain lake canoeing ($77, $52 for children), and in Skagway there's a 3-hour ride aboard the historic White Pass Scenic Railway ($82, $41 for children).

Tour Operators

In just about all cases, tours are run by local operators, not by the ships. In many ports one or two operators have a monopoly so that passengers get exactly the same tour no matter whose ship they arrive on. Some lines do what they can to customize their tours. Seabourn, for instance, never fills it buses more than half full, so everyone gets a window seat, sends a staff member in every bus with a cooler of complimentary drinks, and includes a complimentary refreshment stop as well where feasible. However, many of these local operators have virtual monopolies. Some of their guides speak little or poor English, others are non-communicative, and many insist on stopping for half an hour at bogus "factory outlets" where they pocket commissions on everything sold. The cruise lines can have a difficult time controlling this unless they're willing to pay extra, and complaints of unsatisfactory tours are not uncommon. Jamaica, Italy, and China are notorious for these practices, but they can be found almost everywhere. Local governments can do a good deal through regulation to control these abuses. To their credit, some destinations such as Bermuda, where the Department of Tourism has extraordinary power, have been able to do just that.

Art Auctions

One surprising source of revenue that has become popular recently is art auctions. The idea of buying Picasso lithographs, Norman Rockwell prints, or original pieces by unknown artists appeals to people, so art auctions, actually a form of entertainment with a fair degree of excitement, do very well. One vessel on a major contemporary line we know of sold, $62,000 worth of art on a single 7-day Caribbean cruise!

ET . . . Phone Home

Of course, many people can't tear themselves completely away from home, and they need to call the kids (if they didn't bring them along) or the office to see if they still have a job. There's money to be made in that, too. In the old days you had to go to the radio room to place or receive a call. Now you can call home instantly from the phone in your stateroom via satellite. The cost for this service can run as high as $15 a minute!

We called this chapter "Pieces of Eight"—the traditional term for gold doubloons that the Spanish treasure ships carried from the New World back to Spain. Today's modern cruise line acquires "pieces of eight" in more ways than most cruisers probably realize, as we hope we've illustrated in this chapter.

Different cruise lines have differing approaches to pricing, yield management, and on board revenue opportunities. Successful lines can add 10 to 20 percent or more to the bottom line with their on-board and shore activities. Yet, today, most lines are operating at a loss. Why the huge gap in performance? You may draw your own conclusions. Ours? It's management, no more, no less.

9

Booking Passage
A fresh look at today's travel agent

Of all forms of travel and tourism sold within the United States and Canada, cruising relies most heavily on the travel agency as its distribution channel. Table 9.1 shows the percentage of sales through travel agents for a variety of travel components.

Table 9.1
U.S./Canadian Reliance on Travel Agencies

Travel Component	% Units Sold by Travel Agents
Cruising	95-98
Domestic air	82
International air	90
Amtrak	40
Tours	50-60
Hotels	12
Rental cars	55-60
Attractions	*

*less than 1%

Early Practice

Cruising's heavy reliance on travel agents stems from its historical roots in transportation. Steamship passage was highly regulated by the steamship lines themselves through organizations such as the International Passenger Steamship Association (IPSA) and the Pacific Cruise Conference (PCC). Under the auspices of the Federal Maritime Commission, these organizations set tariff rates for passengers, set commission rates for travel agents, and, significantly, appointed travel agencies. Without these appointments, a given travel agency could not book a cruise and earn a commission. These organizations disappeared in the late seventies as the steamship business completed its transformation from transportation to cruising. Their descendent, the Cruise Lines International Association, is principally an industry marketing organization, not a regulating body.

Bypassing the Agent

In these early times, the cruise industry generated a small amount of direct business, but usually surreptitiously as agents became irate if they felt that cruise lines were bypassing them and dealing directly with consumers, who were felt to be the agents' clients. Probably the biggest bypass program occurred in the sixties and early seventies within the short cruise market in South Florida. Back then the superintendents of service of the large resort hotels could be effectively "influenced" to steer guests to 2-, 3-, and 4-night cruises as either a divertissement from a 1-month or longer hotel stay (common in those days) or as a quick getaway if the weather was cold or rainy. However, as the number of travel agencies grew dramatically and at the same time the heyday of the Miami Beach resort hotel was fading, this practice quietly disappeared.

All the while the strong fear of agency backlash caused by bypass activities was exhibiting a strong, almost negative influence on cruise operators. After all, the prominent South Florida travel agents had their roots in the New York City area (like their clients—the predominant visitor of the time was from Greater New York), and like their New York brothers and sisters, they were the most vocal and aggressive in the country. They were active in ASTA, the American Society of Travel Agents, then and now the dominant agency organization in the industry, and had ready access to the trade press. It was not uncommon to see an article in *Travel Weekly* or *Travel Agent* featuring agents berating a particular cruise line for selling a ticket directly and thus bypassing them. These articles invariably produced stammering apologies from a mortified, sweaty-palms cruise line executive and would strike fear in the hearts of industry executives everywhere. "There, but for the grace of God, go I," was their universal reaction.

As a result, cruise lines were determined to work with travel agents and entered into a unique marriage that's lasted until today. For most of that period, of course, supply and demand have been more or less in synch, and both industries have enjoyed unrivaled growth. Until now it was both inappropriate and unwise to express any dissatisfaction with the travel agent distribution system!

The Renaissance Example

Nevertheless, the ominous signs of discontent began to show in 1995. In March of that year at a Seatrade conference in Miami, the executives of three prominent cruise lines suggested that if the present distribution system—travel agents—couldn't get the job done (presumably by filling their ships) their lines would look to alternatives. And undoubtedly some lines will look elsewhere—some already have.

Ed Rudner, the President of Renaissance Cruise Lines, which does a significant amount of its business directly with the consumer, prefers direct consumer contact because of the knowledge and ability of his reservations personnel. Renaissance operates a fleet of eight 100-passenger vessels deployed all over the world with very flexible itineraries. Few travel agents are prepared to deal with the intricate questions a Renaissance customer is likely to ask. In Rudner's view, the average agent simply doesn't possess the geographical or product knowledge to sell his product effectively. In fact, when travel agents do get involved, Renaissance sales personnel frequently must "undo" the damage of inaccurate or misleading information that well-meaning but ill-informed agents had passed on to the customer. A good argument can be made that in these unique situations direct sales are simply less costly and more efficient.

Direct Business

Renaissance is still the exception, however. The agent distribution channel is still the rule for high-volume, nationally marketed cruise lines, despite the fact that they have numerous opportunities for direct consumer contact, particularly through direct mail to past passengers. When a booking is made through a travel agent, the line only deals with the agent, rarely the customer. In fact, it has no way of contacting the customer as his or her address and phone number are known only to the agent. It's only after boarding the vessel that this information is recorded by the line and stored in a computerized database.

It makes sense to solicit repeat business from a past passenger of the line by mail and most lines do using some form of the "club" techniques that we've discussed previously. Resort hotels do the same thing by sending newsletters to past visitors so they will be motivated to return for another visit.

Keeping the Agent in the Picture

However, almost all of the cruise lines encourage passengers to see their travel agent to make the new booking, even though they could just as easily invite a direct call to the line's reservation department.

Some lines have representatives on board each sailing to sign up passengers for future cruises while the joy and satisfaction of the present cruise is at its peak, and this approach, more prevalent in the premium and luxury markets, can be extremely effective. On a 14-day Seabourn cruise, a couple signed up for over 150 days of future cruises—a very impressive return on a low-cost effort. Seabourn reports that as much as 18 percent of its overall business in 1995 was signed up on board, and the percentage is growing. But here too, the practice is to inform the travel agent who booked the original cruise of the new reservations, transfer the deposits to the agent, and let the agency earn the full commission on the booking(s). In the Seabourn example, if all the reserved cruises were completed, the commission on the couple's multiple-cruise booking will result in a commission of about $25,000 to the travel agent, who didn't have to do anything at all!

Consumer Generated Direct Business

Finally, all cruise lines reservations numbers are published in the trade and consumer periodicals whether the line wants them published or not. As a result, consumers can easily bypass a travel agency by calling and trying to reserve a stateroom themselves. Some even believe they will be offered a lower rate because there is no commission involved, based on their experience of booking hotel rooms directly (where there sometimes is a discount for this), but this is a myth. Because of rebating and group discounts—these people could end up paying *more* than if they had gone through a legitimate travel agency! Some lines encourage this practice (because they do keep all of the commission) and some do not. Frequently, a reservations agent may be well into the booking process before he or she realizes that it's a consumer, not a travel agent on the other end of the telephone. With most nationally marketed cruise lines, the amount of direct business taken this way is minuscule, well under 5 percent of the total cruise business. At Carnival, direct business cases represent less than 1 percent of its overall business.

Electronic Reservation Systems

A further ominous development is the impact of technology. Speaking at the ICTA (Institute of Certified Travel Agents) National Forum in San Antonio, John Lavin, Corporate Director—Travel Industry, for Hyatt Hotels, told delegates that it may become cheaper to have customers book reservations themselves by creating more consumer access to electronic hotel reservation systems. He warned the group that agents "need to create demand, not just manage demand." Coming from Hyatt this is particularly significant. Just a few years ago, the President of Hyatt at the time told another group of travel agents that in the next decade Hyatt expected to get as much as 50 percent of its reservations through travel agencies! Indeed, Radisson and Holiday Inn were already accepting reservations via the Internet in 1995.

The Agency Distribution System— Benefits and Problems

Some cruise lines advertise their toll-free reservation lines to encourage direct bookings, but as we have noted, most consumers, 90 to 95 percent, find it more convenient and economical to use travel agents, at least when buying a cruise. And up to now most cruise lines have been happy with the results. There are of course a few that fault the current distribution system. They believe that agents are not savvy business people or interested enough in selling cruises, and that they do not offer sufficient sales support of their lines, especially since the airlines capped the commission it would pay agencies, which made it eminently sensible to shift agency efforts to selling the products of the companies that are willing to pay them for their efforts.

RCCL's McLeod told us what he thought was going on:

> I think what happened is that the distribution system as a whole said, "the airlines screwed us." We are not going to support the airlines. We are only going to sell those industries that supported us. We're going to sell more cruises, we're going to sell more tours, we're going to sell more leisure travel. We're simply not going to sell airline tickets. If people come into our office and want to buy them, we'll tell them they can call the airlines directly. But they haven't done that. In fact, domestic sales of airline tickets through travel agencies has *increased*! So they obviously are incapable of punishing those they perceive to be their enemies. The reality is that travel agents lack credibility. We need to attract more leisure travelers to use travel agencies. Only one out of every five leisure vacation travel dollars go through agencies. Those figures, of course, are somewhat misleading because they include entrance fees to sightseeing attractions and tolls charged by national parks.

One of the most damnable points that travel agents bring out when consumers ask, "Why should I deal with a travel agency?"

is that they're free, they don't cost you anything. At the same time one of the fundamental consumer axioms heard today is that you don't get something for nothing. What travel agencies need to get across to their customers is that they add value. If an agency says we issue tickets for free and you can pick them up right here, they are positioning themselves as documentation services. The consumer will accept the fact that it might be convenient—it might be better to pick up a ticket at the office, but they'll call the airline first and see what the price is going to be. The fact is that travel agencies were disenfranchised as a distribution system and as a sales arm by the airlines. The airlines have said, "You're a documentation service. You don't sell but you're pretty good at issuing tickets and we'll pay you for that." The reality, of course, is that the airlines have not significantly altered their override agreements for those agencies who can shift market share—those who truly can sell.

McLeod has expressed these same sentiments on many occasions, one the 1995 Summer Cruise-a-Thon, which we described in Chapter 6. In which he opened his remarks with "The distribution system itself has some problems." No doubt many travel agencies feel that the airlines do not appreciate them, and have backed up these claims with lawsuits. They also tried to get Congress to investigate the problem. But the general reaction has been to get on with business and look for more ways to make money to replace lost airline income.

It did not take many of them long to figure out that selling cruises was one of the most effective ways to do this. Cruise sales on the whole have increased since the caps were applied. At the same Cruise-a-Thon debate, Bob Dickinson responded to McLeod by asking, "How can we blame the distribution system when Carnival operates at 112 percent paying occupancy? The same distribution system that *is* selling our cruises *is not* selling the other guys."

Not all of the other guys. Adam Aron, who was not at that debate, told us that he agrees with Dickinson that travel agencies are a solid distribution system, and he, too, points to NCL's increase in sales as support for his view.

Lauraday Kelley is President of the Association of Retail Travel Agents , a group of 2,500 small to mid-sized travel agencies. We asked her what kind of a job she thought travel agencies were doing selling cruises, and if the problem lay with the travel agents or the cruise lines. She told us, "I think it's both. Bob Dickinson is right. Carnival is doing an outstanding job of educating everyone about cruising. And I think CLIA as a trade association could be doing more for the industry. But truthfully there's only so much they can do. I'll probably get crucified by my peers but I agree with Rod McLeod, too. I feel that we travel agents have become too settled in our ways. Of course, we are not marketing experts and we haven't got a lot of advertising dollars to spend. Nevertheless, not all of us, but a good percentage, aren't diligent enough to acquaint our own communities with what we do. We throw a little ad in the paper here or there but that's not enough. My own agency is a case in point. We've been in the same location for twenty years. We are a storefront agency right on the main street with a sign out front. I bet you I have people say to me twice a month, "I never knew your agency was there." "You sell cruises?" "I didn't know what you did."

Part of the reason that the major players see things so differently, we think, lies, first of all, with the travel agencies themselves. To lump all travel agencies into one broad classification is to oversimplify what is in fact a very complex, technology-based, and rapidly growing business. The average travel agency in America in 1994 did in the neighborhood of $2,880,000 annually and employed 5.5 agents. But 33 percent of all agency locations did between $1 million and $1.9 million—about the same or less as the neighborhood McDonald's! Eighty-seven percent have revenues of less than $5 million. The 13 percent with more reaped 46 percent of total agency revenues.

The travel agency industry is for the most part made up of small businesses with very small operating margins. The commissions of a typical $2 million agency, depending on the business mix (between leisure and commercial), might be around $200,000. After overhead (of which close to 50 percent is salaries), a well-managed agency of this size is fortunate if it makes a gross profit before taxes of $45,000. At least $15,000 less then the average McDonald's as a point of comparison. The truth is that 40 percent make less then that: A good many agencies lose money each year and 3 to 5 percent go out of business altogether. You hear very few agency owners boasting about the kind of money they make in this business!

When it comes to full-service agencies, those that do $5 million plus do a better job of selling their services. Their people are better trained, and they often have a different mind set. Phil Davidoff, former President of the American Society of Travel Agents, told us. "Unfortunately, too many travel agents are really order takers, not salespeople. Their activities are limited to that of a fulfillment clerk who provides what is asked for—no more and no less." Now, if you are an order-taking agent, the laws of probability suggest that you're going to get more orders for Carnival than for any other line for a number of reasons. First of all, they're the biggest and therefore the most popular. As we've pointed out before, while most people don't know the differences among the majority of lines, they do know what a Carnival fun ship is and when asked, "What cruise would you like to take?" they answer Carnival. Indeed, according to one independent study more travel agents (92 percent) booked a Carnival Cruise than any other line.

That's good for Carnival but bad for the other companies. In order to increase their market share these lines need salespeople to push their products in frontline agency positions. and they don't have them, as clearly indicated by both Kelley and Davidoff. Thus, for them the distribution system isn't working as well as it does for Carnival.

This is no surprise. Paul Mackey, a securities analyst with Dean Witter who follows the cruise industry, says "The cruise industry, in general, has a big problem and that problem is Carnival. Carnival just owns the business. When you get right down to it it's Carnival's industry."[1] It is much easier for the leader in any business to defend his position than it is for a wannabe to become a leader.

Owner/Agent Bias

Another factor in the equation may be what we call owner-directed business. Here agents in a specific agency have been directed by the owner to push a particular cruise line, perhaps because of a higher rate of commission or a perk of one sort or another (more on this coming up).

---

[1]"Between the Lines," *Tour & Travel News*, October 16, 1995.

Then there is the question of agent bias. If you are a travel agent and the only cruise you have ever sailed on was a Norwegian Cruise Lines offering, and if the NCL agent was just in to see you, you are going to recommend Norwegian before Carnival or Royal Caribbean because you liked it and therefore you can tell your client with confidence that they will like it. This is a bad assumption, but one many agents make. Moreover you know that if you have a problem, your friendly NCL agent will help you out. The others might help you out, too, but you haven't seen them recently. Or if you are a small agency and only sell a few cruises a year, you may not see any cruise line sales rep very often. Out of sight, out of mind!

The area of the country may be another contributing factor. Some lines sailing in the Caribbean get a larger portion of their business from the West Coast or even Europe. Air fares, the state of the economy, and currency exchange rates can all influence a line's clientele. If you are particularly dependent on any one source, you will be hurt more than a line that has a very diverse customer base. Since most of your cruises are sold through agents, your reaction may be that they aren't doing a good job.

If there is a conclusion to be drawn here, it is that Carnival has done a first-class job of educating and utilizing the travel agency distribution system, and it is reaping the rewards. That is not to suggest that Royal Caribbean hasn't done this. Indeed, its sales force, along with Carnival's, ranks very high on all travel agents surveys. Both have been cited for their outstanding sales teams by various groups. Given the nature of the travel agency business, however, the system serves Carnival better and Carnival serves the system better!

Room for Improvement

It should be clear by this point that, despite this controversy and with a few minor exceptions, all of the major cruise lines have chosen to commit themselves, for better or for worse, and their futures to travel agencies as the primary means of distributing their product. Yet they could do things differently.

For an understanding of why this is so, there are some more questions that need more complete answers than we have suggested. How important is selling cruises to agencies? Do the ones who know how to sell or want to sell consciously seek to promote cruises as a preferred form of vacation experience? How good are the front-line sales people at their jobs? If you are a major cruise line with thousands of berths to fill weekly, to what extent can you depend on them to do what needs to be done to implement your marketing efforts?

The answers to these questions are hard to come by. There are over 37,000 full-service travel agencies location within the United States and Canada. (By "full-service" we mean agencies that have airline appointments and thus can issue airline tickets, and that are accredited to sell a full range of other travel products). In the United States alone, there are over 33,000 such agencies, whose average per-location percent of sales revenue is shown in the Table 9.2.

As you can see, with only 10 percent of sales revenue, cruises are far less important to the typical full-service agent than the agent is to the cruise industry. This anomaly is even more bizarre when you consider the mix of business and leisure travel shown in Table 9.3.

Table 9.2
Average Agency Sales Mix

Component	*% of Sales Revenue*
Domestic airlines	50
International airlines	10
Rental cars	7
Hotels	11
Tour packages	8
Cruises	10
Other	4
Total	100%

Table 9.3
Average Full-Service Agency

Component	% of business revenue
Commercial	50%
Leisure	50%
Total	100%

This is the classic way of looking at an agency's business. As you can see, fully half the business is commercial or corporate in nature. A business account is signed up by the agency and then serviced indefinitely or until the account is lost to bankruptcy or another agency, or the corporate client goes direct. The other half of the business is something called "leisure," which, when pressed to explain most agents define as, "you know, everything that's *not* commercial." While the logic is unassailable, it's nonetheless not terribly revealing.

A more telling breakdown is shown in Table 9.4. In this breakout, while commercial business is unchanged, the leisure component is discarded altogether. The second largest component is VFR. Again, this is a service aspect of the business, just like the commercial component. It can't be sold or initiated by the agency, but is rather passively awaited. If business is slow in August, let's say, the agency owner or manager can't call up the Vice President of Sales of a corporate account and suggest he set up a sales meeting in some faraway place and let the agency handle all the travel arrangements. By the same account, the

Table 9.4
Average Agency Location

Component	% of Sales Volume
Commercial	50%
VFR (visiting friends and relative)	30%
Vacation sales	20%
Total	100%

agency can't stimulate VFR business by suggesting that a client visit her mother-in-law in Minneapolis or his fraternity brother in Bismarck, North Dakota.

Putting it bluntly, at least 80 percent of an average full-service agency's revenue is order taking. And it's a full 95 percent of its transactions because of both the low average cost for airline tickets, hotels, and rental cars, and the high degree of canceled, rewritten or double-booked business.

Creating Leisure Business

The other 20 percent of revenue is retail vacation sales: tour packages, cruises, and FIT vacation arrangements, which represent bundled travel components such as air, hotel, and rental car in a customized itinerary for the consumer. Retail vacation business—5 percent on a transactions basis—can be created (sold) rather than simply order takers when someone walks in or calls. Why? Because these kinds of vacations, unlike visiting friends and relatives, are purely discretionary. Furthermore, the majority of prospects for a vacation have only a foggy notion of what they want to do or where they to go. In a study by *Travel Weekly*, agents responded that 68 percent of their leisure clients asked their advice on hotels, 66 percent on package tours , and 56 percent on destinations! As we discussed in the chapter on pricing, prospects have an even hazier concept of the cost of vacation alternatives. As a result, with the exception of an agency's ability to sign up additional corporate business, vacation sales is the one area of a full-service agency's business where there is both opportunity and means to proactively generate revenue.

Order Taking—a Prescription for Lost Business

The fact that vacation sales are only 5 percent of an agency's transactions is quite disquieting, especially when you consider that most travel agents believe that they are overworked and underpaid. A survey conducted in 1995 by *Travel Counselor Magazine* (the official publication of the Institute of Certified Travel Agents) revealed that the average front-line agent makes only $22,700, the average manager $28,700, and the average owner $32,600 per year. We also know that most agents say that the they are able to close only one retail vacation sale for every 10 prospects who call or walk in to inquire about a vacation. This low percentage of completed sales suggests that the vast majority of the successful encounters *are* order-taking scenarios rather than the result of effective selling. But when you think about it, this should be no surprise: After all, 95 percent of their business *is* order taking, isn't it?

The low closure rate also helps to explain the fact that 80 percent of the vacation business bypasses travel agents entirely. That's because most of it goes directly to hotels and resorts where vacationers prefer to make their own reservations rather than suffer the frustration of dealing with ill-equipped agencies.

Let's look at it another way. If nine vacation prospects leave the first agency they call on empty handed, do they immediately rush over to a second agency? If they do and it makes one sale, what about the unfulfilled eight? Do they go to a third agency, and then a fourth? At some point, frustrated that they can't get what they want, they either go directly to the supplier or they give up on the vacation altogether and spend the money on a new home theater, a dining-room set, jewelry, or a new car.

After all, a vacation is a discretionary purchase, which, from the point of view of travel sellers, makes it a tougher industry to compete in than, say, the pharmaceutical business, where medicine is not generally a matter of choice. Intuitively, then, some meaningful percentage of vacation sales, including cruise sales, is lost each year because too many travel agents don't know how and/or don't want to sell. They prefer to see themselves as professional travel counselors (note the name of their magazine), and counselors don't sell, they advise. Those who haven't yet reached the status of counselor in their own minds (because they don't know enough) are simply order takers, ticket printers, or reservation clerks.

The Roots of the Agency Distribution System

There is a certain irony here, in that travel agents in this country started in business in the last century to sell vacations. The first well-known travel agent was Thomas Cook, in Britain. In the mid-1800s he recognized that, with the emergence of railroads and steamships, there was a need for someone willing to make arrangements for people who wished to explore England and the Continent but were nervous about traveling on their own to foreign places. Soon Cook had established himself as a "sales agent" for these new and convenient forms of transportation, and in 1856 he offered his first "Grand Tour" of Europe. At about the same time (1850) the American Express Company was formed in the United States, originally with the purpose of shipping merchandise and money across America and then to Europe. The company soon grew to the point where it also offered travelers' checks and dispensed information on foreign destinations.

Cook's Legacy

By 1920, in the United States and Great Britain there were a host of travel sellers that formulated elaborate FIT vacation itineraries, domestic and world-wide, and sold them to local folks, often to a few couples or an even larger group. On such trips the agent acted as the group's escort and tour guide. When Thomas Cook, a Baptist preacher, organized his very first trip in 1841, he personally escorted a railroad tour for 570 persons from Leicester to Loughborough, England, to attend a temperance meeting!

The Rise of the Traveler

With these new travel services, affluent local doctors, businesspeople, writers, and others with the means to travel had access to a world with which they were totally unfamiliar except through the writings of Marco Polo, Rudyard Kipling, Lord Byron, and Mark Twain, among others. In those far less mobile times, people were born, lived their entire lives, and died without ever traveling beyond a few miles of their communities. The local jeweler, for example, could return to Kansas City and regale his family, friends, neighbors, and business associates with tales of personal experiences traveling along the Appian Way, where noble Romans had set out in chariots to conquer the world and early Christians had fled into the catacombs; visiting Montmarte in Paris and climbing up to the domed Basilica of Sacre-Couer in the steps of Renoir and Toulouse-Lautrec; or sitting in the Egyption moonlight staring at the Sphinx with her great lion paws. This was heady stuff indeed and conferred upon the traveler a certain cachet. The local travel agent, who was himself a mysterious font of information, made all of this possible.

Horseless Carriages

Horses, railroads, and steamships were the only forms of transportation until the automobile, which was introduced first by the French in 1890, when Leon Serpollet, the inventor of the instantaneous steam generator, mounted one of his engines on a tricycle and drove it 295 miles from Paris to Leon. At the same time, steam-powered road vehicles of various designs were being built in the United States. In Lansing, Michigan, Ransom E. Olds built one of the earliest models in 1891, which he sold for $400 to a London patent medicine firm for use in its branch in Bombay, India.[2] In Detroit Henry Ford first realized that if an inexpensive car could be built, everyone would want one, and in 1908 introduced the Model-T runabout—a 20-horsepower, 1,200-pound car—priced at $825 (by 1916, using the assembly line to mass-produce cars, Ford was able to get the price down to $345).

Cars completely changed the way people lived. Small, self-reliant agricultural communities lost many of their businesses and opened some new ones that were dependent on tourists. Touring and sightseeing became increasingly more popular as more Americans acquired automobiles. There were no places to stay, however, which of course lead to the eventual growth of hotels and resorts.

Lindbergh, Pan Am, and the Rise of Commercial Aviation

The end of the first World War marked the beginning of commercial aviation on both sides of the Atlantic. The impetus was the experience gained in military flying during the war and the number of trained pilots and mechanics available to exploit this new form of transportation. The air age got a tremendous boost when a young stunt flyer named Charles Lindbergh, whose act of standing of the top wing of a looping plane thrilled crowds all over the country, decided to compete for a prize of $25,000 offered to the first person to fly solo across the Atlantic ocean. At 7:55 A.M., on May 20, 1927, Lindbergh took off from Roosevelt Field on Long Island, New York, and landed at Le Bourget in Paris 33 hours and 39 minutes later. He thus proved the airplane was a practical means of traveling long distances, and as a result

---

[2]James J. Flink, *The Automobile Age* (Cambridge, Mass: MIT Press, 1992).

investors who had been hesitant to put money into this new form of transportation lined up to back commercial aviation.

Also in 1927, a young World War I pilot, Juan Trippe, founded Pan American Airlines with a mail contract from the U.S. government to fly between Key West and Havana. The DC3, the first popular passenger airplane, was introduced in 1936, and in 1958 Boeing introduced the 707. The jet age was born. The 707 went into service the following year on Pan Am's New York to Paris route.

This new, fast, transatlantic service provided a huge stimulus to both the tourist and the business travel market and sounded the death knell of the steamship business. In a strange twist of fate, however, it is the offspring of that very same steamship business that sustains much of the airline business today. Carnival Cruise Lines alone buys over $150,000,000 of airline tickets each year.

The phenomenal airline industry growth dramatically changed the travel agency business. When the first pure jets began operating in 1958, there were fewer than 4,000 agency locations in the United States When, on October 24, 1978, President Jimmy Carter signed the Airline Deregulation Act into law, there were 14,800 travel agency locations—an increase of 270 percent. In 1995, there were more than 33,000 full-service agencies, an increase of 123 percent from 1978 and a whopping 725 percent from 1958. To put this growth in perspective, during the same 37-year period, the population grew by only 50 percent and the economy as measured by gross national product grew by 198 percent in constant 1958 dollars.

Table 9.5 shows this dramatic growth, as well as the growth of agency penetration of the population over the same period.

The growth from one agency location per 43,750 people in 1958 to one agency location per only 8,000 people in 1995 represents more than a five-fold improvement. It was largely the result of two factors: the incredible popularity and resulting growth in air transportation, and the widespread, easy accessibility of travel perks to these newly powerful distributors of airline seats, hotel rooms, and cruise ships—the travel agents. Domestic airline passenger miles grew from 25 billion in 1958 to 391 billion in 1995, an increase of almost 15-fold. At the same time, the airline industry shifted the bulk of its distribution from city ticket offices

Table 9.5

Event	Advent of Commercial Jet Transportation	Airline Deregulation	Today
Year	*1958*	*1978*	*1995*
# of Agencies*	4,000	14,800	33,000
US population	175 million	223 million	263 million
Population per Agency	43,750	15,100	8,000

* A.R.C. appointed only

and direct phone reservations to travel agencies. In 1958, agents represented only about 20 percent of the domestic airline business; in 1995 the comparable figure was 82 percent.

Deregulation and Travel Agency Expansion
As a result of deregulation in 1978, airlines became free to change whatever they wanted because fares were no longer regulated. This led to a plethora of complex fares and complicated fare restrictions. It was simply cheaper for the airlines to have travel agents figure out the fare possibilities and explain it to the consumer than do it themselves. From a consumer's viewpoint, the travel agent became more and more an advocate for the consumer in the battle to obtain the lowest possible fares, while the airlines were perceived, rightly so, as wanting to maximize yields and so trying to sell tickets at the highest possible fares.

The Lure—Travel Perks
While data on the increased availability and accessibility of travel perks are largely anecdotal, it's very clear to many industry observers (including both authors) that 75 percent reduced-fare agent airline discounts ("A.D. 75s"); free or reduced rates for hotels, rental cars, tours, and cruises; and even totally free familiarization trips served as a huge magnet drawing people into the travel business. It was an especially attractive career for those who already had an abiding love of travel. In fact, love of travel

and of seeing new places is still the most frequently cited reason that people enter the travel agency business in the first place.

Airlines, hotels, tour operators, cruise lines, and other travel suppliers reasoned that if their properties had unused capacity (which they all did at some time or other), why not offer it to travel agents so that not only would they become knowledgeable about the specific features and benefits of the product but also, perhaps, throw in a little "beholding"—wherein agents who had been hosted would make a special effort to steer business to the property to pay back the generosity. Sales representatives of airlines, destinations, hotels, tour operators and cruise lines hear this litany every day. "I can't sell your product if I haven't seen it," the agent will say is the reason for not having booked any business. Hungry to grow their territory's business, the reps succumb with great frequency to this siren song, hoping that new business will materialize. There is some logic to this. But you couldn't possibly see everything. On the other hand, Sears-Roebuck has been selling refrigerators through their catalogs for years to people who have never seen them and haven't even talked with a salesperson.

Sometimes the travel perks help, of course, especially if the agent is conscientious and has a clientele that would be interested in this particular vacation experience if the agent could give them more information about it. More often, however, it doesn't make any difference at all—especially when you are dealing with an order-taking mind set! Even worse are the few agents who arc simply looking for a freebie—that's why they went in the business in the first place! We know because both of us have hosted travel agents on cruises and destination familiarization trips who separate themselves from the group to go shopping or sightseeing on their own and miss what it is we have invited them to learn about. Nevertheless, hope springs eternal—especially among sales reps and sales executives of travel suppliers who are desperate to grow the business and fill idle capacity. And, of course, there's an unspoken competitive force at work here: If I can lure Mary Smith of Mary's Travel to vacation with me, she won't have time to see what my competitor is offering!

Even though the familiarization trips can be nice, the monetary compensation data from the survey of travel agents is somewhat discouraging to would-be and current agents. After all, who aspires to a career where the average pay is less than most college students receive on their first job? But it's not as bad as it looks at first glance. To begin with, motivated and skilled agents can and do bring home pay checks well above the averages. The top 5 percent of frontline agents earn more than $42,000, and some top the $60,000 level. In addition there is always the perceived and real value of travel perks, which amount to nontaxable income for all practical purposes. These perks easily amount to $3,000—$5,000 additional nonfinancial compensation per year, so it's not hard to understand why they are eagerly pursued!

Whose Party Tonight?

Besides the direct compensation, either as money or services, there are seminars, trade shows, and the like, which can take the form of breakfasts, lunches, dinners, cocktail parties, weekend outings, golf and other sporting events hosted by suppliers, and so on. In the larger metropolitan areas, agents frequently have a difficult time deciding where to go because their options are so numerous. At a conservative value of just $50 per week, these additional, nontaxable "social and educational events" can amount to $2,500 per year. It's certainly true that travel agents in remote areas have far fewer opportunities like these, but agents have been known to drive two hours or more, each way, or even fly, to attend a product seminar of one kind or another, practically all of which involve a meal. And the meals at some of these functions can be spectatular. We have attended British breakfasts with lavish portions of smoked salmon imported from Scotland, French luncheons (that took all afternoon) featuring a selection of the best wines in each region, and Italian dinners prepared by chefs flown in from Rome along with their ingredients. Often such events are held at the best restaurants in town and sometimes in even more exotic venues like museums after hours. For the most part, they are sponsored by airlines, tourism boards, cruise lines, and tour operators.

Suppliers again recognize the competitive nature of this whole process. If a Texas city's Visitor and Convention Bureau, in trying to build its tourism business, offers Tex-Mex tacos made with velveeta cheese accompanied by Chateau Schmootz wine at an evening seminar, few if any agents will show up if on the same night the Swiss Tourist Bureau is serving fondue and the Bermuda Department is hosting a champagne and caviar reception featuring the Bermuda Regiment Marching Band followed by dinner and a drawing for a Bermuda cruise. Moreover, if two suppliers both offer dinners on the same evening, the one that will get the biggest attendance, everything else being equal, is the one who has a track record of sit-down dinners versus stand-up buffets, or beef or veal versus mystery meat. If both suppliers are known to offer comparable dinners, other factors will determine which event will out-draw the other:

- Which venue (hotel, restaurant, or private club) has the best reputation or is the most exclusive?
- Which venue has the most central location, including commuting time from work?
- Which suppler will pick up parking costs (valet parking is a thoughtful touch)?
- Which supplier gives away the most elaborate door prizes? These can range anywhere from a bottle of strange domestic champagne to a two-week cruise or two first-class airline tickets to anywhere the sponsor flies. One Caribbean country's tourist office gives a nice door prize to every one in attendance. Needless to say, they draw consistently large audiences.
- Will there be entertainment? A Caribbean steel band is nice, but then so is a Mexican mariachi band. "What, Aardvark Airlines is featuring Neil Diamond? I'm in!"
- Will the supplier's sales representative be offended if I don't attend? Will that work against me the next time an elaborate familiarization trip comes up and the rep with a limited number of places is deciding who to invite?"
- Is the rep gorgeous, handsome, single, well-off, affectionate? Would she/he recommend me for a position with the company?
- The tie breaker (asked by serious agents—and there are some): "What are my chances of actually selling this product in my market?"

A few more points on this important topic. The supplier who offers Velveeta and bills it as a cocktail party will only fool the agents in a city one time. The next time, irrespective of how it's billed or what the invitation looks like, the attendees for the event can be hosted in a phone booth! Also, the menu issue applies to breakfast and lunch, not just dinner. A continental breakfast is a real yawn—who wants to go anywhere for a cheese danish or a toasted English muffin? Belgian waffles with strawberries or Eggs Benedict are much stronger draws. There are regional differences as well. Forget about serving coffee in Salt Lake City because the Mormons don't drink it, or offering anything less than a substantial breakfast in the Midwest, where folks have much healthier appetites than those on either coast and look forward to bacon, eggs, sausage, and biscuits, along with toast and danish. The notions of calories, fat grams, and any propaganda from the American Heart Association apparently have not reached the hinterlands—at least not when it comes to meals hosted by the travel and tourism industry!

Advisory Boards
A special perk for those lucky enough to be chosen is to be a member of a travel agent advisory board. Not all suppliers have these, but those that do usually provide a sweet deal for the chosen few. Advisory boards meet quarterly or biannually, generally over a 2- or 3-day period, and a fine hotel, resort, or cruise ship makes an appropriate setting for the meeting. Accommodations are first-class and totally complimentary, as are the round trip airline tickets and transfers. All meals are on the house and some suppliers even throw in the incidentals bill—which can include gift shop purchases! Along with a few days of wining and dining with the home office big shots and playing a few rounds of golf or sets of tennis, the serious work gets down. This usually starts with a presentation on how nifty the supplier has been in the past and will be even better in the future, of course. Then the agents are urged to give their feedback and opinions on the supplier, 16 competitors, and any unusual market conditions or local occurrences. Travel agents approach this task in a variety of ways, ranging from serious fawning to the truth in such excruciating detail that the executives who invited them, cringing with embarrassment and with beads of perspiration on their brow, are wondering who's brilliant idea this advisory board was in the first place!

The fortunate agents, usually a dozen to perhaps 20 at most, are typically selected for a two-year term to provide fresh input from the agent community. Just how objective is this input is questionable, of course. You cannot help but wonder if the agents are so compromised by the process that they lose all objectivity. Can a dozen or so randomly selected agents truly represent 250,000 agents' opinions? Probably not—it's not a legitimate sampling methodology by any stretch of the imagination. And if a supplier truly wants an opinion from travel agents, why not simply pick up the phone and call some of them? In reality, such a board allows the supplier to neutralize any turkeys in the agency community as well as spread the opulence by putting deserving agents on the gravy train.

Be assured that the mere suggestion by a supplier's rep that an agent <u>may</u> be considered for the next advisory board opening will have that agent jumping through hoops, and not only for the two to four free boondoggles each year but for the prestige factor. Local agents' cocktail conversation is sprinkled with bon mots such as: "Yes, Ethel and I just returned from Fantabulous Cruise Lines' new ship launching in France, Prince Ranier was there, and a few days in Paris at the George V . . . you <u>do</u> know that I'm on their advisory board?"

A curious by-product of the advisory board process is the imperiled agent who has spent his term basking in the sun at Monte Carlo while tasting the Nouveau Boujelais and is now off the board. A sort of post-partum depression sets in when the perks and the prestige have vanished, and the agent is once again "ordinary." Like Rodney Dangerfield, he gets no respect, because he no longer hobnobs with supplier biggies—the airline CEOs, the cruise-line presidents, the tour company owners. He finds he gets few calls, if any, from other advisory board agents. While not exactly ostracized, he may feel like a has been. He has lost a big chunk of his identity. All is not lost, however. At this point of vulnerability, and with a little bit of luck, he can be easily "turned" by a competitive supplier who dangles a position on another advisory board. The word promptly goes out to the office staff. "Forget about selling Abracadabra Cruises—they really weren't that good of a product. Our new friends are Boondoggle Cruises and we're going to push them as hard as we can." Ah, the charm of it all!

There can be no doubt that the domestic airline industry has molded and shaped today's full-service agency. In order to open their doors, agency owners must have received Airline Reporting

Corporation (ARC) appointments—without them they cannot sell any tickets. Appointments involve negotiating an elaborate set of requirements and procedures, ranging from the employment of a manager with at least two years of ARC-appointed agency experience to a safe for protecting airline ticket stock. For readers unfamiliar with the system, the airlines view blank ticket stock as equivalent to real money. (One first-class ticket to Europe is worth several thousand dollars.) Once a name and some flight numbers are written on it, a ticket can be presented and the owner is entitled to fly where ever the ticket says. Now, when a travel agency collects those thousands of dollars the airlines do not present an ordinary invoice for the money in the hope that it will be paid promptly. No, they have a far more sophisticated system. An ARC-appointed agency has signed an agreement with ARC that requires it to submit weekly a list of tickets issued. ARC then deducts the agency commission from the total amount due and automatically withdraws from the agency's bank account the amount due to all of the airlines and distributes it to them. Unlike in other businesses, the agent has no "float" time to use the money from airline tickets to pay the rent or the electric bill. Nor do they have any time to earn interest on these funds, as they are paid out almost as soon as they are received. Of course, the airlines get a float since a ticket issued today may not be used for several weeks or even months. This is one more reason why it is so tough to make money in the agency business, and it's also a reason why smart agents do not extend credit if they can help it. They have to pay for the ticket the same week it is issued, but a customer can easily take 30 days to pay them.

With the advent of airline reservation automation in the mid-seventies, full-service agencies quickly invested in computerized reservations terminals (CRTs). With a computer on every desk, the agency looked, as well as acted, like an airline reservations ticket office. Neophyte agents were schooled in Sabre, Apollo, System 1, or Worldspan—whichever airline system the agency used. This was and still is the primary training emphasis in a full-service agency—how to use that computer to reserve and print out airline tickets and boarding passes. Booking rental cars, hotels, tours and (more's the pity) cruises were all of secondary consideration.

How then does it happen that the agency distribution system—molded by the airlines almost in their likeness—has been able to support the cruise industry so admirably for 25 years, especially when cruise sales, like all other vacation purchases, seem like afterthoughts? There are several contributing factors.

First, while, as we have already made clear, the typical agent is first an order taker, second a counselor or advisor, and third, possibly, a sales person. When it comes to cruise sales, a few thousand agency locations don't follow the norm, and they can be divided into two groups: vacation-oriented full-service and cruise-only.

The first, either for geographical reasons or, God forbid, because they like to make money, do a good job of selling vacations, including cruises. By geography here, we mean the location of the agency. This can be a high-traffic urban location, a suburb, or a small town that folks simply have to get away from and have the money to do it. Midtown Manhattan, a suburban Chicago shopping mall, or Evansville, Indiana, are examples. Then there are places like Leisure City, California, where everyone is retired, affluent, and enjoys traveling.

Location usually isn't enough to ensure success. Agents need an inclination to sell vacations, as well as front-of-the-house personalities, selling skills, and the desire to help people get in touch with their vacation needs. This seems reasonable for someone in a front-line position in a retail store, but trust us, it simply is not the norm. Most agents don't know how to sell, as the data overwhelmingly demonstrate. Moreover, they have an almost universal apprehension about the selling scenario. More than anything they fear rejection, and as a result they are very uncomfortable in any situation where they are likely to encounter it. To make matters worse, because of the reactive nature of order taking and the time needed to service commercial and VFR bookings, these agents frequently view vacation prospects as unwanted. Carnival's mystery vacationer program has for many years sent back report after report from the field about the agents all too commonly ignoring prospects or treating them less than civilly—as if they were somehow intruding on their work day. A prospect walks in and agent Smith bends down to tie his loafers while agent Jones (with exceptional peripheral vision) subtly diverts her eyes to the gray-green glare of the CRT. And Agent Black might look up with an annoyed "Can't you see I'm busy?" look on his face. After all, he is busy re-issuing a profitable $39 ticket to Las Vegas. As for the prospect? "Oh, he's just a shopper, he's really not interested in buying anything," they tell themselves. "He's just out to waste my time, and, after all, I am busy." Of course, they're all busy, but not making any money for the agency. Does it matter? These agents are paid on the basis of salary, with no thought to their contribution to the profit of the company, which is another distinguishing factor between the successful vacation agent and the average agent. The successful ones have some notion, clear or fuzzy, that selling vacations is more profitable than just selling airline tickets. They don't just pay lip service to being in the travel agency business to make money, they are determined to, and do, by focusing on vacation sales and watching their costs.

Probably the best example of this type of full-service agency is Liberty Travel, the sixth largest in the United States. Privately owned, Liberty comprises a chain of 180 agency locations in eight Northeast States and Florida. Its principals, Fred Kassner and Gil Hiroche, run an enormously profitable enterprise. In 1994 gross sales amounted to $1,138,500,000. Plus, their 1,400 full-time agents can and do make an excellent living. In 1993, Brian Kravitz, Liberty's Senior Vice President of Marketing, revealed in *Travel Weekly* that the average Liberty agent is paid on a draw-against-commission basis and the manager, who sells as well, works on salary plus a percentage of the store's net operating profit. In this way special attention is paid to directing business to the more profitable cruise lines and other preferred travel products, which offer both higher levels of commission and high levels of customer satisfaction, which latter results in strong repeat business. Leisure travel accounts for 95 percent of Liberty's business, while business travel makes up the remaining 5 percent. According to Kravitz, "Liberty Travel functions just like any other intelligent, profit-oriented retailer by limiting its product line. This strategy is further enhanced with comprehensive sales training. Each Liberty seller undergoes a thorough sales training program before he or she ever deals with a customer."

There are many other examples, many of which, look like a homogeneous set of locations, like Liberty Travel, but are a very diverse network of agencies. AAA Motor Club travel offices are a case in point. There are 1,036 such offices scattered across the United States and Canada, with 1994 U.S. sales of $1,961,400,000.

While they all appear alike to consumers, they're actually split into 118 separately run state or regional clubs with extraordinarily varying productivity. The productivity of the average AAA location productivity when it comes to cruise and other vacation sales is pretty unimpressive. Viewed by the industry as a sleeping giant for many years in terms of potential, some industry executives have questioned whether AAA is sleeping, or just dead! However, on a national basis AAA appears to be finally heading in the right direction. In 1994, travel was elevated to the status of a core business within AAA, signaling to the various club CEOs that they should begin to put as much emphasis on travel as they do on insurance, travelers' checks, and road service. Moreover, recent management changes at AAA national headquarters in Heathrow, Florida, have resulted in a group of energetic and savvy travel sales and marketing executives who are determined to grow their vacation travel business. In 1994, only 22 percent of AAA club members were aware that AAA ever offered travel service! An example of AAA's new aggressive programs is a national television campaign that repositions the company with the message that AAA isn't just about emergency road service, but about providing to their members a range of attractively priced value-added vacations. Indeed, some of the unique travel benefits the club offers are so attractive that they are encouraging the growth of AAA memberships as well. Graeme Clarke, who heads AAA's new focus on vacation travel, has some has aggressive goals: "We intend to be the premier source of cruise and land-based vacation sales for our members. This goal may, in turn, lead AAA to be the largest vacation provider in the country."

All of these new initiatives notwithstanding, some AAA clubs have been successful selling vacation travel for years. AAA Southern California and AAA Michigan are just two of a number of shining examples with cruise sales that are many times greater than the national average. That being the case, when you consider that overall AAA productivity is about half the national average on a per-location basis, you begin to realize that many clubs and locations generate insignificant numbers of cruise and other vacation sales. But the potential is enormous. If those clubs could emulate the productivity of the successful ones, AAA would become a true powerhouse within the agency community. And why not? AAA members represent 24.8 million households, about 24 percent of the total U.S. and Canadian population. Today, only 11 percent of AAA club members use AAA for vacation sales, but what if the percentage was 22 percent or even 50 percent?

For the successful clubs, the pattern is the same: A specific emphasis on vacation sales that starts from the top and moves down through the individual AAA offices and agents. These clubs aggressively market group departures with special rates and other features, and promote their image as vacation specialists. Industry veteran Bill Figge, Manager of World Travel Agency Service for the Automobile Club of Southern California, says, "With the extreme low percentage of AAA members for travel, we motivate our 205 agents and our 520 auto travel people as well to suggest cruise vacations to AAA members who are then planning their road trips. In other words, we're creating cross selling opportunities to promote vacation travel with our members."

Last but not least are the host of individually owned and operated travel agencies that successfully emphasize vacation sales. They may not be members of a consortium or a marketing organization like American Express or Carlson Travel Network, but they all have a common focus on vacation sales. If they do any significant amount of commercial business, they carefully segregate that order-taking business from the vacation business, even to the point of having a special air desk for VFR travel.

Some agencies even go so far as having a separate cruise-only division to focus resources in that area without the distraction of trying to run two business with one set of agents. The idea, which has become popular in recent years, is that any business should focus on its core competency. More than one competency often means more than one business, and trying to combine them is a common mistake that is almost always disastrous. Have you ever met a top car salesman who was also a top mechanic? We doubt it. Auto dealers understand and make the service division entirely separate from the sales division. The two are treated as different businesses because customers have an entirely different set of expectations for each. Curiously, cruise-only divisions of full-service agencies are somewhat common, but vacation-only divisions are rare by comparison.

CLIA doesn't have a breakout of cruise-only divisions among its full-service members, but it does track stand-alone cruise-

Table 9.6
1995 CLIA Agency Membership

	Number	*% of Total*
Full-service	14,805	66%
Cruise-only:		
Office	4,555	21%
Home	2,990	13%
Total cruise-only	7,545	34%
Total locations	22,350	100%

Source: 1995 CLIA agency membership roster.

only agencies, as Table 9.6 shows. While there may be some leakage of cruise-only divisions in the "cruise-only" category, Jim Godsman, CLIA's President, estimates that at least 85 percent in that category are in fact non-airline-appointed cruise-only agencies, which have been a growing sector of the CLIA agency base, as shown in Table 9.7.

This trend is noteworthy, because the cruise productivity of these agencies is higher than that of full-service agencies, as shown in Table 9.8.

As the data indicate, specialization in cruises results predictably in more productive results: Cruise-only agencies, on average, are more productive than their full-service CLIA counterparts—especially those with offices. Bear in mind that while CLIA has the

Table 9.7
CLIA Agency Membership
(1995 vs. 1985)

	1995	*1985*
Full-service	14,805	12,800
Cruise-only	7,545	500
Total	22,350	13,300
Cruise only % total	34%	4%

Table 9.8
CLIA 1995 Agency Passenger Productivity/Location

Full-service	170
Cruise-only:	
Office	240
Home	67
Average cruise-only	203
Total	181
NACOA agencies	425

largest agency membership of any U.S. and Canadian trade organization, still about 19,000 agency locations are not members (almost half), and the presumption is that they do little or no cruise business. This group includes dedicated corporate agencies, ethnic agencies (which focus on international marketing to and from their clients' home country), and agencies that are in fact suppliers (tour operators, cruise lines, etc., that have captive agencies).

Presumably, too, a small number of agencies do produce cruise sales but perhaps their amount of cruise business is so minimal (random agent bookings) that the owner or manager can't justify CLIA membership (as of writing there is a one-time sign up fee of $95 and annual dues of $180 per location). And, of course, a few owners enjoy their roles as mavericks and refuse to join CLIA, just to be different. These are the folks who pride themselves on always being smarter than everyone else.

Imagine the simplicity of the cruise-only agency. No airline appointments, no expensive airline computer terminals and printers, no demanding corporate clients, no sudden avalanche of airline tickets because some airlines decided to have a fare war, and no worrying about commission caps or whether an airline will decide to pull out of your market and thereby cut into your business—not trying to be a jack-of-all-trades but focusing on a few products and not (literally) the world. Ah, but there are drawbacks. Consider, for example, how cruise-only agencies acquire their business. They advertise and promote and network like other agencies do, but, they have no opportunity, in their offices or via incoming phone inquiries, to convert land-based vacation prospects to cruising. After all, no one calls or strolls into a cruise-only agency to book Las Vegas or a Florida resort. And remember that full-service agencies sell ten land vacations for every one cruise, so that the opportunity to spread the gospel to noncruisers is simply lost unless the agents go out into the marketplace and approach consumers where they live or work. Missionaries do it all the time. So does Amway and Tupperware. It just takes a mindset, determination, and the discipline necessary to focus on that kind of field work. Going door to door on foot helps, but so does direct mail, telemarketing, and even the World Wide Web!

We've devoted this chapter to the travel agencies of today—and what they do and how they do it—some better than others. But that is going to change and it is already changing because the marketplace is changing and the old techniques no longer work as well as they did.

In a 1995 study by Yankelovich Partners and Gannett's *USA Weekend*, only 25 percent of respondents said that a television commercial could get them to try a new product. When you look at magazines and newspapers, the situation is worse. Only 15 percent said they'd be influenced by a newspaper ad, and only 13 percent by a magazine ad. That's terrible considering that cruises are a new product to 93 percent of the population! However, 63 percent said that advice from friends and relatives would influence them.

The same report shows that while image matters, price is equally important. Forty-nine percent said that they would be enticed to buy a new product from a company they trust, but that a price-off coupon would produce the same result! Also, the report pictures consumers as "proactive," with 85 percent saying that they felt they had to look out for themselves because no one else really had their interests at heart. As a result, many were using new ways to shop—catalogs, purchasing by mail through an ad, and buying after watching an infomercial![3]

We could write a whole chapter on why this has happened, but that's not what this book is about. What it is about is selling

---

[3]Kevin Goldman, "Ads Induce Few Consumers to Buy, Study Concludes," *The Wall Street Journal*, October 17, 1995.

cruises and vacations. Larry Wilson of Wilson Learning likes to tell his audiences, "If you do what you did, you will get what you got." Travel marketers can no longer do what they did, because what they are now getting is less and less of what they need to survive.

The most important question to be answered is what can be done to improve the marketing and selling of cruises and other vacation products, and how to do it. In the next and last chapter we describe what we see as the travel distribution system of the future. We've modestly called it "Bob and Andy's Vacation Store."

10

Bob & Andy's Vacation Store

Selling the sea—the way we'd do it

Welcome to Bob and Andy's Vacation Store. It's not real—not yet anyway—but creating it on paper is a good way to illustrate how we believe travel agencies can and should operate to maximize their long-term profits instead of teetering on the edge of insolvency.

Location

Since we both live in the Miami area, we'll put our store on Main Highway in downtown Coconut Grove, one of our more affluent suburbs, and because that's the main drag, our store is in an attractive retail environment with plenty of parking, good signage, and the high probability of walk-in traffic. Shopping is popular in this general area, so we could have just as easily picked one of several strip malls or one of two shopping centers.

The idea is to be seen and easily accessible by as many people as possible. Also, because today's shopper has a limited amount of time, we want to be in an area where people are walking around and shopping anyway so that they don't have to make a special stop to see us. That accounts for the popularity of shopping malls, but we didn't pick one because the rents are high and the best locations go to the big chains. Even so, there's lots of retail shops in Coconut Grove as well as restaurants and movie theaters that attract substantial traffic.

Our store windows are tastefully done with interesting displays (that we'll describe in a moment). They are not cluttered, and we have decided to forsake the 40-odd association and affiliation decals that are too frequently found stuck all over the windows of other travel agencies. Our interior is inviting: One side is designed to evoke the feeling and ambiance of a comfortable living room. We have a carpeted floor, a sofa and love seat, upholstered chairs, and two low coffee tables. On the other side, partially hidden by some planters with real plants (which we water daily) to give us a touch of class, are four work stations: desks, files, and a chair for each salesperson and two additional chairs each for prospects. (Note that we've called them prospects. We haven't lost sight of the fact that in our retail culture an individual is a prospect to whom we expect to sell something when she walks through that door, even if she has been our client for many years.) The computer terminal (optional) is mounted on a side return so as not to intrude on the prospect–seller scenario. We know about the hotel research that reveals that people often feel depersonalized when they see their arrangements being handled by computers, which is why many luxury hotels hide them from the sight of guests checking in.

The desk tops in our store also have a set of manila files representing current trips in process. These files most likely won't reflect the full set of current trip files our agents are working with, but are for show to indicate to our prospects that the salesperson is writing lots of business and is well organized. We're not being deceitful here—we just want our prospect to feel as if he is not out there by himself but potentially part of a large contingent of satisfied vacationers.

Displays

There are absolutely no brochures on display in our office where prospects can get their hands on them without the assistance of one of our counselors. (We use the term counselors; however, we and our prospects know that this is a retail store and the staff are really trained travel sales professionals. If they need personal counseling, there's a psychologist down the street who charges $100 an hour!) Our walls are decorated with a few colorful posters indicative of popular vacation spots such as Las Vegas, Mexico, Disney World, a cruise ship in the Caribbean, or scenes from Alaska and Europe. Nothing unusual or exotic is on display—we left our yak teeth from Tibet and our kangaroo pouch from Australia at home. And that poster a tourist office sent us from Macchu Picchu may be beautiful and serene, but since no one has ever purchased a trip to that destination from us, why should we give up valuable wall space when it could be used to showcase a popular destination or activity?

We prefer posters featuring vacation activities rather than specific destinations although they're tough to find. We know that generic sunbathing, tropical shopping, golfing, sailing, sightseeing, and fine dining scenes allow prospects to visualize what they'll be doing on vacation and more important how they'll feel about it. Our experience has taught us that too many prospects think they want specific destinations only because they think, or know from experience, that their needs will be taken care of there. In reality, we know because it is our business to know, there are many different destinations and vacation products that can fulfill their list of needs—some our prospects may have never thought or heard of—and we may be able to perform a genuine and valuable service by recommending one of these alternatives. We understand that prospects' needs are activity and feeling driven, so the proper visual emphasis in our store should be on these rather than on specific destinations.

To further make this point, our window displays—which are changed every month like our smart retail competitors'—are seasonal and display activities that are hot sellers. In winter, we might feature a lounge chair on a sandy beach, with a tall drink and good book, just waiting for a lucky vacationer. Or we might show a pair of skis with poles, boots, and artificial snow. In the summer, perhaps we'll show a small sailboat or canoe, or a compass and backpack. There might be binoculars, an Audubon guide to birds, and a camera as well. Perhaps we'll display a dining table for four, graciously set with fine china, silver, crystal, and a bucket of champagne. People do love to dine well on vacation, and the scene subtly reminds the one who does most of the meal preparation that there won't be any cooking, table setting, or dishes on this trip. Aren't vacations wonderful?

Another window (if we have two) might contain a mannequin or two dressed in the latest fashion for a game of golf, tennis, or croquet. Perhaps a deck of cards, dice, gambling chips, and a backgammon set. Prospects look at the window and mentally fashion their own dream vacations based solely on their tastes and desires. They quickly visualize themselves enjoying the activities they long to do—and will have the time and opportunity to do when they take their vacation. This is good karma!

Where do all the neat props we put in our windows come from? For the most part (except for a few special items which we rent from a display company) they are on loan from cooperating stores in the area. Credit is given with a tastefully discreet tent card placed in the front right corner of the display. As you might expect, we're active in the community and because we all help each other, we're big on reciprocity. We encourage Connie's Sportswear, Joe's Camera Store, Bill's Luggage Warehouse, and Millie's Bridal Boutique, as well as the movie theater, the Italian restaurant, and the bowling alley, to feature our props such as brochures, bag tags, and travel documents in their windows, giving our Vacation Store the same appropriate credit, of course.

The Back of the House

Of course, we have a back office, with a refrigerator, coffee maker, and hot water for tea, but it's not just for us and our counselors. No, we are prepared to, and always do, offer coffee or espresso, tea, mineral water (with or without bubbles), and a selection of soft drinks to our prospects. We want them to feel at home, to be comfortable, to be looked after, to feel like welcome guests. Trust us, the prospects who have been to regular travel agencies immediately discern and appreciate our warm, hospitable atmosphere. It's good sense to put folks at ease when they're about to make an important purchase decision—spending not just their hard earned money but their very valuable time on that important vacation.

The Front of the House

Our counselors all have what we like to call "front-of-the-house personalities." We all enjoy being with people and get a big kick out of helping them find terrific vacation products. We all are very cognizant of the reality that we are in the happiness-making business, and it shows.

Each of us is a positive individual with a healthy amount of self esteem. We are very good at what we do, and we know it. But we're not cocky or arrogant—we simply have a deep sense of pride in our competency and enjoy doing a job as well as it can be done. We are fearless in a selling scenario because we realize both from our past successes and our mastery of selling skills that we'll likely be successful each time, and those few times we're not don't crush us. Far from it! Unfazed, we learn from each encounter, which enriches our tapestry of experience.

When we are successful, we don't view it as just a completed sale but rather as another satisfied client about to experience a terrific vacation, which we made possible. We know that the odds are very heavily in favor of him being very appreciative and grateful for the service we provided: putting him in the vacation picture that best suited his individual needs. And we derive great satisfaction from the fact that he'll return to us for all his vacation needs and he'll tell his friends and associates.

Why are we so sure? Because we made it easy for him! When he returns home after his cruise, there's a personally addressed envelope waiting for him from the counselor who made the sale. The letter trusts he had a good time (he will 95-plus percent of the time), thanks him for the business, and tells him what a pleasure it was to work with him. It goes on to request that if he enjoyed working with us (of course he did!) would he kindly mail the enclosed, prestamped postcards (just two—so that it seems simple enough) to friends and associates he believes would also like to have the benefit of our vacation services. The postcard we have supplied features a color photo of our vacation store on the front and the hand-written notation:

Dear_____:

I just returned from a terrific vacation arranged by Sarah at the Vacation Store. She did a great job! When you're looking for a fabulous vacation, I recommend you call Sarah at 555-1111. Or just stop in and tell her I sent you.

Regards,

Harry

The letter to concludes by saying that each lead will save him $10 on his next vacation . . . with us, of course.

Significantly, the seed of referrals and repeat business was planted twice earlier. First, when the booking was made Sarah asked if our prospect would like to travel with anyone else—perhaps another couple or a relative. It may not have occurred to the client until she brought it up. "Yes, now that you mention it, wouldn't it be great if the Dickinsons and Vladimirs could join us?" Sarah just received two hot leads! Second, when she delivered the final documents (airline tickets, cruise tickets, hotel vouchers, etc.) she expressed once again her confidence that her client was about to embark on a great vacation and mentioned how much she's enjoyed working with him and how she would appreciate it if he would tell his friends about her. "I'll take care of them personally," she tells him.

The Selling Scenario

Although we hire only people we know will make excellent travel professionals, we still give them sales training. They may be experienced travel agents, but we want them to understand *our* philosophy of doing business and to follow certain procedures that we know will produce the kind of results we seek. Join us now at a sales training seminar, which Bob is leading.

Bob on Power Selling

Good afternoon, everyone. Here at Bob & Andy's Vacation Store we offer a whole range of vacation products. But we like to sell cruises because their high level of satisfaction guarantees us having more satisfied customers than anything else we can offer. Having satisfied customers leads to referrals, which leads to more new business. We also honestly believe cruising is the best value we can offer, and just about everyone who walks through that door is interested in value. Finally, because they're all-inclusive, we make more money and you make more money when we sell a cruise. Clearly it's in both our customers' interest and our interest, and that's why we concentrate on selling them. However, the selling techniques that you will learn today will allow you to sell any vacation . . . or anything else, for that matter.

One more thing. In this session I'm going to be giving you a script almost word-for-word to follow. We don't want you to take this the wrong way. We don't think you're stupid or can't figure out how to talk to customers. On the contrary, we wouldn't have hired you if we didn't think you were bright and articulate. But selling is a skill—one we're not born with. What we want to do is not just tell you how to sell, but to show you, and the best way to do that is to be very specific. Once you understand the principles, of course, you'll be much better off putting all of this into your own words. We don't want you to sound like a robot or as if you're talking from a rehearsed script. So take what I tell you here today and put it in your own words so it sounds completely natural.

Qualifying the Client

The first step in the selling process is to do what we call qualifying the client. In simple language, this step consists of establishing a relationship with the person who has just walked in the door or called on the phone and finding out what he's looking for—his needs and wants. The way to do this is to begin by greeting the prospect properly. You might try, "Hi, welcome to the Vacation Store, you've come to the right place. My name is Bob . . . may I have your name please? May I have your address and your phone number?" The replies are written down on a prospect record sheet—legibly! If the prospect balks at providing the information, don't back down, take control. Ask, "Are you interested in having a great vacation?" This question invariably forces the prospect to say "Yes." After all who would want anything less than a great vacation? "Well, we have them at the Vacation Store. But, as you would suspect, we do so much business here that we simply don't deal with folks we don't know . . . I'm Bob, may I have your name please . . . ?"

A key to this whole process is the verbal question mark and the best way to accomplish this is with a pause. It's important to pause after asking a question. The pause "forces" the prospect to respond. Conversely, if you don't pause sufficiently, you let the prospect off the hook and she doesn't feel compelled to reply. Five to ten seconds is usually more than enough time. If she still don't answer, simply say, "I'm sorry, did you hear the question?" If he says he didn't, just repeat it and pause. If the prospect hangs up (if it's a telephone inquiry) or walks out, celebrate it! You've just flushed out someone who very likely was just shopping for the best rebate and not at all serious about giving you the business. At worst, you've wasted a minute or so of your time. Recognize that there are some people who really don't want to buy or who will be very difficult clients (because they enjoy controlling folks and running them ragged). Good riddance to bad rubbish. You don't have to, and shouldn't want to, deal with everybody. We don't expect you to. Be selective.

The next series of questions is the most important part of the qualifying step. How many in the party? Names and addresses? Who will be making the decision? If the prospect sitting with you is not the only decision maker, simply ask when it would be convenient for all of you—the counselor and the decision makers—to get together? If he's reluctant to set a time, then it's probably best to stop the process at that point, except in unusual circumstances. You're wasting everyone's time if all of the decision makers aren't present. It's important that everyone goes through the selling process at the same time so that no one feels psychologically disadvantaged or that his specific concerns or needs have not been addressed. For instance, you recommend to your prospect a cruise that departs from San Juan, Puerto Rico. He says "fine," but when he takes it home, his wife reminds him that she wanted a cruise that leaves from Miami so they could visit her mother on the way back. Your prospect hates his mother-in-law and was trying to avoid this. This isn't your problem, but you will have spent half an hour selling a cruise that he's not going to be able to buy.

Next you need to settle on dates. Ask questions like "When would you like to travel?" "For how long?" "You say you and your wife would like to go away for a week in March—would the week of the 20th be OK? No? You prefer the 13th? Fine."

Having pinned down the dates, it's appropriate to inquire about activities. You need to know the dates first because if they want to go swimming it would be a mistake, for example, to send them to Bermuda in March—the water is still too cold. If they're golfers, the weather there is gorgeous then, so ask, "What are some of the things you and your wife would like to do on vacation?" Listen to the responses carefully and take careful notes. Probe. The prospect is giving you his recipe for their ideal vacation. Attempt to fill in the blanks if there are any. "Does your wife enjoy shopping? What does she like to buy?" If the answer is antiques, a Caribbean cruise might not be as appropriate as a Mediterranean cruise. "Would you like to play some golf?" If he says yes, find out if they're serious golfers. Some destinations have much better golf courses then others. It can make a difference.

A good series of questions is "Where have you gone on previous vacations?" "For how long?" "Where did you stay?" This goes to the issue of budget without asking directly. The truth is that most people will spend what they need to on vacation in order to buy what they want, if they can afford it. At this point your prospect may have no real idea of what her dream vacation will cost. Nor do you know whether she can afford it. But a good clue is past spending habits. If they went to Hawaii last year you'll know a lot by determining whether they stayed at the Days-Out Inn or the Halekulani in Honolulu, for instance. One tip: don't make any assumptions based on dress, race, or accent. Your prospect may be worth several million dollars, but if he's been puttering around in his garden all day or running errands, he may not look to you like someone who could ever afford a Seabourn cruise. If you don't get a clear answer from this question ("we rented a condo" could mean any price range for example) ask about enjoyable dining experiences. "Yup, Denny's" is a fairly good clue, as is "We really enjoy Le Cirque in New York and their range of older Burgundies is quite marvelous."

At the Vacation Store we keep things very simple. We try to put prospects into one of three bins: budget, mid-range, and top-of-the-line, by asking the kind of questions I've suggested here, listening and observing, and taking notes. It's really quite easy to select among three pretty different lifestyles.

As a thoroughly professional agent there's still another piece of information you need before you are in a position to recommend a vacation that your prospect will really enjoy. It's crucial if you want him to return, and you do, because a lot of our business is repeat business. You need to know what they don't like. "Is there anything you would prefer to avoid?" "What's the worst thing that ever happened to you on any of your vacations that you don't want to run into again?" "Any hassles?" All these questions help jog the memory as well as help prospects get in touch with their vacation needs and priorities. Too many prospects know that they want to get away from the rat race, but they don't always realize how many ways there are to do that. They also may forget that while they may want to visit Germany and drive around visiting old castles, the traffic and speed on the autobahn along with signage in a strange language can be nerve-wracking for all but the most confident drivers. It is not an escape from the rat race—it's just a different rat race! Moreover, to the extent that a prospect consciously thinks about what things he wants to do and his priorities, you can recommend a vacation product that's a close fit. Obviously, the better the fit, the better the enjoyment.

Now step back and take a look at what's been happening here. During this entire qualifying step, you were in total control of the situation. Your prospect did most of the talking and thought, therefore, that he was in control. Importantly, the situation was gratifying for the prospect because you appeared to be (and indeed you were) listening carefully and even taking notes! You were clearly interested in him and that helps to build a relationship which fosters trust.

Features and Benefits

The second step is what we call features and benefits. You have just gleaned a vacation recipe from your prospect. Now is the time to play back your notes. "You said you and your wife wanted to get away from the cold winter and relax and get a tan. You want the possibilities of some night life, good food, and good service. You'd like to play some golf, and she enjoys shopping for jewelry, perfumes, and souvenirs. If I can get you all those things in a casual, hassle-free environment for about the same price as your last vacation, how would that sound?" You've replayed the vacation recipe: the features the prospect is looking for. By doing so you've established credibility with your prospect. He knows that you know what their needs are. You are all now on the same page of our training manual! If the prospect says it sounds good, you can move on to close the sale. If not, something is either missing or misunderstood! You then say, "I'm sorry, what did I leave out?" This question allows you to fill in or clarify the recipe. Once clarified, you recite the amended recipe back to the prospect, ending with the same question: "How does that sound?" If you have the right recipe now, he'll say "yes." If you don't, he'll say "no" until you ask further probing questions like "What did I leave out (of your vacation recipe)?"

Finally, get all the recipe needs out on the table. At the moment he says "yes, it sounds good," you are ready to close the sale.

But, there's another piece to this step that goes along way to mitigating buyer's remorse—that sickening, queasy, unsettling feeling that we all sometimes get when we make what we perceive to be a rash or impetuous purchase decision. This feeling can take all the fun out of the purchase and perhaps even the vacation! You alleviate these symptoms by supplementing the features you've already identified with the extra benefits the vacation you have in mind offers that haven't yet been discussed. A good strategy is to ask, "What if at the same time, I could also give you a place that offers 24-hour room service free? You mentioned that you enjoyed dancing. How about the choice of three different bands and orchestras and a state-of-the-art disco? You said your wife liked shopping, how about duty-free shopping where she can get much better bargains? How about being able to watch continuous movies in your own room for free? You didn't mention it, but what if you had the option of a full gambling casino along with everything else?"

In other words, if your prospect was ready to buy based on features 1 through 8 (which matched his stated vacation needs), chances are he'll be even more eager to purchase after he understands all the extra benefits your recommendation has to offer. He is now ready to purchase, content in the knowledge that you've been in touch with both decision makers' vacation needs, you understand what they are, and you have the product that will deliver them.

What makes this step work so effectively for us is that our office only sells 18 products. Therefore, we expect each of our travel counselors to be conversant with each of those 18 travel suppliers and the features and benefits of their products. We've sampled the products and know them and the kinds of people who enjoy them. As Rod McLeod, Royal Caribbean's Executive Vice President, says, "Product and destination knowledge are the bullets, and the gun is your ability to sell. If you don't have the product knowledge, you're going to be shooting blanks." Of course, you need to know how to sell, too.

That's why we're here today. Vicki Freed, Senior Vice President of Carnival, points out: "The truth of the matter is that product knowledge rarely gets used if you don't have sales training." She's right and we're giving you the training now. It is also our policy to give you the opportunity to obtain more product knowledge. The way we do that is to give you five paid days off in addition to your vacation each year to learn about one of our suppliers. Not only do we give you the time but we pay your expenses for familiarization and inspection trips that you may be invited to attend providing, of course, that it's for one of our preferred suppliers. Additionally, we expect you to attend travel industry conferences, trade shows, supplier seminars, and/or destination and product specialist courses like those offered by CLIA's Sales and Management Institute. We know from experience that knowledgeable sales people are simply more effective and therefore more productive.

You're very likely to encounter a situation where someone asks one of us for the product of another supplier. What we'd like you to say is, "I'm sorry, we don't handle that product" and smile. You can expect two possible responses: either "Oh, why not?" or "Well, what do you sell?" To the first, we reply "Because we've had terrific success with this (generally similar) product." Nine times out of ten they'll be satisfied and inquire about it. If that doesn't satisfy them, we go on to explain that we only sell the vacation products we can recommend with confidence. All retail stores carry only limited brands of merchandise that they're sure their customers will like. Sak's Fifth Avenue and Macy's don't carry every brand of suit or dress made. Their buyers select the ones they consider best, and that's why their customers are loyal to them. We do the same thing. If they ask what we do sell, we reply with the name of one of our preferred suppliers. We hedge our bets a little and supplement our product line up with an additional 30 or so suppliers of exotic destinations such as African safaris, South Pacific resorts, and East Indian sightseeing tours. Two brochures of each of these suppliers are kept in alphabetical order in a tub file. We make no pretext about being conversant with them. They are there just in case. Additionally, two of us are available, schedule permitting, to prepare FIT itineraries (FIT is an industry term originally standing for "foreign independent tour" but today meaning individual customized itineraries) at our regular consulting rate of $75 an hour. Frankly, the rate is too low to make the return we desire but, fortunately, it's high enough to discourage all but the most earnest clients.

Closing the Sale

At this point you go to the phone and close the sale, which is the third step. "I've got just the vacation for you two. You'll be very happy with what I've selected. But, as you may expect, this vacation is very popular, so before we do anything else, let's check availability." This introduces the concept of scarcity—the suggestion that this great vacation dream may evaporate if there's no space. Upon hearing this, our prospect is eager to learn if the space is available. The desire for the product (which is still unknown to the prospective buyer) just intensified.

Because you've predetermined which of the three budget "bins" the prospects are in during the qualifying phase, you can be very specific about the accommodations you are requesting. When you call the supplier's reservations department or use your PC or CRT (computer reservation terminal) to make an automated booking, you have all the information you need, written down, at your fingertips. You don't have to bother the prospect, who is now busy fantasizing about the upcoming vacation and/or concerned about its availability, with mundane, back-down-to-earth issues like names, addresses, and so forth. After making the booking, you say to the prospect "You're in luck, they have the availability. You will need just $400 to secure this reservation. Will you be using a credit card or a check?"

As a matter of policy, our counselors are forbidden to give their prospects an option. If prospects can't pay then, we encourage them to do so quickly in the hope that we can still secure the same space. We don't agree to hold anything. This sense of urgency helps to close the sale (that is, get the money). Of course, we take an option on the space if we can but that's between us and the supplier. We don't give options to prospects—not to be deceitful but because it allows us to give better service to all of our clients. Suppliers love dealing with us because our cancellation rate is many times lower than regular agencies who indiscriminately give out options on suppliers' space on the off chance someone might book. This is a benefit that ultimately accrues to our customers and thereby differentiates us from our competitors. Because we go out of our way to develop this kind of relationship with our suppliers, when we really need a favor for one of our clients we can often get it when others can't.

By this point, please notice that if we've done our job well, the prospect is prepared to purchase the vacation without knowing where he is going! When you get down to vacation needs, destination is frequently not all that important. Sure, if one's primary vacation need is specific sightseeing opportunities like Paris or London, the destination is critical. No matter what, if someone wants to visit Paris on her vacation, no other destination or vacation option can substitute for that. But, on the other hand, the vast majority of vacationers do not have such a specific sightseeing objective, so their vacation needs can be met with, typically, a whole host of vacation choices.

Naturally, you'll tell the prospect what you're recommending when you ask for the deposit. Let's just say, as fate would have it, that your recommendation is a one-week Caribbean cruise. (Say hallelujah because that's what Bob and Andy like to sell!) If you've taken step 1 and qualified properly, and you've taken the second step which has identified and matched features and benefits, then chances are very good—at least fifty-fifty—that you'll successfully close the sale (the third step) that is, get the money. But you might run into an obstacle, some objection you'll need to overcome. Doing this requires an optional fourth step.

Overcoming Objections

Notice that this fourth step is optional. There may well be no re-sistance at all to your recommendation, because after all, it *did* meet the vacation needs of the prospect, which you covered in step 2. Furthermore, step 4 can only occur *after* trying to close the sale. In other words, the sales process itself is not disrupted in any way between the prospect and the seller. This is great karma!

If there is an objection to a cruise, it can only be motion dis-comfiture, a term we prefer to seasickness. Other potential objec-tions to cruising that frequently pop up in consumer surveys—cost, boredom, regimentation, and confinement—simply should not apply here if you have properly taken the second step of match-ing features and benefits. Cost issues have been resolved in ad-vance since you have selected your recommendation on what it will cost in relation to the prospect's last vacation. Remember, too, most folks have a very fuzzy notion of the cost of a vacation (see Chapter 8).

Cost, boredom, confinement, and regimentation have all be-come non-issues because the features and benefits step assured the prospects that all their activity and other needs would be met in a hassle-free environment. So what's left to object to when sell-ing a cruise? The only remaining potential bugaboo is mal-de-mer. In the event this objection is raised, the first thing to do is get in step with the prospect. Empathize with him . . . don't argue. It's poor psychology to be contentious with someone you hope will spend potentially several thousand dollars in your store! Say something like, "I certainly can understand how you might be concerned about sea sickness." (Note that it's not a "problem" but merely a "concern.") "I had (be sure to use the past tense) the same concern until I took my first cruise. Then I discovered that the ship was so large and the ride was so smooth that I couldn't figure out how all those palm trees were moving past the picture windows. Finally, I realized they weren't moving, we were!" At this point, you are of course making direct eye con-tact (if the prospect is in front of you) and speaking confidently as you continue. "Don't take my word for it, as you can well imag-ine, many folks we've done business with have had the same con-cern you and I have had." (You're still talking in the past tense.) "They were so delighted with their cruise and so pleased that they didn't let their concern stop them from trying this terrific vacation that they've willingly offered to answer questions from any of our clients who have this same one. May I give you their names and phone numbers so you can give them a call?" Again, you have a confident approach, your direct eye contact also allows you to look for telltale signs that his reluctance is melting away. Now here's the clincher we've used successfully a number of times. "I'll tell you what, don't take my or anybody else's word for it. I want you both to truly enjoy this vacation. So I'm going to give you an insurance policy." (Pause here for a moment to let this sink in.) "When you pick up your documents, I'm going to give you a set of Seabands®. These are elastic wrist bracelets that employ the principle of acu-pressure. People swear by them and there are no side effects. So you don't need to be concerned any more. Now, will you be depositing by credit card or check?"

This approach, in our experience, works about 80 percent of the time. It's not perfect . . . nothing in this world is . . . but it's pretty darned effective. Occasionally, we've encountered prospects who say: "A cruise is out of the question, I'll get seasick." Rather than trying to end the conversation and throw in the towel, the door-opening response is: "If I can show you a way to have this great vacation and not have to be concerned about seasickness, how would you feel about that?" Usually, they'll relent and be open to considering it. Then you go into your pitch. If they're not open, than of course we want to sell them a tour or another vacation package that is offered by one of our other regular travel suppliers.

Notice, please, that this three- or four-step sales process never involves more than one vacation option. Presenting two or more options is a cop-out. To the prospect it sounds like you're implying that you are not confident or competent enough to select the ideal vacation. You're asking them to select from two or more . . . even though *you're* supposed to be the expert!

We subscribe to the K.I.S.S. theory of selling: Keep It Simple, Salesperson! Folks want and appreciate one recommendation. To present two or more creates confusion, takes more time, and sets up the risk that the wrong choice (or no choice) will be made. No one wants to make the wrong choice—especially concerning one's vacation. Furthermore, if they have to make the choice, what's the point of coming to you in the first place?

I have another suggestion for you. I've covered a lot of ground in this seminar. For a more thorough treatment of these selling steps, we and our counselors frequently watch the videos on how to sell products made by our most important travel suppliers. One of the ones I like best, as you can imagine, is the 60-minute video "Bob live—On Winning Selling Techniques," which Carnival Cruise Lines sells for $15. They offer a money-back guarantee if you're not satisfied. So far as I know, no one's asked for his money back yet!

I also have a confession to make to you. For 13 years, until 1986, I went around the country telling thousands and thousands of travel agents at breakfast, lunch, and dinner seminars and speeches to suggest cruises when prospects inquired about any vacations. I used to tell them that no travel agent was ever killed or maimed for doing this. I was wrong. I was suggesting that they begin the selling the process with the product. As we've said before, prescription without diagnosis is malpractice!

The sales techniques you've learned today start with the prospect, not the product. This is the only intelligent approach to successful selling. Master these four steps and you'll be able to derive tremendous satisfaction in your life because, by putting them into practice, you'll be able to enable folks to be in touch with their needs and then provide them with the means to fulfill them. This process is the essence of sound communications—asking and listening to the other person's response—and conflict resolution. The benefits of this to our personal lives, besides our career, should be obvious to all!

Keeping Score

At the Vacation Store Bob, Andy, and all of their agents keep close track of our sales prospects and sales. Each of us uses a sales contact sheet. This allows us to see how we're progressing, and how we compare to the others in the office, both in terms of the number of prospects and the closure rate. This year, our top counselor is closing about 80 percent of the time, and our rookie (six months in the business) is closing about 30 percent.

To make sure that all of us have an equal chance at prospects, we use the "up" system. Commonly used in men's suit departments and auto showrooms among other selling situations, the "up" system rotates the prospects through the sales force. Among the five, I'll get the first, sixth, eleventh prospect as long as I'm available. If I'm already with someone, or out of the office, I'm out of the rotation until I'm available.

Now you may ask what happens if a client who I've been working with needs servicing while I'm not available? What's the motivation for another counselor to pitch in and help? The answer is the Golden Rule. My co-workers are eager to look after my clients because they're smart enough to realize that there will be times when they'll be out of the office and their clients will need servicing. In addition, we're very much a customer-focused organization. When a customer walks in, he wants immediate service and we are committed to giving it to him. If he indicates that he may want to wait, that's fine, but then it's his choice not ours.

On the wall in the back office, we have a series of charts that show week-to-date, month-to-date, and year-to-date sales for each of us. This visual reminder is very motivational! To keep things very focused, we don't count revenue, we count cabins. A 3- or 4-day cruise counts as one-half a cabin, a 7- to 9-day cruise as one cabin, a 10- to 14-day as two cabins and so forth. This eliminates the question of how many folks are in the cabin and desensitizes us to the quixotic cruise pricing so prevalent today. If Sally sold a cabin for $1,000 and later the cruise line offered a special two-passengers-for-the-price-of-one promotion, she still gets credit for the entire cabin, not half the revenue. Now we know that some travel agents will say that our system doesn't recognize our counselors for selling up—that is, convincing the prospect to buy something more expensive. They're absolutely right! It recognizes them for selling, period! Our theory is that selling up is a myth. We sell what the prospect needs and can afford. We classify folks in three budget categories. Agents who "sell up" don't really go through that discipline. They assume everyone is looking for the cheapest price to begin with. Selling up, in reality, is merely putting the prospects in one of the other two categories they should have been in from the beginning! So we don't encourage it or reward it.

We have weekly and monthly contests to recognize the counselor who sold the most cabins during the period. Of course we have a counselor of the year, as well. We reward these achievements with weekly dinners, monthly fams (familiarization trips), and once-a-year a suite on a preferred supplier. These rewards are over and above our normal compensation and fam policy. Our goal is to motivate with the powerful tool of recognition. The visual reminder is seen by all of us. It gently but firmly allows us to stay focused on our individual (and therefore collective) goals. Unlike many others, we record a sale on the day the deposit is received (normally, the day the sale is made), *not* the day of final payment or the day the cruise sails or returns. This is because we choose to emphasize closing the sale and GTM (getting the money). Any of these other events may occur months later, too far away from the sale itself to effectively reinforce the positive sales behavior we want. Our competitors sometimes ask us how we can control things if someone subsequently cancels and the sale unravels. The answer is simple: we reverse the booking in the week that it cancels.

Our counselors are each compensated differently because each has a different salary history. Sarah, our rookie, with no prior salary history, was hired on a draw against commissions. She's paid $500 a week as a draw—That's $26,000 per year for a sharp twenty-year-old with no prior agency experience. Her commission breakdown is simplicity itself. Here's how we figure it:

Commission per Cabin

Length of Cruise (days)	Commission
2–5	$ 40
6–9	$100
10-14	$150 or 40%*
15–20	$250 or 40%
21+	$300 or 40%

*The smaller of the dollar amount or the percent of commission.

We figure she's on track to sell 400 cabins this year for an expected earned income of about $40,000. As with the sales contests, she and all of the counselors receive full commission credit with the deposit, *not* final payment. This is not too generous, it's simply smart business. It recognizes successful behavior quickly and simply. Again, if there is a cancellation (only 5 percent of the time, on average), the commission income is reversed in the week of cancellation. Every one of us knows how this works, understands the system, and has signed off on it. When the rare cancellation occurs, there are no surprises or recriminations. Rather than cry the one time when a sale is reversed, we celebrate the 19 times that we're compensated many months in advance of final payment.

Our most senior counselor, Sally, has been a travel agent for 15 years. She's been used to a steady paycheck and is, frankly, set in her ways. She has no desire to take any risk on the downside, compensation-wise. We respect her position, of course, but still want to reward her for enhanced productivity. Accordingly, we don't adjust her salary, but rather provide her with a lower level of incentive that kicks in after her performance funds her base salary (and benefits). Her base is $30,000 and we calculate our benefit package off an additional value of $6,000 annually. Therefore, she must sell a sufficient number of cruises each month to "fund" $3,000 a month. The numbers look like this:

The Vacation Store Average Commission

Average revenue/cabin	$2,000
Average commission rate	16%
Average commission income/booking	$320

If Sally sells 400 cabins a year, she'll generate $128,000 of revenue for the Vacation Store. Our guideline is that compensation (salary plus fringe benefits) should equal 40 percent of commission revenue, so

$128,000 commission revenue × 40% salary and fringe benefit contribution

$$= \$51,200 \text{ Contributing to salary/fringe}$$

Per booking this works out to:

$320 × 40% = $128 contribution to salary/fringe

To fund Sally's $3,000 compensation per month, she needs to sell 24 cabins per month or 288 each year. Accordingly, our incentive begins with the 25th cabin Sally sells each month. Her incentive is 50 percent less than Sarah's per booking for each booking beyond 24:

Commission per Cabin

Length of Cruise (Days)	Commission
2–5	$20
6–9	$50
10–14	$75 or 20%
15–20	$125 or 20%
20+	$150 or 20%

*The smaller of the dollar amount or the percent of commission.

The reason the incentive is less is that Sarah is willing to take downside risk and Sally is not. If we have a slow month (August is usually troublesome), Sarah may not earn her draw, reducing our labor cost, but Sally's base compensation is fixed. There's an important stipulation: The base sales quota of 24 cabins rolls each month. In other words, for example, if Sally sold 18 cabins in January, she has to sell 30 in February, in this same example, before she qualifies for the incentive. If she sells 28 cabins in February, then she'd have to sell 26 cabins in March before the incentive goes into effect. This ensures our Vacation Store will not inadvertently overpay Sally for uneven sales activity. It also discourages Sally from unfairly "loading" one month's sales activity.

So, if Sally sells 400 cabins a year, the same as Sara, her compensation is as follows:

24 cabins × 12 months = 288 cabins = base quota

400 cabins – 288 quota = 112 incentive cabins

average incentive: $50/cabin

total incentive $50 ×112 cabins = $5,600

Sally's total salary and incentive earnings =

$30,000 salary + $5,600 incentive = $35,600

Sally earned only 11 percent less than Sarah for the same number of cabins sold. With each additional cabin, however, Sarah earns 100 percent more than Sally.

Which leads us to Jack. In the business ten years, Jack is a bit of a gambler, but not completely. He was willing to cut his monthly salary of $2,500 (the same as Sally's) in half in exchange for a richer incentive. With not-quite-Solomon-like precision, we partially split the difference and created an incentive that was 90 percent of Sarah's that kicked in at the 13th booking: Jack responded and sold $1,000,000 worth of cabins. At an average rate of $2,000 a cabin, that amounted to 500 cabins a year. His compensation is as follows:

Base cabins 12 months × 12 cabins/month = 144

Incentive cabins (500 –144 = 356)

Incentive: 356 cabins × $90 cabin = $32,040

Jack's total compensation = $15,000 salary + $32,040 incentive = $47,000

Had he sold 400 cabins, he would have earned $38,040—more than Sally but less than Sarah for the same amount of business sold. On incremental business, because he was willing to take a salary cut, he receives 80 percent more incentive than Sally (90 percent versus 50).

So here's how our compensation sorts out:

The Vacation Store—1995 Results

Employee	Booking	Base Salary	Incentive	Total
Sarah	400	$0	$40,000	$40,000
Sally	400	$30,000	$ 5,600	$35,600
Jack	500	$15,000	$32,040	$47,040
Andy	600*	$0	$60,000	$60,000
Bob	600*	$0	$60,000	$60,000
Clerk	0	$18,600**	$ 4,400***	$25,000
Total	2500	$63,600	$202,040	$265,640

*Our productivity is blended so that Andy, who is also our main rainmaker (sales and marketing director) doesn't feel too bad.
**A clerk magnifies our usefulness.
***The clerk gets a year-end incentive based on the overall profitability of the Vacation Store. It's meaningful: Almost 25% of his base pay.

You might be thinking: Whoa! How can a six-person agency afford to pay so well. The answer is because of its fundamental productivity: five counselors are averaging $1,000,000 in sales each, over twice the norm of the so-called leisure travel agent. Let's look at the overall Vacation Store profit and loss statement for the year:

Vacation Store P&L

REVENUE:		
	Gross Cruise Revenue	$5,000,000
	Cabins Sold	21
	Average Commission Rate	16%
	Gross Commission Revenue	$800,000
	Year-End Override Incentives	$ 25,000
	(1 point retroactive on 50% of	
	the business)	
	Total Revenue	$825,000
COSTS:	Compensation	
	Salaries	$ 63,600
	Incentives	$202,040
	Total Compensation	$265,640
	Fringe Benefits (20%)	$ 53,000
	Rent (1500 sq. ft. @ $20/foot)	$ 30,000
	Utilities	$ 24,000
	Marketing Budget	$200,000*
	($80/cabin × 2,500 cabins)	
	R&D (seminars/fams	$ 25,000
	@ $5,000/counselor)	
	Travel & Entertainment	$ 25,000
	Postage, Accounting, Misc.	$ 24,000
	@ $2,000/Month	
	Client Gifts, Champagne, Lunches,	$ 75,000
	Limos, etc.** @ $30 per cabin	
	Total Cost	$731,640
PROFITS		$ 93,360
	Profit reinvestment	$ 13,360
	Profit distribution to owners	$ 80,000***

*We target to negotiate an average of $15/passenger, or $30/cabin, as marketing co op money from our six preferred cruise-line suppliers. That gives us additional marketing funds of $30 x 2,500 = $75,000 for a total marketing budget of $275,000.
**The value depends on the length of the cruise as well as how easy the client is to deal with. Let's face it, some clients exact a charge against psychic income! In those instances, we scale back or eliminate client gifts.
***This gives Andy and Bob total annual income of $100,000 each.

This profit and loss statement represents a very fat marketing budget. As a result, we expect the $275,000 to generate sufficient traffic to support the sale of at least 3,000 cabins in the next year. This raises an interesting question: Can the five of us sell an average of 600 cabins apiece without being run ragged? That amounts to almost three bookings per day per counselor. The answer is probably yes with an average sale and service time of two hours per booking. Don't forget, we have a clerk to help us, as well. But even if we add an additional counselor, on full incentive like Sarah, and she or he sells all the additional cabins, the additional profit to the Vacation Store is still significant:

Incremental Revenue

500 cabins @ $2,000/cabin =	$1,000,000
Commission @ 16% =	$ 160,000
Override Bonus @ 1% on 50% of Overall business	$ 5,000
Total Incremental Revenue	$ 165,000

Incremental costs

Compensation 500 cabins @ $100/cabin	$ 50,000
Fringe @ 20%	$ 10,000
Client gifts @ $30/cabin	$ 15,000
R & D (seminars, fams etc.)	$ 5,000
Travel & Entertainment	$ 5,000
Postage/Accounting/Misc.	$ 5,000
Total Incremental Costs	$ 90,000
Incremental Profit	$ 75,000

If we do the additional business ourselves, without hiring a counselor, we would make an additional $40,000 for a total of $115,000.

In all the calculations, we assumed that 100 percent of the actual vacation products sold were cruises. You may suspect that we are unduly biased (Who, us?). We did this to assist cruise-only agencies by using unit cost and revenue data pertinent to their operations. In actuality, there are over 7,000 cruise-only agencies, but, at the moment, there are only a hundred or so vacation stores. To adjust the data to include land-based vacation packages, use the following average package prices and commissions. You'll quickly understand why we want to sell every cruise we can!

Average Unit Sale Data (per Booking)

	Land Package	Cruise
Revenue	$1,000	$2,000
Blended commission rate	13%	16%
Average commission/booking	$130	$320

As you can see, the unit commission revenue for a land vacation is less than half that of a cruise vacation. Accordingly, incentive payouts have to be scaled back disproportionately to ensure that the land vacation sale contributes an adequate contribution to overhead. Using Sarah's full incentive as a reference, here's how we would compensate a land vacation:

Length of Stay (Days)	Land	Cruise
2–5	$ 5	$40
6–9	$ 10	$100
10–14	$ 50	$150 or 40% of the commission
15–20	$100	$200 or 40% of the commission
20+	$150	$275 or 40% of the commission

The land incentives of the other folks are prorated from Sarah (who was on 100% incentive) in the same base as the cruise incentives detailed above.

Importantly, incentives—cruise or land—are only paid on sales of preferred suppliers' products, of which we have the following in our store:

Vacation Store Preferred Suppliers

Cruise:	1	Mass-market
	2	Premium
	4	Niche (luxury specialty, Hawaii, Riverboat, Exploration)
	<u>1</u>	Luxury
Total Cruise Lines	8	
Tour Operator:	1	Hawaii, West Coast
	2	Major airline captive (including Las Vegas, Orlando, & other domestic U.S.; Europe; South America)
	1	Caribbean
	1	Mexico
	1	Pacific Rim
	1	Canada
	1	Africa
	<u>2</u>	European (budget and escorted)
Total Tour Operators	<u>10</u>	
Grand Total	<u>18</u>	

We have brochures available on 34 other products because they have some brand recognition or as a safety net in case of lack of availability (much rarer in practice than perception), or because some few folks have asked for the off-the-beaten-path destinations that they prefer, such as India and the Galapagos.

We don't pay incentives on these 34 products because:

- There's not enough volume to earn override commissions (override commissions fund most if not all of the incentives).
- We want to stay focused on selling a few products—so we know them better and direct prospects to them to drive up

commission revenue. All our preferred suppliers give us the opportunity to increase the percentage of commission we can earn if we improve our sales volume with them to stipulated levels.

- We want to reinforce the appropriate behavior—which is selling preferred suppliers, not order taking obscure products.

Oh yes, beyond the 52 products, incentives are a non-issue— there is no sale. We just simply tell folks "Sorry, we don't handle it." (Anyhow, the request for other products as we have pointed out, is very, very rare.)

Marketing Efforts

Advertising

As you might suspect, we don't just wait for the business to come to us. We advertise our Vacation Store, using co-op supplier dollars with the brand-positioning slogan, "Greater Miami's Best Vacation Store." We like preemptive positioning! Our Yellow Pages ad catches the eye—it was designed *after* we looked at what the regular agencies were doing. Andy writes a gratis travel column for the local paper and a three-minute travel advisory for one of our radio stations in exchange for plugging the Vacation Store with publicity at the end of the column. This gives us free exposure in each Sunday's travel section and on the air, while at the same time positioning Andy and our other counselors as "travel experts."

Reciprocity

We do business with a good number of folks: accountants, lawyers, insurance agents, electricians, print shops, the local Fed-Ex office, restaurants, delis, coffee services, florists, and so forth. Because we do business with them, we let them all know that we expect them to do business with us . . . and tell their friends about us, too! We do the same thing. We send them additional business based on our referrals, and we make certain that we get credit for their new-found business. This creates an obligation if you will, which reinforces our relationships and motivates our vendors to help us even more. To aid in the process, we created a one-panel, envelope-stuffer-sized promotional piece, in color, that speaks to the advantages of using the Vacation Store. It says in part:

Bob & Andy's Vacation Store: Who Needs Us?

If you're a person who doesn't know how important a good vacation can be, you don't need us.

If you don't believe a vacation can provide some of the most exciting and memorable experiences in your lifetime, you don't need us.

If you don't care whether you end up with an average vacation at an average price, you don't need us.

But if you don't fall into any of those three classifications, then you're our kind of client:

Someone who can't stand mediocrity in travel or anything else. Someone who takes a vacation, not because they have money to spend, but because they have wishes to be filled. Someone who demands a really terrific vacation and a good value at the same time.

That's what Bob & Andy's Vacation Store provides. Travel consultants who listen to you to make sure you get what you want.

Trained professionals who know what they're talking about and provide superior service and sound advice

Courteous folks who will be pleased to assist you by phone or in person.

Find out for yourself why everyone calls us "Greater Miami's Best Vacation Store."

Our brochure has a photo of Bob and Andy and our staff to personalize the business. The bottom quarter of the piece is our business card, which can be cut off and appropriately filed by the prospect.

Networking

We've inventoried all the organizations that each of the six of us belongs to, as well as those of our close friends and relatives with whom we have some influence. In our community, that process gave us a list of 42 organizations, including church parishes, garden clubs, Rotary, Kiwanis, the Jaycees, a bowling league, Toastmasters, and three local PTAs. One of us has been designated as the lead salesperson for each group lead—responsible for creating as much exposure and group and individual business as possible.

Our company belongs to the local chapter of the Executive Association. This organization exists solely to promote reciprocity business and business leads among 100 noncompeting member companies. Not only is the business good, but the social opportunities have allowed us to become personal friends with a lot of nice folks.

Business Promotions

We scouted the local beauty parlors and determined which one was the best for our purposes. We found Madge's, an established, stable, salon with middle to upscale clientele, including a number of trendsetter types. We approached the owner and offered her a free cruise for two for each 15 cabins sold from leads through her shop. We stock and maintain a brochure holder, next to the beauty parlor's magazine table, promoting our favorite cruise line. The brochure has a sticker that invites a prospect to bring it in when she's ready to book for a free cabin upgrade. This allows us to track Madge's progress. The cost? At a maximum, 6.25 percent of sales as a commission to Madge, who in effect is acting as an outside agent for us with practically no other overhead. Now that she's returned from her first cruise (and juiced), she's talking about putting a group together! There is also a very popular deli in a strip shopping center a mile away from us—we're doing the same thing with a brochure rack strategically placed by the cash register. The gregarious owner touts our cruises to customers he feels would enjoy them (who wouldn't?).

Once every two weeks, a popular restaurant several miles from our store has a drawing for a free lunch for two. We set up the display, and we buy the lunch, of course. In exchange, we receive all the business cards submitted for the drawing—leads we would never have had otherwise. The patrons of the restaurant are exposed to our name, phone number, address, and our slogan as "Greater Miami's Best Vacation Store." The restaurant owner appreciates both the business and the fact that he's offering his clientele a chance to win something for nothing. We'll stop the promotion when the number of new leads dwindles. Then we'll experiment with $50 and $100 discount coupons with a very limited (two-week) redemption window. This will be timed to coincide with a slow booking period. Again, the restaurateur is motivated to offer his clientele an exclusive deal. And it will be exclusive to him for at least a few weeks on either side of the promotion window.

We always participate in the local annual bridal fair but continue the promotion year-round by utilizing a joint effort flyer promotion that includes the top florist, photographer, limousine company, bridal store, and tux rental firm in the area. The flyer extols the virtues of each of us and touts the years of experience we have working together to ensure fabulous weddings and honeymoons (that's where we come in)! These flyers are prominently displayed at each of the participating firms. It's practically free exposure and gets great leads. Also, there's a sort of Good Housekeeping seal of approval aspect to all this: The Vacation Store is being associated with some of the best stores in town!

Because we don't display brochures in our store, we have plenty of wall space. In addition to attractive vacation posters and a beautiful world map (so we can show people exactly where they'll be visiting), our eye-catcher is a photo display of happy, smiling clients, captioned with their names, having fun on their (mostly cruise) vacations. This is a subtle but effective third-party endorsement both for our store and for our terrific vacations.

We give our customers a $10 bill when we present their travel documents, asking them to kindly buy an extra photo of themselves from the ship's photographer for us to display. They are invariably flattered and frequently comply with two or three pictures! In addition to posters of gleaming white ships in exotic locales, vacation prospects see friends and neighbors—real people—enjoying themselves. To a first-time cruiser, this display makes the cruise experience more tangible and accessible, silently transmitting the message, "They're having fun, they chose to cruise, so can you."

We have a separate section of the display for groups. These photos, too, are captioned with the names and residential areas of each individual and the group name and sailing date. All photos mention the ship and itinerary (Alaska, Lower Caribbean, Bahamas, etc.). They are rotated seasonally to emphasize products that are likely to be booked at the time. For example, family travel photos are prominent in the first half of the year, Alaska travel in the fall and winter, and the Caribbean year-round. At all times, however, we try to show the diversity of our clientele to increase the chances of having all prospects relate to the photos.

Sales Representatives

We see very few sales reps, mainly because we deal with so few suppliers. This saves time for us and for the reps of the products we don't sell. They appreciate our honesty, which enables them to use their time elsewhere, where they can possibly be more productive. When we do initiate an appointment with a sales rep for one of our 18 preferred suppliers, we have specific objectives that we review by telephone, ahead of the meeting. We want to give the rep every opportunity to know what we want to accomplish at the meeting so that he or she can prepare whatever answers may be needed or obtain approvals from the home office. In other words, we don't use the meeting itself to ask the questions, but to obtain the answers!

This process applies as well to a scheduled sales call where we're looking to the supplier to help us sell more of its product. Then we have an annual goal-setting and co-op budget request meeting—each September or October, or a subsequent meeting if necessary, to discuss a mid-course correction on the year's plan, say in April after reviewing first quarter sales activity, or a meeting to discuss new projects, unanticipated in the previous budget process.

Sometimes the reps will call us to set up a meeting. When that happens we use the same technique. What is the purpose of the meeting? Is there anything we should prepare in advance to ensure that the meeting successfully achieves your objective(s)? How long do you think the meeting should last? This allows both of us to schedule our time appropriately. Sometimes these meetings don't need to occur. The rep might say that she'll be in the area next week and she'd like to give our staff a product update. We'll ask on the phone: "What's new?" The answer frequently, is not too much. The rep is either just making a courtesy call or trying to hit a sales-call quota.

Reps like to spend time in their star agencies—those that embrace their product to the virtual exclusion of direct competitors. On those visits, they feel at home, supported and unthreatened. Conversely, cold calls or sales calls where the agents are order takers with no control over their business, represent over 95 percent of all sales reps' accounts. On these calls, sales reps feel either threatened (their fear of rejection) or disheartened (encountering agents who need to get in control of their business and make a difference) or both. After days or weeks of being in this sort of hostile environment, a safe harbor, an oasis, looks pretty good! From our perspective, though, if a call is really unnecessary, and we are pretty busy with prospects, we will take control and politely but firmly decline the appointment. We like our reps, but we're not their nursemaids. After all, we *do* have a business to run!

The Home Office

We make it a point to personally know key people in the home offices of our preferred suppliers. The more important the supplier is to our business, the more people in the home office we want to know and the better we want to know them. Even more important, we want them to know us and our agency very well. Some of these suppliers may do business with 20 or 30 thousand agencies. We don't want to be lost in the crowd—just another travel agency in that vast field of 40,000. We want to stand out and be recognized as practically a dealership of the company's products.

We want our extraordinary sales performance to be recognized, appreciated, and rewarded. On a per-location basis, we strive to be one of the top 20 outlets for at least 5 of our suppliers, and certainly among the top 100 for the 15 others. When favors are needed, we want to hear "You bet!" When fams and inaugural cruise cabins are being passed out, we want them— and with accommodations that match our performance.

We want to know what makes their senior management tick. How they think, what's made them and their companies successful. We want to pick their brains! What's new? What's hot?

What are other successful agencies and vacation stores doing in other parts of the country? What are their suggestions to improve sales for us? From experience, we know that we will be treated better when these executives know us. Let's face it, our Vacation Store's success is riding on the successful relationships we have with a few key suppliers (five suppliers account for 75 percent of our business). Our company is our people, and their companies are all about their people as well. The truly successful companies know, appreciate, and build successful, person-to-person relationships. It's a two-way street.

Imagine how flattered we are when a senior executive of a major cruise line or tour operator calls us and thanks us for the business or asks our advice, and actually listens to what we have to say. Imagine how we feel when he recognizes us in a sea of faceless agents at a conference or invites us to sit with him at his table at a ship or agent's function? All of this is psychic income: gratifying, special, and never taken for granted. We make friends with these folks where the chemistry allows and treat them as such. Some, unfortunately, are either too stuck up or arrogant to notice us. It seems "beneath" certain travel executives to waste their time with "lowly" travel agents. Others seem to have the personalities of dead cod!

All the way through the home office, in each and every department, there's a key employee or two who makes things happen—who beats or bypasses the system, perhaps, but gets things done! These folks are invaluable, whether in reservations, air/sea, groups, accounting, guest relations, marketing, sales, or wherever. We discover many of these folks by accident, encountering them through the years when the occasional problems arise and they are able to solve them. When we stumble on them, we write down their names, and titles, and send thank you notes to their bosses. All concerned appreciate the acknowledgment of superior service. It motivates our suppliers to go the extra mile again and reinforces the Vacation Store as a caring, thoughtful marketing partner. These people are immediately added to our "key employee" list that we maintain for each and every supplier. This list is distributed to our entire office staff, properly filed and regularly consulted by all.

When the opportunity presents itself, we make it a point to visit our suppliers' home offices. This allows many of the employees whom we have known only by telephone to meet us (and vice versa) and put a face to the voices they've been dealing with on the phone over the years. When the spirit moves us, we create and present a plaque to a deserving company or department.

Well, there you have it: All of this is what makes the Vacation Store tick. We all enjoy what we do—providing terrific vacations for appreciative customers. We are well compensated and have the option of expanding our business and earning greater incomes. We are very optimistic concerning the future of our company, as we believe the vacation business will be a truly growth industry for many years to come. Moreover, we recognize that 80 percent of all vacations are booked directly by customers with suppliers. There is an enormous opportunity here to garner increased business as we *know* (not just believe) that we can provide prospects with better vacations than they are likely to discover on their own, and at no additional expense.

A Look Ahead

As cruising continues to enjoy the highest satisfaction ratings of any vacation alternative, our strategy of focusing on cruises is right on target. In our view, cruising will continue to be the largest growth sector of the vacation business. Capturing only 2 percent of today's North American vacationers, it has the clear prospect of growing fivefold or more in our lifetimes.

We certainly appreciate that the cruise industry is experiencing some choppy seas as we write this (including the dramatic bankruptcy of Regency Cruises in 1995). Nevertheless, we are confident that the industry as a whole will be able to navigate to calmer waters. Of course, we recognize that everyone won't make it. A few will sink and others will be able to grab hold of a life preserver.

Here are some positives we see:

- Old, uninspiring vessels are being retired or repositioned outside of the North American market, and gleaming new ships are coming on line in every shape, size, and price point—literally something for everyone. New designs and technology result in higher levels of spaciousness, openness to the sea, and smoother rides—motion discomfort is pretty rare these days. The addition of new ships will allow for the creation of new itineraries as well as new ports or embarkation—enhancing both variety and convenience.

- The industry is beginning to hit critical mass: a sufficient number of past passengers and new cruisers each year that will help fuel a chain reaction of new demand.
- With expansion, the large, well-financed cruise lines have the possibility of becoming truly branded—household words— that will help create top-of-mind awareness to this still too obscure industry.

However, cruising is not without its challenges:

- A surplus of underfinanced, poorly positioned or nonpositioned, "me-too" cruise lines will assuredly fall by the wayside.
- The cumulative effect of individual lines' market share strategies will inhibit the market expansion of the industry.
- Many lines tend to overpromise the cruise experience— especially when lower than anticipated yields (remember the pyramid) put inevitable pressure on cost and result in product underdelivery.

At the end of the day, the customer, the marketplace, will determine the composition of the cruise industry—its size and scope, its winners and losers. We believe there's an inherent fairness about all this. Cruise lines and other leisure travel providers exist solely to provide for customers' vacation needs. Only the buyers, not the sellers, should decide who does it right and who missed the boat. That's the way it should be, and we expect to have fun watching it all play out!

Glossary of Cruising and Vacation Terms

add on   a supplementary charge added to the price of the cruise, usually to cover air fare or other expenses that are not included in the price of the cruise.

affinity group   a group traveling together from an organization formed for another purpose such as a church, civic group, or club.

agency distribution system   the network of travel agencies that sells the majority of cruises, tours, and airline seats.

agent bypass   a business strategy where a supplier sells directly to the public, bypassing travel agencies.

air/sea   a package that includes the cost of both the air and the cruise as well as transfers between the airport and the port.

aft   towards the back or stern of the vessel.

Association of Retail Travel Agents (ARTA)   a trade association of small and mid-sized travel agencies.

American Society of Travel Agents (ASTA)   the major trade association of travel agencies in the United States. Allied memberships are also available to cruise lines and other travel suppliers.

ashore   on land.

baggage allowance   the amount of baggage carried by the cruise line at no charge.

basis two   double occupancy. Cruise prices are quoted basis two, which means on the basis of two persons sharing a cabin.

beam   the width of the ship at its widest point.

bearing   the compass direction toward a point to which the ship is headed—usually expressed in degrees of the compass.

berth   a bed on board a ship.

bilge   lowermost spaces inside of the ship.

bon voyage   a French term meaning "have a good trip."

booking   a telephone or automated request to a cruise line requesting a reservation for a passenger.

bow   the front of the ship. It's pronounced to rhyme with "how."

bridge   the part of the ship from which the captain and his officers command the ship.

bulkhead   upright partition dividing the ship into compartments (a wall.)

cabin   the rooms in which passengers sleep. Also known as state-rooms or bedrooms.

cast off   to let go of the lines that moor the ship to the pier.

category   a price gradient of similar cabins from the most expensive to the least expensive, or vice versa.

Centers for Disease Control and Prevention (CDC)   an arm of the U.S. Department of Health and Human Services that conducts sanitation inspections of international cruise ships.

charts   maps of the ocean, harbors, etc., used by sailors.

chief engineer   the officer in charge of operation and maintenance of the machinery on board a ship—everything from the engines to the plumbing and air conditioning.

chief steward   the officer in charge of the cleaning and maintenance of all rooms and public areas aboard a ship—reports to the captain.

come about   to turn the ship around.

companionway   interior stairway.

Computer Reservation Terminal (CRT)   the computer terminal on a travel agent's desks that is part of the system developed originally by the airlines to make reservations. Apollo, Sabre, and World Span are the largest of these. Today hotel, car rentals, and cruise lines can be booked on the same system.

consortium   a group of travel agencies who join together for the purposes of earning override commissions and consolidating support services such as accounting and advertising.

course   the direction in which the ship is headed.

cruise director   the individual in charge of all activities and entertainment on a cruise—reports to the hotel manager.

cruise fare   the actual cost of the cruise, not including port changes, tips, air fare, etc.

Cruise Lines International Association (CLIA)   a trade promotion association consisting of cruise lines and travel agencies.

davits   structures on the ship that hold, raise, and lower the lifeboats and tenders.

deck   the equivalent on a ship of a floor on a building.

deck plan   an overhead diagram that illustrates the location of cabins, public rooms, and other spaces on a deck.

deposit   a partial payment of the cruise fare required at the time of booking.

disembark   to leave the ship.

dock   a place to tie up a ship, also called a pier, quay, or wharf.

drill   a safety test ordered by the captain. Ships often have lifeboat and fire drills.

draft   the distance from the waterline of the ship to the bottom of the keel—in other words, the number of feet below the water at which the ship will touch bottom.

duty free   refers to items that are sold free of import (duty) taxes.

embarkation   the process of boarding a ship.

fantail   the overhang at the rear of the ship.

fam   familiarization trip, offered travel agents to visit cruise ships, hotels, and destinations.

first sitting   the earlier of two meal times on a ship, also called main sitting.

flag state   the flag of the country in which a ship is registered.

food and beverage director   the officer in charge of all food and beverage preparation and service—reports to the hotel manager.

fore   toward the front of the ship, the opposite of aft.

Foreign Independent Tour (FIT)   technically, an international prepaid independent trip where the itinerary and accommodations are specified by the traveler. In common usage, any agent-prearranged individual trip.

galley the kitchen on a ship.

gangway the ramp, bridge, or stairway used to get aboard and disembark from a ship.

gangway crawler a battery-powered device that crawls up and down a gangway, used to transport wheelchair-bound passengers on and off ships.

global positioning system a navigation aid operated by the United States government that tracks satellites and from them determines the latitude, longitude, and altitude of the ship.

gratuities also known as tips. Waiters, busboys, and room stewards receive the majority of their compensation from gratuities on board most cruises. Different lines provide guidelines, but passengers are free to tip whatever they feel the service warrants.

Gross Registered Tons (GRT) the way the size of ships is computed—it has nothing to do with weight. One gross registered ton equals 100 cubic feet of enclosed revenue-earning space (volume) on a vessel.

guarantee the cruise line's promise that the passenger will sail on a particular voyage with a specified price or type of cabin at an agreed rate. In some cases the accommodation may be improved at no additional cost.

guarantee share fare acceptance by some lines of a single booking at the same rate as a double occupancy with the understanding that the passenger is willing to share the cabin with a stranger of the same sex.

heavy seas rough water.

helm the ship's steering apparatus.

hotel manager the officer on board a ship in charge of all passenger services—reports to the captain. On British ships this person is called the chief purser.

hold the interior space in which a ship carries its cargo.

hull the frame and body of the ship not including the superstructure.

International Council of Cruise Lines a Washington-based association of cruise lines that works with and lobbies government organizations that regulate and control cruise-line operations.

inside cabin a cabin that does not look out on to the ocean.

Jones Act the wrongly used name for the Passenger Services Act of 1896, a U.S. law that prohibits ships that are registered outside of the United States from carrying passengers between two American ports without stopping at a foreign port.

knot a unit of measurement used to express the speed of a ship— equal to about 1.15 land miles per hour.

latitude the distance north or south from the equator expressed in degrees. One degree equals 60 nautical miles.

lines the ropes that tie a ship to the dock. The largest of these are known as hawsers.

longitude the distance east or west from the prime meridian at Greenwich, England, expressed in degrees. At the equator 1 degree equals sixty miles, but at the north and south poles it equals zero.

mal-de-mer French for seasickness.

manifest a list of the names of the ship's passengers, crew, and cargo.

master the captain.

midships toward the middle of the ship.

muster to assemble the passengers, crew, or both.

nautical mile 6,080.2 feet. This is longer than a mile on land, which is only 5,280 feet.

open sitting seating anywhere in the dining room as opposed to an assigned table.

outside cabin a cabin with a view of the ocean.

override extra commission paid to travel agents as an incentive or bonus for selling.

pitch the motion of a ship forward and backward in heavy seas.

port the left side of the ship facing the bow (front).

port charges fees levied by cruise lines, which include taxes/fees assessed by governmental and other agencies; costs incident to entering/leaving ports, such as pilotage, tendering, and line handling; costs incurred while in port such as dockage, stevedoring, and other port-related functions; and other corporate costs and expenses associated with the foregoing.

preferred supplier a supplier of a travel product that has been selected by a travel agency to recommend to its clients. Usually preferred suppliers offer agencies overrides in return for meeting certain sales goals.

prospect a prospective or possible customer.

purser the officer on the ship who handles all financial matters and is also in charge of the information desk—reports to the hotel manager except on British ships, where he or she is the hotel manager.

roll the side-to-side motion in heavy seas.

Safety of Life at Sea (SOLAS) a set of rules of the International Maritime Organization (IMO), part of the United Nations, that becomes mandatory in 1997, applying to the configuration and equipment all ships must carry to prevent and control hazards at sea such as fire.

second sitting   the later of two meal times aboard a ship.

shore excursions   tours and activities that are offered to passengers (usually at a charge) when the ship is in port.

single occupancy   when one person occupies a cabin instead of two.

space ratio   a measurement of how spacious a ship is calculated in cubic space per passenger. Gross registered tonnage divided by the number of passengers a ship carries (double occupancy) equals the space ratio.

stabilizers   retractable "wings" that extend from the sides of a ship underwater to reduce motion.

staff captain   second in command on board.

starboard   the right side of the ship as you face toward the bow.

stateroom   another term for cabin or bedroom.

stern   the back of the ship.

stripes   the designation on a ship's officer's uniform of his or her rank. The exact number of stripes each officer carries differs by cruise line, but the one with the most is always the captain.

superstructure   the part of the ship located above the main deck.

tender   a small boat used to transport passengers to ports when the ship is not able to dock.

tour conductor's ticket   a free cruise ticket issued to the leader of a group of sufficient size traveling together.

transfers   transportation between airports and/or hotels to the ship.

travel agent   an individual or company that sells cruises, tours, and other travel products to the public and is generally compensated by the travel suppliers whose products he or she sells.

Travel Industry Association of America (TIA)   a nonprofit association of government and private organizations whose purpose is to promote travel to and within the United States.

Visiting Friends and Relatives (VFR)   travel that is not vacation sales or commercial.

upgrade   to provide a better class of service such as a more desirable cabin.

wake   the tracks of agitated water produced by a ship's movement.

Index